THE COSMIC CANCER

EFFECTS OF HUMAN BEHAVIOR
ON LIFE OF OUR PLANET

THE COSMIC CANCER

REVISED AND EXPANDED EDITION

DAVID LOUIS SUSSMAN

iUniverse®

THE COSMIC CANCER
EFFECTS OF HUMAN BEHAVIOR ON THE LIFE OF OUR PLANET

iUniverse books may be ordered through booksellers or by contacting:

iUniverse
1663 Liberty Drive
Bloomington, IN 47403
www.iuniverse.com
1-800-Authors (1-800-288-4677)

ISBN: 978-1-4917-4556-4 (sc)
ISBN: 978-1-4917-4558-8 (hc)
ISBN: 978-1-4917-4557-1 (e)

Library of Congress Control Number: 2014916841

Printed in the United States of America.

iUniverse rev. date: 9/25/2014

For
Claire
Ellen, David, Rona, Michael
and particularly those most affected by the outcome:
Caitlan, Daniel, Emma and Nicholas,
their contemporaries and successor generations

CONTENTS

PREFACE

Edward O. Wilson, eminent entomologist at Harvard University and exponent of socio-biology, published a book a few years ago entitled *The Future of Life*. His concern was that human lifestyles were pushing all species toward disaster, as indicated by the current rate of extinction of flora and fauna throughout the world. He attributed this modern phenomenon to human behavior patterns—mainly our abuse of the natural environment. Although I read the book avidly, the title alone served as catalyst for adding coherence to my own ideas on the subject.

As we humans have only the *illusion of choice*, a theme that permeates much of this discussion, it's necessary to explain how it happens that I have "decided" to set down my thoughts on our modes of conduct and their impacts on the outlook for living things on Earth. My explanation of purpose is paradoxical to say the least, as a member of a species lacking choice or purpose, but there's no alternative: as evolution has bestowed on *Homo sapiens* both outsized braininess and sexiness, at the same time it has made us masters of self-deception, so it's natural to behave as if we have the power to chart our own course, appearing to make not only day-to-day decisions, but even planning for posterity.

For most of my adult life humanity's missteps have evoked a sense of profound impropriety—incessant hostility and war, our common home despoiled, human numbers exploding to levels only possible at the expense of natural capital accumulated over eons. Along the way arose a sense of identity with nature, under assault by this rogue species spawned perhaps 5-7 million years ago when the first glimmer of the hominid line split from a common ancestor with our primate cousins. My "epiphany" occurred at Bear Mountain Park, in New York

State, at the age of twelve. To gain respite from the ordinary turbulence of our family life, my father would pack my mother and the brood of six or seven siblings into the old Hudson Terraplane and wheel over to the park on a Sunday morning. Once there we would picnic and have the run of that beautiful rolling and verdant terrain. On one of these occasions—a pleasantly warm and otherwise glorious summer day beneath a cloudless and brilliant sky—I lay down under an enormous spreading shade tree, when I suddenly melted into the surroundings, and have never been the same since. Later in life it became clear that the sense of connectedness derives from the inclusion of all things in a unified eternal and ubiquitous nature—the material and operational dimensions within the range of human observation or comprehension, as well as those that may lie beyond.

In my youth, images of magnificent creatures tromping regally through bucolic rain forests of Asia and Africa were seared into my consciousness through literature and films. Living in a city seemed an aberration, an anemic choice of habitat for humans, whose life experiences would be so greatly enhanced were we to live in the jungle along with its other unfettered inhabitants. Going to a zoo with my parents and siblings was a painful experience, as it seemed to me that perfectly innocent cousins, whose bizarre behaviors could easily be understood with a little role reversal, were incarcerated for no reason other than perverse pleasures of misguided people.

The spontaneous auto-assembly of matter into cells with progressively more complex structures that learned self-replication is the miracle that is probably a singular occurrence in cosmic history. As such a rarity, life is too precious—all of it, even houseflies, although practicality compels us to sometimes send them off to fly heaven—to ignore the waywardness of the one species that has emerged whose practices will affect the future of all living things. This deep and abiding fascination and reverence for life is the impetus for attempting what is essentially a treatise on human behavior.

My personal history doesn't appear to lend authority to an inquiry into human behavioral underpinnings, characteristics and consequences: no educational or professional involvement in sociology or any of its derivate specializations, only stages as young (and compliant) warrior, student, engineer, college teacher, farmer, international business consultant, (inept) basketball player[1]. In fact, rather than attempt to surreptitiously poke a foot into this arcane discipline, I'm rather inclined to keep my distance, as most of its practitioners have stubbornly failed to take into account the most fundamental basis for social phenomena, our multi-million year evolutionary history.

There are multiple paths to understanding, not only the institutional approach of formal education, a system that in some circumstances stultifies thinking. In my days as a teacher, engineer and manager, in some cases students and colleagues who were regarded as anything from oddball to incompetent defied the conventional path to understanding and, in fact, led the search for knowledge. While guiding a class of aspiring engineers in a two-semester foundation course, I was permitted by the college president (who recognized the potential value of unconventional learning) to accept a consulting job that would spill over into the second semester, leaving my students to fend for themselves for the first month or so. In preparation, the students and I discussed only where they "needed to go," but without a prescribed structure for getting there. Upon my return I learned that they had met as a group during scheduled class sessions, with one or another taking the lead in discussing the topic of the day. Their "progress" would have been awesome had I not realized that they dance best who follow their own inner rhythms.

In truth I have been a student of human behavior for over seven decades, starting from the day at age five when I pondered why my aunt apprehensively observed my doings while sitting on the bathroom potty of her Coney Island apartment. Subsequently, in the course of my work and other interactions with people, what lies beneath behavioral patterns has been an unremitting fascination. It's now lamentably evident that behaviors in most all civilized societies have pushed us close to the brink of extinction, along with other species, as violent confrontation and despoliation afflict virtually every corner of this once beautiful planet.

As un-anointed social analyst for starters, certainly the breadth of issues addressed here appears presumptuous, at the very least.

However, it's clear that all dimensions of life among humans, as well as other species, are manifestations of an underlying strategic endowment honed through millions of years of evolutionary history, which may still be in a state of flux. Only a few characteristic behaviors have been singled out for scrutiny, which I believe clearly illustrate the unfortunate paths that humanity has taken.

You may notice an apparent inconsistency in alluding to my own and others' personal behavioral choices against the assertion that choice is illusory. However, self-consciousness and temporal awareness provide a kind of simulated independence from nature, so in everyday life we cling to the delusion that what we think or do is a matter of choice, which makes life in a sense livable. Otherwise, many of us would give up even the pretense of acting morally, finding in our lack of control an excuse for anti-social behavior, indulging in self-interests or simply accepting what the fates have to offer.

From the outset I have to point out that in everyday life a trend toward misanthropy, more distrust than hatred, has gradually ripened with life experiences. Although enamored with life in any form, humans have been a great disappointment. This may seem inconsistent with the assertion that we are not in control of our destiny, and therefore can't be blamed for our shortcomings, either singly or as a group. In our usual state of consciousness we certainly *feel* that we can choose. This is the context in which we ordinarily function, while the underlying influences are obscured by our perceptual limitations.

To feel uneasy about one's own species is discomfiting, but to this I must admit. For anyone who cares to notice, humanity has inflicted great harm to our planet and to the many other species that have accompanied us on this journey through the eons. What would we think of a passenger on a train who hogged all the seats, imposed his obnoxious ways on the others aboard, and in the end dispatched to oblivion a good number of them for pure enjoyment? Or one who fouls his home by treating it as an open sewer, discarding wastes and toxins to watercourses, land and air? So, here in the twilight of my life, I can only hope to shed some light on the hazardous path that humanity has taken, and, in some small measure, to influence corrective adjustments. This may likewise be delusional, but it may be an early inkling of the kind of alteration in human consciousness that may bode well for the future of life.

What follows, then, is merely a minor manifestation of a chain of cosmic forces extending from time immemorial, so aptly expressed by Omar Khayyam in 1120 C.E. (Quattrain 71)[2]:

> The Moving Finger writes, and having writ,
> Moves on: nor all your Piety nor Wit
> Shall lure it back to cancel half a line,
> Nor all your tears wash out a Word of it.

According to the gospel of Luke (23, KJV[3]), during his crucifixion Jesus asks forgiveness for his tormentors. Nothing more cogently identifies humankind as unwitting instrument of nature, directed by forces beyond the control of any living organism.

But we are so accustomed to functioning as if we have some say in the matter that it seems essential for communication to slip over occasionally into the vernacular, predicated on the view of ourselves as thinking and deciding independent agents. Besides, this seemingly insignificant compulsive endeavor might serve as a transcendental flap of a butterfly's wing in the chaotic[4] global social system. If you "choose" to listen, I beg your indulgence for one who really can't help himself.

ACKNOWLEDGEMENTS

I am deeply indebted to Reg Morrison, who graciously agreed to review an early manuscript, and whose critique of content and structure was instrumental in helping me to reorganize and improve the presentation of the first edition; and also for allowing me to "stand on his shoulders" while peering at the subjects of his seminal work on human behavior, "*The Spirit in the Gene, Humanity's Proud Illusion and the Laws of Nature.*" Michael Sussman also reviewed the original and this expanded and revised manuscript, providing invaluable suggestions for improvement. Had I followed their advice to the letter, this would undoubtedly have been a much better piece of work. Those listed in the bibliography were mainly involuntary participants in the process of shaping my own thoughts on matters of human behavior, whom I thank profoundly for sharing their ideas through their published works. None of these individuals can in any way be held responsible for errors, omissions or misguided conclusions, which are strictly of my own doing.

INTRODUCTION

Every one of us has exactly two parents. We probably have four grandparents, but not necessarily; in fact, we could have only one maternal and one paternal grandparent if our parents brought us into this world incestuously.

If we assume the normal pattern of parenthood, five generations back we would have 32 ancestors. Go back 10 generations and there would have been 1,032. Fifteen generations ago our ancestry, numbering 32,728, would have trouble finding seats in a sports arena. Beyond this our parentage begins to assume the proportions of the modern industrialized state—33 ½ million at 25 generations. At 50 generations, approximately a millennium, the numbers approach the astronomical at a little more than 1,000 trillion!

Modern humans have a history of about two hundred thousand years (perhaps 8-10 thousand generations). It's clear that the assumption, at this juncture, of two distinct parents for each ancestor of anyone alive and doubling the number of progenitors in each generation backward in time is patently untenable. In fact, there were only about 100 million humans in the year 1,000 CE.

Over the span of modern human history there obviously has been a great deal of mixing and matching. How closely any two of us alive today are related can only be approximated, but through the advancing art of genetic mapping, much more accurate relationships with both contemporaries and recent ancestors from whom genetic samples are available may be known. However, this would only be possible for relatively few of the numerous generations since the onset of our brand of humanity, *H. sapiens*. Considering intermingling of genetic strains brought about by war, migrations, pilgrimages and the like, for all but the most isolated human populations, each of us is of uncertain parentage beyond a relatively minor span of history. We stand on the shoulders, or under the foot, of our ancestors, the great majority unknown. To sort out the amalgam of genetic and cultural strains, of which each of us is comprised, becomes increasingly difficult in the deep recesses of time.[5]

Recent experience tells only a very small part of the story and is woefully incomplete at best, and in fact can be highly misleading: inferences drawn from analysis of behavior in a current social milieu fail to take into account the great river of history that resides in each of us. As Scottish biologist Richard Dawkins points out (*River Out of Eden*), we are all progeny of an unbroken string of survivors, those who had what it took in their respective eras to stay alive at least to the point of producing offspring. In another work (*The Selfish Gene*), Dawkins explains the relevance of kinship to what is commonly considered altruistic behavior.

Steve Olson (2002) explains how race and other stereotyping of human populations tend to overstate divisions among us. We are much closer genetically than meets the eye. For example, he points out that every one of European origin living today had at least one common ancestor within the last few thousand years. If altruism were linked to kinship, one would anticipate far less strife among national and ethnic groups. The fact that we are more militant and contentious than might be expected is, to say the least, a disappointment, which compels us to think about the potential benefits of spreading knowledge about human relationships to the minds of every child in the world. Perhaps in this way the brutality that has been all too prevalent in human relations from time immemorial could be reduced or even eliminated.

No two humans are genetically identical, except for the original genomes of identical twins formed from a single fertilized egg. Of the roughly three billion base pairs that make up the human genome, about a tenth of one percent varies between any two individuals. So 99.9 percent of the genome is the same for all humans[6], the variations responsible for physical and (as subsequently explained) behavioral differences. Genetic variation also distinguishes one species from another, so it should not be surprising that there is a characteristic behavior pattern for all species, including humans.

An outgrowth of our complexity is that we are not one-dimensional. We exist at many levels, sometimes at the peak of the mountain and at other times in the vale of tears. So it isn't possible to continually survey the human scene as if we are in a gigantic zoo. But at times, not only the emperor loses his clothes, but also everyone in sight, and movements and gestures of the passing gallery take on the aspect of a primatorium.

There is little doubt that culture also greatly influences behavior. "It is incontrovertible that human beings are a product of evolution, but with respect to behavior that evolutionary process involves chance, natural selection, and, especially in the case of human beings, transmission and alteration of a body of extra-genetic information called 'culture.' Cultural evolution, a process very different from genetic evolution by natural selection, has played a central role in producing our behaviors."[7]

But what *is* culture? The term is commonly used to represents the creative endeavors that largely distinguish human society from those of more primitive species—e.g., the arts, scholarly pursuits, altruism, etc. In a larger sense, it is the essence of civilization, the human organizational invention arising from the need to ameliorate internal conflicts that would otherwise be resolved with blood and tears (Freud 2006), and also to manage relations with the external world. Culture is the behavioral superstructure that a society erects over its genetic and economic underpinnings, which codifies and otherwise institutionalizes behavioral norms, organizes for greater efficiency in securing needs and wants, and creates avenues for the "higher" pursuits that expand the range of human capacities. Dawkins (2006) identified the *meme*, the conceptual or ideational equivalent of a gene, as the instrument for spreading cultural norms through a society and contributing to cultural evolution in an analogous manner.

While the imprint of genetic evolution in the species, in isolated populations and in the individual can be seen in the genomic record, cultural influences are more ephemeral. There are undoubtedly cultural strains that influence behaviors of groups unified by ethnicity, nationality and even ideology, some historical aspects accessible through artistic and scientific documentation, but most lost in the mists of antiquity.[8] So the "choice" herein is rather to deal with behaviors from a contemporary sociological perspective, with only general references to the river of life experiences from which they derive.[9]

We are inclined, by our own experience of birth and death, to insist that there is a beginning and an end to everything. But suppose that there isn't any *isn't*, only what *is*. An omnipresent and timeless nature may be the only game in the universe, which, despite all our attempts to intervene, has always been and continues on its merry way without being constrained by our limited perceptions. "God" *may* have created and may even be controlling things out there, but our rational faculties don't lead us inevitably to its existence.

The delicious part of this mélange is that our fate is not sealed, despite our attempts to plan and control. We are not free agents, nor is the future predictable:

> The best laid schemes o' mice an' men
> Gang aft a-gley, [often go awry]
> An' lea'e us nought but grief an' pain,
> For promised joy.[10]

Nature plays her tricks with the billiard balls of life (see Chapter 1), games of chance that obviate predictions about how an organism, including any of us, responds to physical and emotional interactions. For an observer this is the most interesting part of the panorama. This is what makes immersion in the currents of life a worthwhile endeavor.

There seems little doubt that humankind has now reached a state in which its numbers and consumption patterns have remarkably altered its habitat, comprised of virtually every corner of Planet Earth. Pundits have warned of imminent danger of extinction. In fact, the rate of extinction of other species is now greater, from all evidence, than it has been since the disappearance of the dinosaurs 60 million years ago. There is little doubt that we are the culprits. Mass extinctions in the past have been associated with cataclysmic environmental events. This is probably the first instance of extinctions at such a scale resulting from the lifestyle of one of Earth's inhabitants, and there is little doubt that these other species are so many "canaries in the mineshaft," harbingers of what's in store for humanity itself.

Something has happened to the feedback loop. Normal instincts of self-preservation, even in the absence of will, would be expected to inspire individual countermeasures to avoid catastrophe, which would be reflected in the collective response. But knowledge about symptoms of imminent danger such as urban mayhem, children murdering children, alienated people reeking of hatred and seeking to inflict violence, even hysteria in music and other art forms, do not appear to register or elicit any serious response that would tend to alleviate them. We have "selected" a path that we know to be wrong, but continue its traverse because we are powerless to correct, driven by forces stronger than rationality. Our dual personality disorder is epitomized in the words of *Pogo*, Walt Kelly's[11] comic strip character: "We have met the enemy and he is us!"

A reading of any period in the annals of humankind reveals the same litany of wanton disregard for the health and welfare of others, whether of kindred beings or those other species whose presence enriches the tapestry of life that billions of years of evolutionary honing have produced. And yet there is more. It's not sufficient to destroy those whose extermination either materially or symbolically advances the quest for power and possession, but there is all too prevalent in the record instances of a diabolical step beyond, a sadistic streak that seeks to inflict pain for the sheer pleasure of witnessing its effects.[12]

What makes the humans species unique is, at the same time, a badge of dishonor. Most characteristics are shared to some degree by other species—bipedal primate cousins and birds, stereoscopic vision of many mammals. Consciousness of self, on the other hand, as surely fashioned over the eons by natural forces as a giraffe's neck or an octopus' tentacles is, in humans, quantum leaps beyond that of any other species. This characteristic not only magnifies the individual's own significance, but also provides a channel for imposing one's will on others through psychological devices from simple rejection to the use of terror. Images of past and future traumatic events are employed to heighten the impact of both physical and emotional assaults, providing for the power-seeker a very effective mechanism of dominance. In many instances potentially subservient beings are destroyed in the process, but there are others to fill the gap, whose servility is thereby intensified.

A review of recent human history provides many examples of the use of terror for the purpose of dominance. Any place we start is like coming in at the middle of the movie. Annihilation of native Americans in the 19th century by the military and vigilantes; the enslavement and cultural destruction of Africans from the 17th to the 20th centuries; the holocaust in Europe of WWII; Vietnam, the Balkans, Rwanda, Burundi, Sierra Leone, Mexico. It's only necessary to mention the sites of such atrocities—modern media are proficient at disseminating the gory details to every corner of the globe.

No, it's not easy to love humans. On the other hand, it's quite easy to find us contemptible, both individually and collectively. The inclination to go beyond mere dominance, to inflict pain and suffering gratuitously or as a means of gaining and perpetuating advantage, is all too prevalent. As if the exercise of dominance is not sufficient, a lasting reminder is often applied to indelibly imprint the subjugated with the desired degree of subservience—the Nazis did this literally by branding their victims. The hapless participants in this ancient dance play their parts faithfully, like well-seasoned veterans of a long-running theatrical tragedy.

The truth is that it's all beyond our "poor power to add or to detract." We live under a grand illusion of independence from natural forces, exacerbated in western industrialized countries by a material cocoon, woven with the threads of exhaustible capital resources whose limits we deny. We do what we do what we do, deluding ourselves that we could do otherwise under the circumstances.

So are we to blame for our shortcomings? There is the fundamental issue of the motive force behind what our rational capacities tell us is out there. There seems to be order in the universe, as far as we can tell, some rules for nature's expressions that are immutable—conservation of energy, the Uncertainty Principle, relativistic time dilation and the like. At first glance it appears that there is some structure to the universe, which from our perspective of cause and effect, demands acknowledgement of a prime mover or designer. Why, for example, are there neat mathematical forms that uncannily describe the behavior of physical processes? Why do inverse square laws have a perfect "2" for the power of distance?

The apparent order in the universe coupled with our propensity for mysticism suggests to us that (a) there must be a creator for what apparently exists, who is (b) omniscient and (c) omnipotent, and who loosened the reins to attribute choice to humans, a gambit that provides clever exploiters a framework to expand political influence. Choice allows for good and evil thoughts and deeds, with gods and their earthly interlocutors ready and willing to accordingly praise or condemn, and with monumental consequences. Who could more effectively gain our attention and allegiance than those whose judgments conduce to eternal Eden or hell?

Feedback, aside from its function involving mere survival, may yet have its effects in altering the nature of humanity to a more sustainable path, even though it may well be true that we are not in control. Since cultural modifications often spread like wildfire, in sharp contrast to the sluggish pace of physical evolution, we may yet see humanity transmuted into a species at one with its environment, in harmony with nature and all of her mysterious inclinations, and before we would otherwise consign ourselves and our planetary wards to oblivion.

In fact, we have witnessed time and again how culture has engendered redeeming qualities that militate against total depravity and loss of hope. Too many individuals have been acculturated to transcend narrow parochialism and to act magnanimously and heroically, even to the extent of sacrificing their lives for ideals—heroes made, and not born.[13] There are undoubtedly legions unsung, which have brightened the landscape over the millennia. During the World Wars of the 20th century the prevailing sentiment of Americans who answered the call to military service was predominantly to save the world for democracy.[14] Women and men were inspired to put their very existence on the line for a principle—abhorrence of totalitarianism—and suffered over a million casualties.[15] In the 1960s many Americans rose to challenge apartheid, facing physical danger and death in the cause of promoting equal opportunity for their fellow citizens. If only this were the norm!

For millennia philosophers have pondered the issue of man's uniqueness in nature—the capacity to choose (free will) as the central characteristic that separates man from beast. Almost invariably the conclusion is that a human being does have the capacity to chart one's own course, to opt for the "road not taken" for example.[16]

Buddhist tradition ostensibly skirts the issue by emphasizing awareness, leading to better "choices": introspection concerning impacts of past and current influences on one's attitudes that condition experience; concentration of attention to objects at hand; cultivation of the deepest levels of consciousness, which unifies all things and obviates the significance of choice.[17]

Recent behavioral research increasingly attributes actions and attitudes to conditions in the brain and other parts of the body that are described in biochemical and biophysical terms, in other words, as responsive to natural imperatives. However, the scientific community seems reticent to cross the line by acknowledging some justification for the proposition that all human behavior, as well as that of all other organisms, is strictly a function of matter/energy interactions. Why this is so would be puzzling, if it were not for the realization that they are merely acting out their destinies under the influence of the very phenomena that they relegate to irrelevance. Scientists are constrained culturally to follow a code of conduct that insists upon adhering to rigorous methods involving hypotheses and experimentation. Questions concerning mechanisms of human behavior for many of them are not only too large, but also too hot to handle. However, progress in the field of neuroscience is gradually allowing these issues to find their way to respectability.

What settled the issue for me was Desmond Morris' "*The Naked Ape*," published in the 1960s, which presented humanity as nothing more (or less) than a primate in clothing. Although he refrained, from modesty and sensitivity, to bind humanity inescapably to its animal roots, he made it clear through unbridled observation and analysis that there is no reason to suppose that we humans have transcended our natural underpinnings.

Why assign to humans the epithet "Cosmic Cancer?" So long as we "choose" to restrict our presence to our mother planet and the stratosphere, though we may continue on our path of excess and violence, our impact is negligible in the unimaginably vast reaches of space. Now we have not only undertaken missions to the other planets of our solar system, but some space probes have already penetrated into the reaches beyond. Space flight has become a commercial venture: scientists and adventurers see the planets and galaxies as the new frontier to be conquered, oblivious of the devastation we have wrought on our own planet, perceiving no harm in extending it to whatever bodies in the cosmos might have the misfortune to encounter us as guests or even settlers.

The proposal that humanity has cancerous behavioral characteristics is not original, although conceived independently. Dr. Alan Gregg (1955), proposed that the explosion of human population is analogous to metastasis, preempting my claim to discovery, although at that time he focused upon what was occurring on our own planet:

> "I suggest, as a way at looking at the population problem, that there are some interesting analogies between the growth of human population of the world and the increase of cells observable in neoplasm (cancer). To say that the world has cancer, and that the cancer cell is man, has neither experimental proof nor the validation of predictive accuracy; but I see no reason that instantly forbids such a speculation ... What are the characteristics of new growths?... they exert pressure on adjacent structures ... within closed cavities (they) exert pressure that can kill, because any considerable displacement is impossible.... Metastasis ... describe(s) another phenomenon of malignant growth in which detached neoplastic cells ... lodge at a distance from the primary focus or point of origin and proceed to multiply without direct contact with the tissue or organ from which they came. It is actually difficult to avoid

using the word colony in describing this thing that physicians call metastasis."

James Lovelock (2000), a British atmospheric chemist, postulated the Gaia hypothesis—that Earth is a single, self-regulating, living organism. Earth's internal management system, in a manner suggestive of homeostasis in humans, regulates interactions of biota and biosphere with Earth's other physical elements (land, seas and atmosphere), with the capacity to maintain conditions supportive to all of life. His concept is supported by knowledge about life's origins, apparently a singular event about 4 billion years ago, shortly after Earth's formation, in which self-replicating molecules developed in the primordial mix of organic material in water. For billions of years these simple organisms were the only life forms, until environmental conditions propitiated the formation and replication of the first pre-cellular DNA (deoxyribonucleic acid), which gradually evolved into single, self-replicating cells that derived sustenance from their ocean surroundings. Gradually, over millions of years, the string of genetic coding increased in complexity and length, providing for the production of nutrients from basic materials and replication of cells with multiple forms and functions.

All of the resultant life forms, except for bacteria and archaea, share the same fundamental structure, chemistry and building blocks. Andrew Knoll (2004), Professor of Natural History and Earth and Planetary Sciences at Harvard University: "It's pretty clear that all the organisms living today, even the simplest ones, are removed from some initial life form by four billion years or so, ... the first ... much simpler than anything that we see around us. But they must have had that fundamental property of being able to grow and reproduce and be subject to Darwinian evolution." Plants and animals are comprised of eukaryotic cells, which have a nucleus that allows for the production of multi-cellular organisms. Our cousins, the bacteria and archaea, are comprised of prokaryotic cells without a nucleus (most are unicellular), and are therefore "condemned" to a relatively simple life, although symbiosis between prokaryotes and eukaryotes (with cell nuclei, such as humans) is essential for continuation of life, as we know it.

As a component of Gaia, humanity would do well to observe its own responsibility to self-regulate. But the truth is that we do not observe the "rules," and have created problems for ourselves and for the rest of life. Humanity appears to be an element of the system out of control, much like cancerous metastasis. As a consequence of our special natural endowment, we have the propensity to procreate beyond sustainable bounds, to expand numerically to the point that in order to maintain our accustomed mode of existence we seize the space and resources of other communities, human and otherwise; in some cases we send our excess population packing so that they are not only someone else's problem, but also that their presence and further expansion in that remote setting does not adversely impact upon our standard of living. The solution is before our noses, but unrecognized or otherwise dismissed: to adjust our fecundity to the available resources so that the standard of living is not only maintained, but also is open to non-materialistic advancement.

Attempting to intervene in nature's inexorable but uncertain trajectory while, at the same time, acknowledging that none of us has any say in the matter is a fundamental paradox, something like being condemned to a life sentence behind bars without the possibility of parole but continuing to dream and plan what we will do when released. Nature plays the cards that it has dealt to all of us who share the vast majority of the human genome, and to every other particle of matter/energy in the cosmos. Part of our hand is the illusion of control. The paradox is perhaps akin to what Lewis Carroll had in mind as he created *Through the Looking Glass* in 1872, as Alice climbs through the mirror over the mantel and then becomes privy to what lies beyond her ordinary consciousness.

Is humanity approaching a dead end? Is evolution over?

The evolutionary process of beneficial genetic modification conferring selective advantage may be arrested or at least attenuated as human culture has progressively intruded and integrated with the physical side of nature, imposing survival influences such as legal and moral codes (e.g., ethics and religious strictures), social safety nets and other public programs that result in survival outcomes different from what nature "red in tooth and claw" alone would produce.

As for any species, there exists a set of morphological and behavioral characteristics that distinguishes *H. sapiens* from all others, predicated on genetic and cultural traits that are too interdependent to be considered in isolation; *civilization* is a cultural phenomenon that has now permeated the most remote segments of human society. However, cultural variations adopted by groups distinguished by ethnicity, nationality and even ideology are only skin deep, in some cases literally. Traits that unite us are much greater than those that divide us.

Part I reviews the state of our species in its current level of development. As discussed in Chapter 1, on the historical map "we are here." Our strategic legacy, comprising factors of morphology and behavior—perhaps its most notable aspect consciousness of self in space and time—evokes the delusional assumption of choice, and, in turn, our inclination to blame and praise. Thus is humanity almost certainly doomed to an early demise, as nature exacts its penalty arising from widespread employment of this ruse by some of us to exercise control over other people and resources.

Chapter 2 is a review of inordinate growth in human population, already far beyond numbers that can comfortably be accommodated by the sustainable capacity of the one planet available to the vast majority of humans living now and, more than likely, in the future. Population *growth* is not strictly an imperative, and yet is so fundamentally a conditioned response to nature's prodding that it is treated as part of the foundation for humanity's behavioral repertoire.

Of the extensive litany of egregious behaviors deriving from our condition, a few are singled out for examination in Part II, which appear to be most unfortunate and yet possible of correction. They are intended to illuminate and to suggest solutions to these imperfections in the human constitution—our collective predilection to almost invariably do the wrong thing, with devastating, if not fatal, consequences. The principle criterion for selection is their impact on prospects for the continuation of life on Earth. It may appear at first an eclectic array of topics, but they are unified by their indubitable contributions to the mayhem that humanity has spawned and by their potential for accelerating the demise of our species and other innocent bystanders.

The failure to cherish and to properly nurture youth is a universal characteristic, doting mothers notwithstanding, virtually assuring a buildup of ignorance and hostility in future generations (Chapter 3). A derivative effect of endemic political machination is the endorsement of *rights* of potentially devoted followers, rather than inculcation of *responsibilities*, thus setting faction against faction in pressing for perquisites, arousing social disharmony and ultimate disintegration (Chapter 4). Civilization has destabilized sexual expression through codes and standards that have little bearing on maintaining social order, conducive to rampant sexual abuse on a global scale. Media moguls have channeled the sex drive into a force to generate profits, with attendant aberrations and resultant social tensions (Chapter 5). Religionists and politicians have learned and conspired to inject large doses of mysticism into the affairs of an already excessively prone species, greatly impeding social maturation (Chapter 6). The pursuit of knowledge has been largely relegated to specialists whose primary identity is "scientist" rather than "member of society," and who peer with laser-like intensity at ever subdividing areas of knowledge with little concern for larger consequences, a type of myopia that will shortly, barring a perceptual transformation, complete the great job it has been doing in despoiling Planet Earth (Chapter 7). A general assumption prevails that items that are worn, out of fashion or simply no longer coveted can be discarded without consequence. Industry and commerce assume the "right" to discharge effluents to land, air and water, leaving problems of pollution to "others." Meanwhile, mountains of trash accumulate to foul the environment, the stratosphere, and even the heavens (Chapter 8). Our tendency is to take conflict to the bloody stage, a proclivity to wage war to the death rather than settling differences with less draconian methods; a consequence of our insensitivity— unlike most other species—to signals leading to more benign modes of resolution (Chapter 9). An "Edifice Complex" prevails, whereby bigness and concentration defy the sensible benefits of diversification and avoidance of risk, and which produces inordinate and dangerous disparities in distribution of wealth and income (Chapter 10).

Many other human foibles could be fruitfully scrutinized in this fashion, but a sampling will illustrate sufficiently how human behavior patterns are recapitulating the previous five great extinctions[18] in Earth's history, which this time around will likely include us. Patterns of human behavior, honed during eons of physical and cultural evolution, are wreaking havoc on our planet.[19] As a component of the biosphere, *H. sapiens* plays out its role as nature dictates, in its current form with disastrous consequences. Our behavioral repertoire, derived from the strategic plan devised by nature for our species through interactions of individual organisms with their external environments, is largely shared with all people throughout the world. How these inclinations are manifested is crucial to attaining a decent life for posterity.

Although paradoxical under the assumption of the absence of choice for all living organisms, including humans, this examination is an element of discourse with the potential for altering human activity to a more sustainable path. Awareness of our inability to choose is a liberating factor, contributing to greater comprehension of the roots of behavior. The primary need is for enhanced depth perception, greater concern for the far-reaching consequences of individual and collective attitudes and actions. Acknowledging where we have gone astray is the first step toward developing a more wholesome behavioral repertoire.

Part III (Chapter 11) assesses the outlook for the future of life on Earth. Nature's bequest to humanity—who we are—is the primary determinant. This is even truer as human impact already alters climate, land, sea, and air qualities and is responsible for the sixth great extinction of species. The likelihood of constructive behavioral changes depends upon the breadth and depth of sensitivity to the devastation we are wreaking on the only planet we will most likely ever occupy and to what extent we embrace identity with nature: no lesser perspective will suffice.

PART I

THE HUMAN CONDITION

CHAPTER 1

A MATTER OF CHOICE

Most of the time, as we wend our way through life, events seem to follow a logical pattern. If it rains, we get wet; if the sun is shining, it's a warm summer day and there are no immediate household impediments, we may decide to go to the beach. If the number one team in the league is playing against number ten, almost certainly number one emerges victorious.

Occasionally events take an unexpected turn. Although there are showers in the area, a patch of clear sky follows us overhead, so all but we are drenched. Conditions are perfect for a sojourn at the seashore, but we decide to read a book. The number ten team annihilates number one.

Would the unexpected outcome be explained if we only knew all of the antecedent conditions and circumstances? Are we really free to choose, and if we cannot, is the future foreordained?

Although these questions have been debated for millennia, as information accumulates concerning the origins of human behavior, that choice is an illusion becomes ever more plausible. Furthermore, its contraposition with determinism is a false dichotomy: absence of free will does not imply a predetermined future. There is too much indeterminacy built into the natural world, with humanity as a component, for our future to be cast in stone individually or collectively. The same uncertainties affecting human life apply to the matter and energy of which all things are comprised. Although no organism is in control of its destiny, neither is that destiny foreordained. Alternative trajectories for life are not predicated only on either strict determinism or free will. Even if all uncertainties arising from antecedent events could be resolved by greater observational and reasoning powers, the behavior of any organism at a given time and place is essentially unpredictable within certain ranges. Indeterminacy remains and, as far as we know, is a fundamental characteristic of nature, and everything that exists in its domain.

The proposition that choice is illusory may be wrong, but it has the potential to vastly improve the landscape on Earth. If accepted, even tentatively, it would lead to a number of healthy developments. For one thing, we would function with humility rather than pomposity, and perhaps forever relinquish claim to hegemony over other forms of life that has been so destructive of our fellow Earth-mates and the planet in general. Secondly, it would discourage the practice of blaming and praising—manipulative devices intended to coerce vulnerable souls to do another's bidding—and acknowledge that no one can fundamentally be held accountable for anything. We would be more prone to respond objectively to threats, without absolving anyone of the responsibility to do the right thing. Menaces to society could be dealt with, even harshly, not from malice, hatred or vengeance, but to allow for orderly societal functioning and progress.

CHOICE

In "Free Will," a chapter of *13 Things that Don't Make Sense* (2008), author and physicist Michael Brooks describes investigations of neuroscientists concerning the effects of electromagnetic brain stimulation on motor responses of subjects. He cites the work in the 1990s of Itzhak Fried, a neurosurgeon at Yale University School of Medicine, who was able to elicit motor responses in epileptic patients by stimulating brain sites with electric charges. Responses at certain sites were first sensed as "urges" at low stimulation, followed by action with greater stimulation. Patrick Haggard, professor at University

College, London's Institute of Neurological Sciences, has done similar experiments, convincing him that "there is no such thing as free will" since these studies seem to link actions with physical brain phenomena.[20] In the conclusion of a study of "free won't,"[21] described as "inhibition of prepotent action," the authors state that "our results suggest the "free won't" may be no more free than free will."

Psychologist Steven Pinker believes that "free will is a fictional construction, but it has applications in the real world." The supposition (and fear) is that general dissemination of this knowledge could jeopardize our entire social structure, built upon the idea of individual responsibility, and that it would lead to dismantling our legal and cultural structures and institutions. In a Time magazine article (Jan. 29, 2007) Dr. Pinker, Johnstone Professor of Psychology at Harvard University, discusses the origin of consciousness. He alludes to behavioral links with areas in the gray matter of the human brain, leading to his speculation on the identity of mind and matter. He asserts that recent studies indicate behavior predicated on evolved physical processes, that all of our thoughts and actions are manifestations of material events in the brain. Consciousness must have evolved in the same manner as any other feature of an organism, and must be made of the same stuff. "Although neither problem (the easy: to distinguish conscious from unconscious mental computation; the hard: explaining how subjective experience arises from neural computation) has been solved, neuroscientists agree on many features of both of them, and the feature they find least controversial is the one that many people outside the field find the most shocking ... the idea that *our thoughts, sensations, joys and aches consist entirely of physiological activity in the tissues of the brain* (italics added)." He dismisses the idea that consciousness resides in an ethereal soul that uses the brain like a PDA[22]. "Scientists ... have amassed evidence that every aspect of consciousness can be tied to the brain ... For many non-scientists this is a terrifying prospect. Not only does it strangle the hope that we might survive the death of our bodies, but it also seems to *undermine the notion that we are free agents responsible for our choices*—not just in this lifetime, but in a life to come" (italics added). Popular media do not often deal with such esoteric subjects, particularly when the conclusions could shake some of our most fundamental ideas and beliefs.

Aside from those with dubious claims of extrasensory perception, most of us, like Missourians, have to be shown. All we are sure about is what we are *told* by our senses. Our sensory apparatus receives physical information, which is processed by organs and their components obeying the laws of nature. However, not only is our sensory apparatus subject to its own physical variability, but also the information it receives is transmitted across a nebulous void. The human body (and every other physical entity) never actually touches anything. Our cells, as those of any other physical object, are comprised of molecules and atoms, each of the latter's nuclei surrounded by orbiting electrons of uncertain character, expressed alternatively as waves or particles, depending on the method of observation. The laws of physics preclude two electrons in precisely the same location: forces of repulsion would rise to the infinite if the distance between any two reduced to zero (this is also precluded by Pauli's Exclusion Principle). So physical contact is impossible. For other sensory impressions we rely on intermediates. Sound, for example, is a complex of pressure waves processed mechanically by the tympanic membrane (eardrum), which activates a mechanical linkage that signals the auditory nerve, which in turn sends chemical and electronic pulses to the brain. Whatever humankind has discovered from observation is physical in nature. Metaphysical perceptions only arise, so far as we know, from the peculiar human imagination, a trait acquired through long history of evolutionary development.

PHILOSOPHICAL UNDERPINNINGS OF FREE WILL

Philosophers from the ancient Greeks to recent times have pondered the existence of free will. Flora and fauna evolving and functioning under omnipresent laws of nature would appear to lack the ability to choose. However, before revelations concerning the composition of the genome and discoveries of neuroscience in the 20th century, almost invariably philosophers ultimately came down of the side of man apart from nature in some measure, and thereby "allowed" choice.

Hegel traces human consciousness through its evolutionary stages, and at some point proclaims the existence of free will. "As a free will, a being 'for itself' a person has the consciousness of being something determined, insofar as one is a 'free will', and as something indeterminate insofar as 'free will' is an abstraction, a universal. It is by virtue of being a 'free will', a being who is 'for itself', that a person gains consciousness of his duty to self to endow his free will with external concrete determination such that it can realize individual freedom." Mind is regarded as the goal of nature, from which it is derived; whatever is in nature is manifested in higher form in the mind. But once created, mind rises above the limitations of nature and becomes free to exercise itself through art, religion, and philosophy, and to create its own reality (Kowalski 2004).

Kant also postulates morality predicated on the existence of an autonomous free will, from which moral action derives and which is universal among humans as an outgrowth of our commonly shared rational faculties. Rummel (1975): "For Kant, freedom is an independence of the will of motivations, character, and external causes. It is more than just the power to choose. Freedom is the power to fulfill our moral oughts (ought implies can), to will as reason directs, to be a first cause of events."

David Hume (1993) combines liberty with causality deriving from natural imperatives. He posits two types of liberty, the choice of whether or not to act according to determinations of the will. One is "hypothetical," a characteristic of everyone who is not otherwise constrained (incarcerated). Another type is "liberty of spontaneity": a person may enjoy "liberty of spontaneity" but still be denied "hypothetical liberty." What you would prefer to do (spontaneity), and what you have capacities or means to do (hypothetical), are two different things.

John Locke, in *An Essay Concerning Human Understanding* of the 17th century, proposed the *tabula rasa* or blank slate theory for human development, in which the rules for acquiring and interpreting information are derived from sensory exposures. The mind, character and soul are thereby free and self-defined under the constraints of an immutable human nature. Sigmund Freud also alludes to the concept of *tabula rasa* in his psychoanalysis, where environmental history plays the major role in the development of personality and character. In *Three Essays on Sexuality* (1915), Freud outlines the stages in child development (oral, anal, phallic, latency period, and genital), each responding to libidinal urgings that largely determine the adult personality, and presumably, choices.

The existence or absence of choice has politico-religious implications. Paul, the disciple of Jesus, parlayed the ancient idea of free will into a formula for expanding the reaches of Christendom. His appeal was to co-opt the minds of those whose sufferings could be relieved only by willfully accepting Jesus as the savior of mankind and following his precepts. There could be no promise of heaven against the threat of everlasting hell if one did not have choice. "Jesus saith unto him, I am the way, the truth, and the life: no man cometh unto the Father, but by me."[23] Accept my word or suffer the consequences. It is well within your powers.

Charles Darwin believed that the combination of heredity and environment determine all feelings, thoughts and actions. Although some philosophers argue for "soft" determinism—a notion of freedom somehow compatible with unbridled cause and effect—in one of his notebooks Darwin confessed that "one doubts [the] existence of free will" and concluded that *humans deserve neither credit nor blame for their actions* (italics added). Viorst (1998) points to tacit acknowledgement of his material perspective on humanity: "Thought, however unintelligible it may be, seems as much function of organ, as bile of liver. This view should teach one profound humility; *one deserves no credit for anything. Nor ought one to blame others* (italics added)."

On the other hand, proponents of the existentialist philosophical movement[24], whose central theme is the uniqueness of the individual, postulate that a human being is free to define oneself. Paul Sartre (*Existentialism is a Humanism*): "man first of all exists, encounters himself, surges up in the world—and defines himself afterwards." Definition is dynamic: one can choose a course of action, to be magnanimous rather than cruel, but that was yesterday. Today is another story.

It's axiomatic that you can't build a solid house on a shaky foundation. Philosophers through the 19th century had little awareness of the evolution of human development, DNA or links between physical, chemical and biological processes in the body and behavior. They otherwise might have been less prone to think of humanity as somehow insulated, and even isolated from nature.

Do we really need science and inconsistencies in politico-religious dogma (Chapter 6) to tell us that the will is not free? How could it be otherwise? Life for humans is a process begun with a sexual encounter that, even if willfully undertaken, certainly could not, in the wildest of our imaginings, have involved the willfulness of the zygote produced. Does a child decide to be born? Even granting the infusion of will from the time of conception, certainly the mere fact that the all-important choice—to be or not to be—is denied by definition to any living being obviates the significance of choice in the course of a human life. Even the Buddha's concept of reincarnation does not attribute rebirth to the will of the unborn.

What we call *choice* is the behavioral response of an individual to one's external environment. For such a complex organism, the environment is both immediate and remote. The immediate environment is everything within range of the senses, including what is available through the appurtenances of modern technology. The remote environment consists of the range of images and scenarios derived from knowledge, experience, conjecture—all of the conceptual mechanisms within the human mental arsenal.

The compactness of that great human invention, mathematics, can be called upon to succinctly express the proposition that behavior follows from a virtually infinite stream of antecedents that brings the organism to its present state, upon which its response to an external stimulus is completely dependent, but indeterminate (for those not mathematically inclined, the next four paragraphs may be skipped without missing a beat; they are simply an imperative arising from the author's own history).

So differential behavior (the instantaneous response to a stimulus) might (audaciously) be expressed in the following mathematical form:

$$\frac{dB}{dt} = \Psi(g, \Delta g, e, s)$$

dB	differential behavior, or instantaneous response
dt	time differential
g	genetic endowment
Δg	genetic mutations during lifetime of organism
e	environmental, or experiential history
s	spiritual bequest
Ψ	stochastic (probabilistic) function

This is intended only to emphasize the relationship between instantaneous change in behavior of an organism over time, as a function of genetic endowment, genetic mutations that occur within the cells of the living organism, environmental or experiential history, and perhaps a spiritual[25] bequest.[26] It should also be noted that the relationship is random (stochastic)[27], meaning that within a range of possibilities for the determinants of behavior to be expressed, at any instant the precise value can't be predicted. One source of randomness, even though it is generally perceived as relevant only to subatomic particles, is quantum effects. "Until the past decade, experimentalists had not confirmed that quantum behavior persists on a macroscopic scale. Today, however, they routinely do. These effects are more pervasive than anyone ever suspected. They may operate in the cells of our body."[28] Chaos is another factor. It isn't strictly random in nature, but rather generates indeterminacy in the functioning of biological systems.[29] The character of an organism, at any instant of time, is a product of the cumulative effects of the above factors—it's history. The equation states that, in the same sense that "we are what we eat," we are what we have accumulated as a consequence of genetic makeup (parental endowment plus postnatal mutations), the sum of our experiences and perhaps the infusion of a spiritual component that provides some moral (or immoral) foundation.

Behavior of an organism is considered a continuum, comprised of differential elements that only in the macroscopic scale of time reveal a pattern that we can discern. It may well be that macroscopic responses are, in fact, more discrete in their elementary nature, perhaps packaged in small elements, or "quanta," related to minimal neural response intervals. It can be argued that triggering of synapses, which control neural functions, is inherently digital in nature.[30] It is also possible that only a finite sequence of neural operations constitute a meaningful experience, which thereafter becomes an incremental effect of an organism's history. In either case, the response to a stimulus is essentially instantaneous, and subsequent responses are conditioned by all previous differential behaviors, with environmental feedback further conditioning the elements suggested in the above function: more concretely, life doesn't exist in a vacuum.

Consider a newly born human infant. It has a genetic endowment, and some limited experiential history in the womb. Piaget[31] and others tell us that the character of a child is substantially formed at a very early age by the nature of, and before there is any chance of willfully having an influence on, her surroundings. Nor was the child's genetic makeup of her own choosing. So the factors that formed the child's character were essentially beyond her control.

The infant had no parental choice, maternal or paternal. The external environment certainly is not under the control of so helpless a creature. Whether or not she is yet the recipient of some spiritual bequest is uncertain; even if so, it is not of her own doing. So, the child controls none of the factors upon which her response (or choice) is predicated. At this point it's probably not very controversial to assert that free choice is not an option for a newborn infant.

In a subsequent instant, not long after the first, the infant remains a product of her history. This is an inescapable fact, even into adulthood. Every differential behavior evokes its own external response, which form part of the child's experience. There is a virtually continuous interaction between the infant and her external environment, so that at any instant of time none of the factors that could influence behavior are under her control. Neither the older child, nor the adult that carries the same historical baggage, is completely free to choose a course of action. At any instant of time, the child (or any other organism) exists, molded only by her endowment and history.

Yet, in the United States and other countries, despite having experienced abuse and other destabilizing exposures, children of any age can be tried as adults for homicide and other violent offenses. The US Department of Justice estimates that about ten percent of homicides are committed by youths less than eighteen years of age. Many were formerly sentenced to life imprisonment with no chance of parole, but the Supreme Court ruled in 2010 that the practice was disallowed for juveniles except those convicted of murder. Thousands of children who committed lesser offenses are still sent to adult prisons. In some states courts can waive juvenile offenders as young as thirteen to be tried as adults. If a child is to be held accountable for anti-social behavior, at what point in life is this justified? The evolution of behavior is a continuum, so there is no point in time at which it can be attributed to moral turpitude.

The history of any organism invariably involves phenomena with elements of randomness, so that up to the instant of exposure to a stimulus, within a range its character is fundamentally indeterminate; its environment is similarly affected by randomness. This is what makes life, as we perceive it, interesting. If we had evolved in a deterministic universe we would be automatons, with immutable models wired into our brains rather than what passes for reasoning.[32]

Our rational faculties don't lead to the existence of freedom to choose; only injection of moral standards by an interventionist god or other creator could render us responsible for our choices. Considering the litany of abhorrent acts committed by humans throughout history, the mayhem inflicted on the rest of life by this most dangerous creature ever to walk the earth, this seems highly unlikely. Only a malevolent deity could have conferred such a property on humans, a possibility that is anathema to believers.

What should be comforting is at once a source of unease, if not terror. What demonic forces will be unleashed if no one is responsible for anything, even the most heinous crime? Religionists and sociologists are terrified that if the word gets out, a species totally unprepared for its consequences could easily run amok. What mayhem would result if unrepressed masses got the notion that they can't, or at least shouldn't, be held responsible for anything?

Intuition tells us that we can calmly accept this information without panic (although not without a program for a change in our priorities). If a child is caged at an early age, abused continually and deprived of all that children need to grow up secure, sane and otherwise healthy, it's clear that barbarous acts committed could not be held against her. On the other hand, a person reared with all the support elements necessary to allow for identity with, and full participation in, her social milieu would be most unlikely to commit antisocial acts, but is similarly undeserving of praise or blame.

We can live content in the knowledge that we are devoid of free will while pursuing our everyday lives as if we did. At the same time, we are likely to be, in a sense, more compassionate knowing that no one is really responsible for bad behavior. We can punish, and even commit miscreants to the most severe penalties under extreme conditions, but with understanding and never with malice or hate. If we are able to adopt as our goal enlightenment of populations around the world, this can be a liberating process. The more people are disabused of their mythical notions the more likely it is that rational processes will lead us to a better way of life. Man does not live by bread alone. We are multidimensional and so can live in the day-to-day world while at the same time being acutely conscious of our inescapable identity with nature.

SPIRIT[33]

The spiritual quality is defined as a moral foundation divinely conferred on the individual human being, an endowment that bestows magnanimity, compassion and good will, along with their behavioral consequences; however, the individual remains free to elect among socially abhorrent behavioral options, such as malignancy, oppression or dishonesty.

An omnipotent force either has the power to direct the future of everything, and free will (choice) does not exist—so that the spirit is superfluous—or it confers the power of choice upon its creations and thus relinquishes omnipotence.

If human morality, the aspect of our spiritual characteristic that purportedly causes us to behave altruistically rather than exploitatively, is the essential quality that separates man from beast, we can speculate on the precise point in human evolution that this quality was conferred. Whether the nature of the evolutionary process is continuous or punctuated, there is general agreement that reproductive success of a trait introduced by genetic mixing or mutation is the basic mechanism. Could the spirit have *evolved* under the guiding hand of a creative force? Paleontology tells us that we derive from very simple organisms whose behavior could only be instinctive, responding to external stimuli as determined only by their genetic endowments. Speciation is generally attributed to physical isolation of a segment of a population that changes genetically to the point that fertile breeding between the original and isolated population is no longer possible. The omnipotent force (or the spirit-conferring creator) would have had a very difficult time deciding at what point in the evolution or speciation process the offspring of a remote ancestor qualified for human-hood, and thus to be infused with moral fiber. Was it at the point of the genetic mutation, or when the mutation was first expressed in the body of an offspring? How about siblings, some of whom received the non-mutated allele from the sex cell of the parent and some who did receive the crucial mutant? Some are on the path to human-hood, and thus conferred with moral fiber, and others free of the terrible onus and thus at liberty to continue their beastly ways without fear of retribution.

It is possible that the spirit (or choice) is granted incrementally to the individual, perhaps as zygotes mature, so that in each step toward the fully accountable state only a portion of omnipotence is relinquished.

Or, spirit could be granted at the species level, perhaps in a linear process. If there are so many variants in the genetic makeup of humans as compared with our remote non-human ancestor, then the buildup could have occurred in direct proportion to the percentage of transitional variations realized at a particular stage of the process. Human spirituality could have grown in intensity as we approached the fully modern human state. During the transition phase, the standard by which the omnipotent force would then either absolve the individual of blame or exact retribution would perhaps be proportionately adjusted.

As evolution is an endless progression, we humans may still be only partially held accountable for our thoughts and deeds. If spirituality is conferred only at the fully developed state, we may still lack the property. However, we may be at the end of the evolutionary trajectory, in which case we may already enjoy (or suffer with) all the morality we will ever have. A cursory review of recorded human history, invariant over time in its behavioral gamut of tyranny, mayhem, murder and exploitation, leaves one with the impression that this is one gift horse that should be looked in the mouth.

In any case, the capacity of the omnipotent force both to set behavioral benchmarks and to exact retribution seems logically inconsistent—lack of omnipotence would appear to nullify the capacity to punish transgressors.

But it isn't necessary to conjure up the notion of spirit to understand altruism. In fact, the concept of spirit is a distraction from a more comprehensible and supportable basis for cooperation. A practical way to comprehend the incidence of moral behavior is reciprocity. In an enlightened individual, capable of sensing the infinite stream of behavioral ripples that emanate from any thought or action, the rational faculty invokes operational morality based upon analysis of consequences. Essentially something like the *quid pro quo* concept embedded in the Golden Rule acts as a guide for individual behavior and for conditioning the external environment, fostering development of individuals who similarly sense the benefits to be enjoyed when they and their neighbors are mutually well-intentioned.

INDETERMINACY

Uncertainty surrounding future events is the delicious part of human existence. It is the flavor and spice of life. However, even the genius of Albert Einstein, as expressed in a letter of 21 March, 1942 to Cornelius Lanczos[34], could not fully accept it: "You are the only person I know who has the same attitude towards physics as I have: belief in the comprehension of reality through something basically simple and unified ... It seems hard to sneak a look at God's cards. But that he plays dice ... is something that I cannot believe for a single moment."

Einstein's collaborators and friends, Banesh Hoffmann and Helen Dukas (1981) expressed his unwillingness to accept indeterminacy in physical processes: "We see here Einstein's vivid way of looking at and expressing dissatisfaction with the quantum theory, with its denial of determinism and its limitation to probabilistic, statistical predictions. He was himself a pioneer in the development of the quantum theory, but he remained convinced that there was need for a different understanding."

Despite Einstein's reservations, virtually all of the scientific community now accepts the reality of indeterminacy. George Johnson (1995), a science journalist of the New York Times, in his masterful exposition on the common roots of science and mysticism, very neatly categorizes and sums up the sources of uncertainty in physical processes. Uncertainty is perceived as randomness, whether or not the underlying mechanism is random. First is apparent randomness arising from complexity of a system that we cannot adequately model or analyze. Second is *chaos*, a characteristic of complex systems: a salient feature of chaotic systems is that they are critically dependent on initial conditions—a minor difference or change in distribution of particles or temperature in China can cause tidal waves on the east coast of N. America. Even if the system is essentially deterministic, the final outcome is basically unpredictable. Third is quantum uncertainty, as explained by Heisenberg, which operates at the subatomic level. Johnson asserts (citing scientific authorities) that micro uncertainty can produce macroscopic effects.

In a 1998 conversation with Dr. Jeffrey Mishlove[35], Professor Murray

Gell-Mann, Nobel Laureate in physics, describes the link between the principle of indeterminacy, which occurs at the subatomic level, and free will that humans seem to experience. Uncertainty is a fundamental characteristic in the domain of the ultra-small. The rules of quantum mechanics govern the behavior of minute subatomic particles, which are usually described in terms of probability, rather than having definitive characteristics such as energy and momentum.

As a rule in the scientific community, specialists in one field are loath to express their views concerning others. However, Gell-Mann, ventures to extend his understanding of physical processes to the domain of behavioral science by linking indeterminacy, as a fundamental characteristic of matter and energy, to the behavior of organisms, including humans. If the mind/matter duality is an illusion, then choice is not logically possible since matter—fermions, bosons and their more elementary forms—are not attributed with any sort of choice, even though there may be variations in the way processes are carried out because there are inherent uncertainties in nature.

However, Gell-Mann doesn't "actually adopt the point of view that our subjective impression of free will, which is a kind of indeterminacy behavior, comes from quantum mechanical indeterminacy." He suggests that it has other derivations, such as partial information, but mentions the link as a "logical possibility ... quantum mechanics gives us fundamental, *unavoidable indeterminacy* (italics added), so that alternative histories of the universe can be assigned probability. Sometimes the probabilities are very close to certainties, but they're never really certainties."

According to Gell-Mann, the fundamental basis for indeterminacy in behavior of the universe is quantum-mechanical uncertainty. An organism, a component of the universe, must be similarly affected. Even though this form of uncertainty is operative at the subatomic level, which might involve a photon (the fundamental unit of electromagnetic energy) exchange within the human brain, there are macroscopic implications. One mechanism might involve small quantum-mechanical fluctuations amplified in some cases by the classical phenomenon of chaos, where the outcome of a process in a complex system, say the human brain, is highly sensitive to changes in its initial state. There are also uncertainties in the information transmitted. A further source of indeterminacy in behavioral response to a stimulus from interaction with the outside world is that the information received is affected by the sensory characteristics of the receiver.

There is an understandable hesitancy in Gell-Mann's assessment of a possible link between free will and physical processes, as he is stepping outside the bounds of disprovable propositions that Karl Popper (2002) insisted as necessary for a scientific theory. "A theory which is not refutable by any conceivable event is non-scientific. Irrefutability is not a virtue of a theory (as people often think) but a vice." To scientifically test that all human behavior is linked to physical processes rather than an essential spirit is probably beyond the realm of possibility.

Berkeley computer scientist James Crutchfield suggests that there are macroscopic effects of inherently uncertain subatomic phenomena, estimating "that the gravitational pull of an electron randomly shifting position at the edge of the Milky Way, can change the outcome of a billiard game on Earth."[36] Couldn't a photon from Betelgeuse (a star in the constellation Orion) trigger a neuron that can affect the behavior of an organism, even one in the shape of a human?

As a product of natural processes, it's unlikely that humans can ever discover all of nature's secrets. We can only view phenomena at the subatomic level as inherently probabilistic, in accordance with discoveries of quantum mechanics, which would appear to preclude absolute knowledge. In one explanation of quantum phenomena (Niels Bohr's "Copenhagen interpretation"), matter is characterized by Schrödinger's probability waves so that at the subatomic level particles only reveal their nature when they have to do something. Furthermore, according to the *multiverse hypothesis*, it's possible that there are an infinite number of parallel configurations of the universe that give rise to alternative realities that are only manifested when observed. Doesn't it follow that there is no objective reality, or more to the point, no objective reality upon which the future is predicated?

"Quantum mechanics ... establish(ed) that the predictions of science are necessarily probabilistic. We can predict the odds of attaining one outcome, we can predict the odds of another, but we generally can't predict which will actually happen. This well-known departure from hundreds of years of scientific thought is surprising enough. But there's a more confounding aspect of quantum theory that receives less attention ... no one has been able to explain why only one of the many possible outcomes in any given situation actually happens. When we do experiments, when we examine the world, we all agree that we encounter a single definite reality. Yet, more than a century after the quantum revolution began, there is no consensus among the world's physicists as to how this basic fact is compatible with the theory's mathematical expression."[37]

BLAME AND PRAISE

If there is no objective reality, can the absence of free will be far behind? Should people be castigated for misdeeds or praised for good deeds?

Paul Watzlawick (1976) suggests three possibilities: (1) reality has no order and confusion reigns, with life a "psychotic nightmare;" (2) we invent an order and then delude ourselves into thinking that there is something out there for us to choose; or (3) there is an order created by some higher being with whom we long to communicate. Watzlawick asserts that if we believe that choice, as any other event, is predetermined from all causes in the past, then free will or choice is an illusion. Even if one thinks there is an alternative, that thought is an echo from the past events. "It does not matter how I choose, for whatever I choose is the only thing I *can* choose. There are no alternatives, and even if I think there are, this thought itself is nothing but the effect of some cause in my personal past." Whether as perpetrator or recipient of an action, the event is determined by antecedent events even though "I may call (it) causality, the Being, the divine experimenter, or fate."

Two tenets of psychoanalysis support the contention that free will is illusory: that what we do or think is strongly influenced by past events, and that we are driven primarily by instinctive needs and unconscious impulses. John Bargh and Ezekquiel Morsella (2008) point out that "There are a multitude of behavioral impulses generated at any point in time derived from our evolved motives and preferences, cultural norms and values, past experiences in similar situations and what other people are doing in that same situation." These impulses provide unconscious motives, preferences and behavioral tendencies in response to perceptions about others' behavior. " There certainly seems to be no shortage of suggestions from our unconscious about what to do in any given situation." If unconscious impulses are such influential factors in behavior, can the will be operationally free?

A study at the University of Minnesota[38] found significant similarities between twins raised in separate homes with different parents, strongly supporting the importance of genetics in determining physical appearance and other attributes, such as personality and abilities. Correlations were indicated for all twin pairs raised outside their genealogical, biological, and ancestral groupings. Orphaned, fostered, or adopted children's behavior or inheritable traits could be activated by environmental factors or adopted parents, but only within the limitations of their genes. The study found that identical twins (monozygotic, or genetic clones) separated at birth and reared in different family settings had about an equal chance of being similar to the co-twin in terms of personality, interests, and attitudes as one who has been reared with his or her co-twin, concluding that similarities between twins are attributable to genes, and not environment. The similarities and differences in behavior patterns of identical twins point decidedly toward the identity of mind and matter: each of us is an organism whose response to the external environment is determined by our genetic and experiential history following the dictates of nature's biological rules.

"Prevailed upon by my informational 'nose,' *I too make choices I cannot help making, given the prevailing landscape of information* (italics added). Regardless of the careful reasoning I may marshal in support of my actions, the choices I make are ultimately animal choices. In fact, the only thing that distinguishes humans in the arena of animal behavior is our naïve belief that our decision-making processes are primarily cortical and rational and therefore unlike those of all other animals. ...We may agonize over alternative courses of action for as long as we like, using whatever combination of reason and intuition we feel is appropriate, but *our final decisions still represent the inevitable reactions of our particular genetic makeup to the peculiar patterns of perceived information investing us at the time.* In other words, *the choices we make are those we cannot help making in the circumstances* (italics added)."[39]

But there is a tendency to insist that people have to be held accountable for their actions that in spite of genetic disposition or unwholesome experiences, some standards of behavior have to be maintained to keep us on the straight and narrow.

If humans and other living organisms are not responsible for their behavior, is blame a legitimate concept? Do individuals or groups who despoil the earth or who commit crimes deserve condemnation? Do heroes merit special recognition, or are they merely doing what comes naturally, under the circumstances? It would be quite a departure from the ordinary reaction to good or evil deeds to recognize that behavior is not under the control of the perpetrator. Inescapable subservience to the dictates of genetic instructions would appear to preclude choice, and thereby absolves every individual from responsibility for actions. That's not to say that societies don't need institutions that praise or punish, but they can function more effectively with more comprehensive understanding of behavioral underpinnings.

The illusion (or perhaps more accurately, self-delusion) of free will and the duality of mind and matter are essential to humanity's survival. "It has been argued that something called 'genetic determinism' is a suspect concept in that it offers too easy an excuse for past actions. ... This argument fails to account for the fact that we could only take *cynical* advantage of those excuses (that behavior is genetically determined) if the central proposition were *untrue.* As it is, however, even that degree of free will remains unavailable to us, and for very good reason. If we were not continually at the beck and call of our genetic code, and if we did not instinctively believe in the duality of existence (the body and the spirit) and act accordingly, then our mythically driven civilization would grind to a halt. In other words, our delusions of spiritual autonomy are essential to the survival of our species ... a proper understanding of our genetic subservience would also rob us of all our heroes and villains, since they too are governed by their genetic imperatives and no more worthy of reverence or condemnation than the rest of us."[40]

The vagaries of nature allow that any person at any time can act within a range of possibilities. It's only a question of the degree of possible variation (which can be thought about in statistical terms, for example the bell curve) and time. The monkey at the keyboard will eventually tap out an etude of Chopin. If the synapses line up in a certain way and a photon from Alpha Centauri happens to impinge upon the sensory apparatus at the proper time, almost anything can happen in the cranial recesses of an individual, with behavioral consequences. Princes might beg, and paupers disseminate good tidings.

Darwin explains that the underlying imperative for individual behavior is essentially security and survival. Constrained by that framework, behavior is indeterminate, normally within ranges that do not raise eyebrows, but occasionally off the wall, the equivalent of rare celestial alignments that cause earthquakes and tidal waves.

The absence of free will, and the indeterminacy that characterizes future events, does not recommend passivity. We do what we do what we do. We are compelled to play out what is in us, and hope that it leads to something better.

So evil, obstinacy and other despicable traits are to be pitied rather than despised. When we regard self-serving politicians, antisocial behavior of criminals, pompous assertions by scribes, insensitive treatment of fellow species by hog-butchers or terrorist acts of fanatics, we can best try to correct their waywardness, but not blame them for their transgressions from good sense. As Jesus admonished while suffering crucifixion, "forgive them, for they do not know what they are doing."[41] Pity them, and put them away if necessary, but humbly, because they are only blindly subservient to the forces of nature.

WE HAVE NO CHOICE

Although counterintuitive, there's no reason to assume that humans are endowed with free will or choice. Certainly it "feels" as if we can choose, but so far as we know this can only be one of the traits that nature has bestowed through the process of human evolution. The importance of widespread acknowledgment of the true capacities of *H. sapiens* can't be overstated, particularly regarding the matter of choice—the basis for assigning blame and dispensing praise that are so effective as social polarizers. Our failure to acknowledge the absence of choice is an impediment to social progress and a grave threat to life. This illusion is behind much violence among humans, mass extinctions of other species that have shared our trek across the eons, and devastation of the planet that is our common home. Recognizing our limitations does not have to diminish the richness of life's tapestry; instead, it has the potential to transform us into a much more tolerant and accommodating animal, with positive benefits for the quality of our lives and for those of our travelling companions.

The absence of choice does not imply a deadening determinism for human life. "The uniqueness of our dictatorial genes guarantees our unpredictability and the ultimate failure of anyone who attempts to control our behavior. Thanks to the autonomy of our DNA, we remain indomitable and therefore free in the only sense that matters to us."[42] The material unity of matter and mind, coupled with the inherent variability in physical processes, assures the unpredictability of individual or collective human fate.[43]

CHAPTER 2

FECUNDITY TO A FAULT

At this point in time (2014) there are about 7.3 billion humans on Earth. In the course of one lifetime, the proverbial threescore and ten (70) years, human numbers have increased to this level from about 2.3 billion, an average rate of growth of a bit over 1.5 percent that has produced over three times as many alive now as compared with seven decades ago. Projections by the United Nations Population Fund (UNFPA) indicate that there will almost certainly be 9 billion or more of us by mid century and perhaps as many as 12 billion by the year 2100.

By the most conventional measure of prosperity, in the face of this expansion, world real per capita growth in Gross Domestic Product (GDP) has averaged a little more than 2 percent over this span[44]; nevertheless, 21 percent of people in the developing world in 2010 (1.22 billion people) had an income at or below $1.25 a day in 2005 prices.[45] According to the World Bank report, this represented an improvement from 43 percent in 1990 (1.91 billion) and 52 percent in 1981 (1.94 billion). However (as economist/philosopher Kenneth Boulding once said of believers in indefinite growth on a finite planet), anyone who believes that $1.25 per day is sufficient to allow for a person to live decently, to reach for any significant level of personal growth, is "either mad or an economist."

Despite the apparent improvement, income *disparity* is growing.

Even when people are not destitute, they may feel poor on account of their status relative to others and barriers to upward mobility:

"In Eastern Europe and the CIS countries the per capita income of the highest quintile is 7 times that of the lowest quintile, in Russia 14 times. In industrial countries the per capita income of the highest quintile is 7 times that of the lowest, and in Japan only 4 times. In Lesotho the per capita income of the richest 20 percent is 22 times that of the poorest 20 percent. For South Africa the figure is 19 times, and for Kenya 18 times."[46] In the US, the top 300 thousand people had about as much income as the lowest 150 million.[47] The top group's average income in 2007 was 440 times that of the lowest group, nearly twice the disparity that existed in 1980.

Increasing income spreads between "haves" and "have-nots" are a reflection of excessive world population. Producers of goods and services, abetted by their political and religionist collaborators, salivate at the surplus wealth to be skimmed from growing minions of workers and consumers ready and willing to play their respective roles. Rather than work to attenuate the looming threat of unsustainable population growth, they seek optimality with respect to their own corporate objectives. Technology has permitted global marketing reach, while disseminating information that ironically has the impact of reducing fertility.[48] Overall, these developments have been positive for powerful market players, permitting concentration and more capital-intensive production. The result is global widening of income disparity[49] and increasing numbers of destitute people in some regions, whose procreation rate tends to increase with the degree of uncertainty in survival of their offspring.[50]

Conventional measures of prosperity distort the true impact of changes in income distribution. Subsistence farmers, for example, have little cash income, but through hard work and good husbanding practices can maintain a simple but adequate lifestyle. As land is divided among siblings, increasing numbers are forced to seek wage income, usually at the lowest rate permitted by the supply/demand relationship. This now appears statistically as an increase in the wages of low-income workers, whose life qualities have actually deteriorated as a result.

While on the surface things are getting better according to World Bank indicators, most of the reduction in poverty in the decades since the early 1980s is attributable to rapid growth in China.[51] GDP in that country has been growing by over 9 percent per annum and should surpass the US economy within a year or two. However, on a per capita basis US income is far higher than China, and is likely to remain so despite China's overtaking the US in GDP. In addition, the relationship may also be distorted by China's manipulation of the official rate of currency exchange to the US dollar.[52]

Much of the improvement in income is attributable to spending on the credit card. Budget deficits in the world's largest economies feed into consumption of the integrated global economy. In 2010 projected budget deficits for some of the leading economies, as a percentage of their GDPs are as follows: Germany 6.5, Italy 6.2, US 9.0, UK 7.1, Japan a staggering 170. Deficits in the US are projected at about the same level for the second decade of the 21st century, although recently some apparent improvement was spurred by extraordinary intervention of the Federal Reserve Bank.[53] .

Advocates of a hands-off policy on world population argue that there is little evidence that present numbers can't be sustained by tapping Earth's resources, that alarmists on population have been "crying wolf" for decades without the predicted catastrophes. They point to the power of the global economic system to adjust to change, substituting one material for another in short supply, for example.

Jeffrey Sachs, Director of the Earth Institute at Colombia University, and architect of "shock therapy"[54] for economies of the former Soviet bloc in the 1980s, apparently believes that the trend toward increasing poverty in the Third World can be overcome. In developing his exposition on the theme, a plan to put an end to global poverty, to reduce disease, armed conflict and environmental degradation within 20 years, he proposes market solutions.[55] According to Sachs, it is the responsibility, as well as in the self-interest of industrialized countries, to assist the less-developed countries in achieving a path to peace and prosperity by helping them to develop market-based systems for production and consumption. More mouths to feed and bodies to clothe does not factor into his calculus.

Little has been reported concerning a link between climate change, which many experts predict will have dire consequences for the future of life, and human population. However, in its *State of the World Population Report* of 2009, the UN Population Fund does suggest that human numbers may be relevant: "Although its role is difficult to quantify amidst the many factors contributing to emissions growth, population growth is among the factors influencing total emissions in industrialized as well as developing countries. Each additional person in a population will consume food and require housing, and ideally most will take advantage of transportation, which consumes energy, and may use fuel to heat homes and have access to electricity." The report points out that the impact of population on emissions is greatest for those countries with the highest levels of per capita energy and material consumption—the industrialized countries. For those countries with population declines, for example Japan and Italy, the International Energy Agency projects emissions to be lower in 2030 than today.

How do we know that the world is overpopulated? To borrow the phrase of Supreme Court Justice Potter Stewart (regarding pornography), it's not easy to define but we know it when we see it. One only has to observe the multitudes of desperate people around the world, who will never have access to the dream world of poverty alleviation that Sachs suggests is just around the corner, if only ... That the prerequisites for his rosy scenario are impractical and unachievable does not seem to faze Prof. Sachs, nor does the fact that sustaining 7 billion or 9 billion or even 12 billion humans on Earth with anything like a decent standard of living is a pipe dream.

EXTINCTION

Indicators of excessive human population are in plain view. For one thing, the rate of extinction of species that have for eons shared the development path along with humans is the highest since the dinosaurs disappeared 60 million years ago. Some estimates have the extinction rate as much as 100 times the background rate, which would occur in the absence of human impact. "Although the extinction of various species is a natural phenomenon, the rate of extinction occurring in today's world is exceptional—as many as 100 to 1,000 times greater than normal."[56] Fossil evidence confirms that many large mammalian species occupied North America at the time of the human appearance about 12-20 thousand years ago and rapidly became extinct (before entering from Siberia across the land bridge that existed at that time, it's very likely that no human had set foot on the American continents, although this is in dispute as studies suggest some European origins for that era).

Most paleontologists believe human intervention was the cause. Humanity has continued to adversely affect survival prospects for many species, large and small, albeit not through the same mechanisms as the early Americans. Most threats to the continued existence of other species is the result of habitat intrusion, as massive numbers of humans seek living space and exploit the remaining land for crop production, mining resources and disposal of human wastes. As brilliantly explained by Rachel Carson (1962), whose pioneering work has been advanced by many others, much of the extinction is attributable to contamination of Earth's land, air and water.

FOOD SUPPLY AND SPACE

Although cultural patterns differ in this regard around the world, most people seem to enjoy a little breathing room, enough space around them to be able to sit quietly and take in the beauty of nature. While the US population has trebled in the course of one lifetime, Mexico's has quintupled in the same time span. Between 1960 and 2010 Pakistan's population nearly quadrupled to 180 million. The UN projects that Pakistan will add 66 million people within the next 15 years, and become the fourth most populous country in the world, behind India, China and the United States. By that date, the average land area per capita for Pakistan compared with the US will be (sq. km. per capita): US 0.024, Pakistan 0.003. In other words, Pakistan will be *eight times* as densely packed as the US.

It has been argued that there is plenty of room left on Planet Earth for many more humans, that if all the current world population of about 7.3 billion moved to Australia, the average allotment would be about a quarter acre. To put that in perspective, Australia's ecological footprint (see definition below) was 7.8 hectares[57] or 19.2 acres per person. In other words, to maintain their lifestyle, the average "Australian" would need 76 times the area allotted.

The available land surface area of the six habitable continents (excluding Antarctica) is about 45 million sq. miles, if water surfaces are excluded. However, only about a quarter is arable, or about 12 million sq. miles—the remainder is too frigid, arid or mountainous for ordinary cultivation. This leaves about an acre per capita, but only about half is actually under cultivation, a square of about 150 ft. on a side. If the human population increases to 9 billion by mid 21st century as predicted by the UN Population Fund, this will be reduced to a plot of about 135 ft. on a side. About an eighth of the world's population is chronically malnourished or starving, which should indicate how adequate the land available is for food production.[58] In the United States, about 1.2 acres per capita is required for food production, while population growth projected at 2050 (500 million) will reduce available land to 0.6 acres per capita.[59]

The most obvious indication of an impending food crisis is the increase in prices. During the period 2000-2012 the World Bank global food price index rose by 104.5 percent, an average annual rate of 6.5 percent. Of the trends driving the strain on food supply and consequent price increases, actual and anticipated population growth is the central factor. By 2050 UNFPA (UN Population Fund) projects a global population of 9.2 billion—many more mouths to feed and less arable land for food production. Some impacts of inordinate population growth[60]:

- Increasing prices for fuel and the consequent diversion of food crops for fuel production (biofuels); higher oil prices affect cost of food production at many levels, from farm to consumers (currently 20 percent of the US corn crop goes into ethanol production, a figure likely to rise to 32 percent by 2016);
- Greater demand for meat, dairy and fish in developing countries with high and increasing populations and rates of economic growth, e.g., China and India;

- Climate-related decrease in food production, e.g., drought in Australia, cold weather in US and Europe; high rates of erosion and desertification of croplands attributable to intensity of cultivation;
- Export restrictions by some major grain producers, imposed to secure domestic supply;
- Inelastic production system—slow response of production capacity to increases in demand for foods; IFPRI (International Food Policy Research Institute) estimates that aggregate agricultural supply increases by about 1-2 percent for each 10 percent increase in price, and by even less when prices are volatile.

The United Nations Food and Agriculture Organization (FAO) reports that, despite its 12-year concentrated effort, hunger continues as a fact of life for large numbers of people throughout the world. "A total of 842 million people in 2011-13, or around one in eight people in the world, were estimated to be suffering from chronic hunger, regularly not getting enough food to conduct an active life."[61] This figure is lower than the 868 million reported for 2010-12. The total number of reported undernourished has fallen by 17 percent since 1990-92, but doesn't account for those subject to sporadic hunger, a number that could be much higher.

"Scientists and development experts across the globe are racing to increase food production by 50 percent over the next two decades to feed the world's growing population, yet many doubt their chances despite a broad consensus that enough land, water and expertise exist."[62] The US Office of Global Food Security estimates that global food production has to increase by 70 percent before 2050 to feed the growing population.

By some estimates the problem of hunger is not the lack of sufficient food production. In fact, the World Health Organization shows average consumption of food increased (in kcal/day) from 2,358 per capita in 1965 to projected levels of 2,940 in 2015 and 3,050 in 2030, which would represent an increase of almost 30 percent over the period.[63] Rather, hunger and malnourishment are linked to poverty. The United

Nations Millennium Development Goals (MDG) report of 2013 indicates that the proportion of undernourished people in developing regions decreased from 23.2 percent in 1990-1992 to 14.9 percent in 2010-2012, and suggests the target of halving the percentage of people suffering from hunger by 2015 appears to be within reach.

But will the situation really get any better in the future? World leaders often evoke the green revolution of the 1960s and 1970s as a model for progress. The original "revolution," inspired by the work of agronomist Norman Borlaug, was predicated on the introduction of new crop varieties, increased use of fertilizers and irrigation in Asia and Latin America to stave off famines. Impressive increases in yields and reductions in maturity periods were realized, and greater resistance to climate extremes and disease.

However, the new technology required hybridized seeds, which are sterile. Farmers could no longer save seeds for the next planting cycle, but rather had to purchase them from suppliers. Farmers were also faced with increased costs of non-renewable fertilizers and pesticides. Herbicides were needed because the more intensive fertilizer application also stimulates weed growth. High yields and the use of artificial fertilizers often led to degraded soils. As groundwater supplies are depleted from overexploitation, irrigation becomes an increasing problem. Larger farmers operating on a commercial scale generally profited from the "revolution," but small farmers were primarily disadvantaged. Furthermore, the green revolution is probably not replicable in much of Asia and Africa, if only for the lack of irrigation—only about 7 percent of these farmland are irrigated. Another downside is that rents for land producing higher yields became too costly for tenant farmers, denying many of them a livelihood.

Genetically modified organisms (GMO) are another issue, promoted as the next revolution in food production that will stave off world hunger. However, there is widespread concern that GMO are a health hazard. Borlaug stated in a 2002 interview that biotechnology (that is, the use of genetically modified crops) was an extension of the green revolution.[64] Even though the World Trade Organization has declared the practice illegal, the European Union has established rules limiting the use of GMO. Some member states have invoked the "safeguard clause" (Art. 23 Dir. 2001/18/EC) to restrict use or sale of GMO, but must justify the action on grounds of risk to human health or the environment.

A report of the US Department of Agriculture in 2014[65] suggests that land resources are, in principle, adequate to feed twice the current world population, which would amount to about 15 billion people. It's not the capacity to produce the necessary quantities of food, but practical considerations of political will, insufficient investment in modernizing agriculture and disinterest in sustainable land management practices that will "threaten food security in Third World countries and in some, contribute to poverty and famine (analogous to the contention that anyone could lift 500 pounds if they only had the muscles)." This doesn't account for the amount of arable land to be taken out of production, as population increases, for residential, commercial and industrial uses Furthermore, "local and regional food shortages are likely to continue to occur unless mechanisms for equitable food distribution, effective technical assistance and infusions of capital for infrastructure development are implemented in some developing countries." In other words, as stated in an earlier report in 1999, that there is adequate land "does not imply that all will be fed."[66]

Although countries with poor quality land, incapable of sustaining even subsistence agriculture, and which are most greatly afflicted by endemic poverty and hunger, could theoretically be assisted through proper planning and cooperation at the international level, such rosy scenarios, even if political impediments were removed, are unlikely to be realized beyond a few decades at most. Resource constraints, particularly fossil fuels and fertilizers such as potassium and potash, which are needed in virtually every component of industrialized agriculture that now produces the bulk of the world food supply, will most likely preclude adequacy for the world's growing population after they are largely exhausted. Food production will also be adversely affected by climate change and diversion of food production to biofuels).

Much of the global food supply is energy-intensive. Petroleum derivatives are used for fueling farm equipment and also in the production of fertilizers. Without adequate supplies of fuels and lubricants derived from fossil deposits (e.g., natural gas, gasoline, diesel and greases) much of global agriculture as currently practiced would come to a (literally) screeching halt.

Large shale oil fields have been discovered in North America, the Bakken Formation and Williston Basin in Dakotas and Saskatchewan and the Utah/Colorado formation. As early as 2008 the US Geological Service (USGS) announced that the Bakken discovery "has potential to eliminate US dependence on foreign oil." In April 2013, the United States Geological Survey (USGS) estimated oil and gas reserves for the Bakken Formation the Three Forks Formation in North Dakota, South Dakota and Montana at 7.4 billion barrels (BBO) of undiscovered, technically recoverable oil, which represents a doubling of previous assessments (much less than the 300 billion first announced). At the current US consumption of about 18.5 million barrels per day (mbd), these deposits would be depleted in a little over a year. Oil shale of Utah/Colorado contains trillions of barrels, but the technology to extract liquid hydrocarbons from kerogen, a rock-like solid containing organic compound in which it is embedded, is extremely difficult and energy consuming. According to the USGS "It is impossible to substitute unconventional oil (e.g., shale) for high flows of sweet oil—high energy requirements, low flows and oil often of low quality."

Exploitation of shale oil and gas deposits has altered the outlook for energy production in the early 21st century. A process call "fracking" is employed, using high-pressure fluid to fracture rocks in subterranean oil-bearing layers in production of oil and natural gas, in the United States in particular, but emulated in Europe and other countries. This technique has dramatically altered the availability of fossil fuels. The International Energy Agency (IEA) indicates that US oil production in 2013[67] was 12.3 million barrels per day, or mbd (consumption 18.5 mbd), up from 9.2 mbd in 2012, the increase largely attributable to exploitation of shale deposits, making it the largest fossil fuel producer in the world. However, the IEA also predicts that US output will plateau after 2020 and the nation will lose its top ranking at the start of the 2030s. The agency's chief economist, Fatih Birol: "We do not expect this trend will continue after 2020s. It will come to a plateau and decline as a result of the limited resource base of light tight oil." The IEA report states that fracking will not change the energy status in the long run. "The US moves steadily towards meeting all of its energy needs from domestic resources by 2035. But this does not mean that the world is on the cusp of a new era of oil abundance. Light, tight oil shakes the next 10 years, but leaves the longer term unstirred. The Middle East, the only large source of low-cost oil, remains at the center of the longer-term outlook."

In terms of proven reserves of oil, OPEC countries top the list with about 1,200 billion barrels. Russia and the United States are far behind, with 80 and 26.5 billion barrels.[68] To put the US number in perspective, with consumption of 18.5 mbd, US reserves would be exhausted in about four years. However, it's likely that reserve estimates will increase over the next few years as more shale oil deposits are identified for exploitation. World oil consumption is about 90 mbd, or about 33 billion barrels per year. At the current consumption rate, assuming global reserves are about 2.5 trillion barrels, the last drop would be consumed in about 75 years.

Of course, these estimates are highly suspect: the last drop of oil would be extremely expensive to extract, and estimates of reserves will change. There are also huge deposits of coal and natural gas, the latter possibly to become the fuel of choice when costs of oil extraction inevitably increase as the "lowest hanging fruit" is picked first, and as the detrimental impacts of coal consumption are taken into account. Another factor cited by Birol is the state of the oil infrastructure, old and rusting and in need of huge capital investment.[69] There is another cost that is treated as an externality (somebody else pays the bill) by the fossil fuel industry. While fracking is allowing for extraction of oil deposits by breaking up rock formations in which it is embedded, at the same time aquifers that supply water to the host communities are being contaminated. Dangerous chemicals are mixed with large quantities of water and sand and injected into wells at extremely high pressure. Residents of areas where the technique has been employed allege that their drinking water supplies have been contaminated and have reduced capacities as a result of fracking.[70] What is perhaps of even greater concern is the effect on communities afflicted with shale oil disease. As the last economically viable drops of oil are extracted, drillers and wildcatters will pack up their gear and seek other fields to conquer, leaving in their wake despoiled and devastated cities and towns that will likely never return to their pre-boom, often near pristine state.

A presentation prepared by the Society of Petroleum Engineers, Gulf Coast Chapter[71] shows how crude oil production increases are more than offset by steep declines in production of key existing fields in many producing countries, and that new discoveries are generally smaller than existing fields. Significant new finds, such as the Tupi field in Brazil, are in ultra-deep water and in unusually difficult drilling conditions so that extraction will be very expensive.

In a 2009 news article Tom Whipple, a retired CIA analyst and columnist, predicts major changes in American agriculture resulting from depletion of fossil fuels:[72] "With shrinking amounts of increasingly expensive fossil fuels, the American way of agriculture is going to be severely tested. Throw in some climate change and our food producers are going to have trouble keeping up with the demand. Many are worried about depleted soils, and the vast amounts of energy required to grow, store, process, and transfer food raised thousands of miles from the consumer ...." Whipple associates the decline in agriculture with the outbreak of social unrest as foods become scarce and expensive. In contrast to the 1960s "This time riots will be for food and jobs rather than for civil rights and against the draft. The unrest will change everything."

Lester Brown, of the Earth Policy Institute, links the prospect of peak oil production with world food security, as modern agriculture depends heavily on the use of fossil fuels either directly or through the power grid for operating cultivating and stationary machinery.[73] Natural gas is the source of ammonia as the foundation of nitrogen fertilizers. Production and distribution of the other major fertilizer components, phosphate and potash, also depend heavily on fossil fuels. In fact, the entire food system is largely energy-dependent. Only 20 percent is consumed in cultivation, and the rest in distribution, processing, packaging, marketing and preparation in home and food service outlets. "In short, with higher energy prices and a limited supply of fossil fuels, the modern food system that evolved when oil was cheap will not survive as it is now structured."

Over the next few decades, and almost certainly by the end of the century, agriculture in the US and other major food exporting countries will undoubtedly hit a wall. Fourteen industrialized countries, including the US, are responsible for about 67 percent of global food exports. If some degree of political stability can be maintained throughout the world during this period of transition to a more sustainable system of food production, we may be able to work our way out of this mess. But with nearly a billion people already near starvation, increasing population and the prevalence of armed conflict and terrorism, the problems seem almost insurmountable. If it's not too late to start to convert to more local production of foods using renewable resources, there is certainly no room for delay.

In the early part of the 19th century the sole source of energy was biofuel, mainly wood. After the end of World War II, fossil fuels became the primary energy source. In most of the decades since that time, about 80 percent of global energy consumption has been fossil fuels. A very large part of the human population *would not exist* had it not been for exploitation of these energy sources (physically, we are essentially what we eat). What happens when the (energy) wells run dry?

WATER

One of every six humans lacks access to potable water, and one-third lack adequate sanitation.[74] Millions die each year from water-borne diseases. The supply of potable water is significantly reduced by pollution and contamination from agricultural runoff, untreated sewage and industrial effluents. It *is* true that much fresh water is wasted. Agricultural use, which accounts for about 87 percent of fresh water use globally, is widely inefficient, with much irrigation water lost to evaporation and runoff as a result of poor planning. Water is usually underpriced, with subsidies diminishing pressure for conservation. Nevertheless, demand for clean water increases with growth of human population, with about one third currently experiencing water stress.

There is widespread concern that availability of fresh water will reach crisis proportions in many parts of the world in the near future. Per capita availability of water in Asia, heretofore an abundant resource, declined by 40-60 percent between 1955 and 1990. Availability of clean fresh water is expected to be severe within the next decade or two. Other parts of the world are even in worse condition, e.g., Africa, where desertification and population increase will create stress, scarcity and vulnerability in huge swaths of the continent by 2025.[75]

FOREST COVER

Another obvious sign of overpopulation is the loss of forest cover. The annual net loss of forest area between 2000 and 2005 was 7.3 million hectares, an area about the size of Sierra Leone or Panama, down from an estimated 8.9 million hectares between 1990 and 2000.[76] Now each day an estimated 100,000 acres (40,400 ha.) of rainforest disappear (about 14.8 million ha. per annum) and an equal area degraded, with as many as several hundred species going extinct. Loss of forests from agriculture (64 percent), logging (18 percent), fuel wood (10 percent) and ranching (8 percent), is accompanied by increases in atmospheric carbon and loss of topsoil to erosion. Tropical forests, which provide habitats for a myriad of species, have experienced an increasing rate of deforestation, 8.5 percent higher in 2000-2005 as compared with the 1990s. Even though natural reforestation and plantings may make up the difference, much of it still represents a considerable loss of biodiversity, as plantations do not reproduce the diverse habitats lost to a multitude of species when the primary forest that they replace was destroyed.

MIGRATION

During the decade of the 1990s, according to the Census Bureau, 33 million (13 percent) people were added to the US population, and in the first decade of the 21st century another 28 million (12 percent).

About half of this growth is "natural," and the rest attributable to immigration, more than 1 million legal and a half million or so undocumented. By most estimates from 12-20 million undocumented persons reside in the US early in the 21st century.

The territory that is presently the continental United States has been a destination of migrants since the original newcomers crossed the land bridge from Asia that existed about 15,000 years ago. In more recent times, waves of immigrants arrived from Europe, in the 16th century from Spain and France. In the early 17th century English migrants established the first permanent settlement in the New World at Jamestown, Virginia, followed by Pilgrims and Puritans ostensibly fleeing religious persecution. In addition, thousands of English convicts were sent abroad as indentured servants. Large numbers arrived from Northern and Western European in the 19th and early 20th century, including about 4.5 million from Ireland who were fleeing famine, about 5 million Germans who settled in the Midwest, and thousands of Asians lured by the California gold rush. Almost a million African slaves were brought to the US up to the early 19th century.

Although often attributed to other factors, more accurately migration-motivating social tensions in other guises are usually rooted in absolute and relative economic deprivation. The problem of excessive migration becomes more apparent in periods of economic recession. Although the developed countries are havens for refugees driven from their mother countries by oppression, most migrants leave their home countries because their economies are incapable of absorbing their increasing populations while providing a decent living standard.

Migration to the US and other developed countries has to be regarded as just one part of a global phenomenon attributable largely to the wide disparity in income distribution around the world. Much of the global migration is linked to economic liberalization, income disparities among nations, increased access to transportation and demographic imbalances between developed and developing nations. Some migration is the result of geo-political changes such as the breakup of the former Soviet Union during the 1990s. Although the primary impetus is undoubtedly economic, many seek asylum from persecution and other forms of terror.

On the surface the number of migrants as a percentage of world population does not seem overwhelming. International migrants represented 2.5 percent of population in 1960 and 2.9 percent in 2000, about 175 million. A report of the International Organization for Migration (IOM)[77]: "The most significant changes in recent years have been an increased concentration of migrants in the developed world and in a small number of countries. There have also been significant shifts in the poles of attraction for labor migration, for example to East and Southeast Asia, and a remarkable contribution of international migration to the population growth of receiving countries experiencing low fertility levels [to serve as low-paid workers]."

According to this report, 17 million refugees [ostensibly fleeing persecution] in the world represented 9.7 percent of all international migrants in the year 2000 as compared with 4.5 million or 5.5 percent in 1970, the majority having found asylum, not in the industrialized countries, but rather in the developing countries of Africa and Asia.

The IOM assists from about a half to one million migrants per year, but to put this in perspective, census figures confirm that in the early 21st century about 1.5 million immigrants arrive annually in the United States alone. At this point the US has the highest rate of population growth of any industrialized country by far. Why is this a concern, for a country purportedly the wealthiest in the world?

So long as the United States, as titular world leader, fails to acknowledge through public policy that population is a global concern, little will likely be done about it. The US Congress has been wrestling with this issue for over a decade, but fierce political infighting stands in the way of resolution. A rate of population growth of one percent or so for the country or world does not seem excessively large with economic growth typically in the 3 percent or greater range in the US and even larger in some of the developing countries. However, conventional measures of economic growth don't take into account costs of resource depletions, notably petroleum, which the world will shortly have to face, nor do they consider environmental degradation.

Furthermore, economic growth, even by conventional measures, is unlikely to match what has occurred in the past.[78]

It seems compassionate to permit the downtrodden of the underdeveloped countries free access to the industrialized and ostensibly prosperous nations such as the United States. One argument in favor is that migrants take up places in the economy that are shunned by its citizens. Even in the unlikely event that this is true, can the US or any other part of the world comfortably accommodate nearly one billion people worldwide who are living on the brink of starvation, all facing only bleak prospects at best, and who would surely opt for better opportunities if given the chance?

Countries in North America, Europe and Africa are experiencing serious tensions, to the extent of murderous attacks, between their own unemployed citizens and workers from South Asia, Africa and Latin America, mainly undocumented, who are competing for low level jobs. In the US for example, "recent studies have begun to document, in rising levels of detail, the tension that has emerged between immigrant groups and lower-skilled American natives ...."[79] Physical and psychological violence against Mexican immigrant workers is increasing as the debate on illegal border crossings escalates into a political football.[80]

Expectations of migrants, legal and undocumented, go largely unfulfilled. Despite attempts to provide minimum work standards, the law of the market often controls: an excess of supply tends to drive down the wages of unskilled workers with little economic leverage. Particularly for the 12-20 million undocumented workers in the United States (2014 est.), conditions are dire: they lack employment benefits such as vacations, health and unemployment insurance, breaks and rest periods; most are forced to live in overcrowded tenements with poor sanitation, inadequate nutrition and medical services. Agricultural workers are subject to serious health impairment, including neurological damage from excessive exposure to pesticides and herbicides. Their children are often unable to attend school as they work in the fields to supplement family income.

In the mid-term election year 2012, the administration of U. S. President Barack Obama placed a temporary moratorium on deportation of some children of illegal immigrants. This policy change provided that for people under 30 years of age who entered the United States before the age of sixteen, who were not considered criminals or security threats and who were either successful students or served in the military, and who could prove that they were living in the country for at least five years, would be eligible for a two-year deferral from deportation. They could apply for work permits.

One apparent, unforeseen consequence of this policy is that it was interpreted as an amnesty for children—that they would be permitted to enter the country without being subject to deportation. The ensuing flood of unescorted children—over 50,000 in 2014—who journeyed primarily from Central American countries of Honduras, El Salvador and Guatemala, posed extreme hazards for the children and a crisis for immigration authorities. To what extent these children suffer physically and mentally during their journeys is unknown, although at least one was discovered deceased near the Texas border. While immigration advocates in the US identified these children as refugees fleeing a high incidence of crime and violence, more likely the families of these children, some still undocumented residents, are motivated by economic opportunity that is unavailable in their home countries.

The fundamental problem is the failure of world leaders to promote sensible family planning. The need was apparent decades ago when there were numerous indications that global population increases were unsustainable, e.g., environmental degradation, growing destitution. As matters now stand, it is very unlikely that the current world population can be accommodated with anything like minimally acceptable standards of living for all.

Rather than rely on the rest of the world to produce low paid workers, a far better course for industrialized populations is to learn to do what they have to do for themselves. With unemployment rampant in these countries, there are undoubtedly sufficient numbers willing and able to do whatever jobs are necessary, so long as they are paid a living wage. Highly skilled workers in demand by these countries would much more fruitfully serve needs in their countries of origin, even if not specifically in the areas for which they were trained. There is really no need in the receiving countries, which have the wherewithal to upgrade capacities of their own populations to fill whatever jobs are necessary. The claim of insufficient workers is essentially a ruse to increase the supply of potential employees to a level greater than demand, for reasons that are all too obvious. At the same time, prosperous nations would serve their own long-term interests by taking the lead in uplifting the status of indigent populations throughout the world, which would tend toward population stabilization.

Promoting excessive growth in population, or its tacit equivalent, ignoring or opposing family planning measures, is a dangerous and destructive game. Endemic episodes of violence, arising from the poverty and ignorance of economic deprivation, occur when, as in any market including labor, too much supply compared with demand has the effect of depressing wage compensation. The situation is exacerbated in a global economy geared to rapidly depleting cheap fossil fuel, with inevitable economic recessions and depression that have the greatest impact on massive numbers of humans living in dire conditions.

Michael Klare[81] explores the relationship between economic downturns and increased civil unrest and ethnic strife. "As people lose confidence in the ability of markets and governments to solve [global crises], they are likely to erupt into violent protests or to assault others they deem responsible for their plight, including government officials, plant managers, landlords, immigrants, and ethnic minorities ... It is entirely possible ... that, as the economic crisis worsens, some of these incidents will metastasize into far more intense and long-lasting events: armed rebellions, military takeovers, civil conflicts, even economically fueled wars between states."

Violent protests erupted in Cameroon, Egypt, Ethiopia, Haiti, India, Indonesia, Ivory Coast, and Senegal as a consequence of rising food prices in 2008. Civil unrest in Indian-controlled Kashmir resulted from allegations of discrimination in jobs, housing and land use. Nomadic shepherds around the city of Agra (location of the Taj Mahal) closed roads and railways as a protest against infringement on their means of livelihood, leading to civilian deaths as police fired into the crowd.

Impoverished citizens in Assam violently resisted the influx of even poorer, mostly illegal immigrants from Bangladesh. Economically driven unrest occurred across much of eastern China in 2008, protests by workers over sudden plant shutdowns, lost pay, or illegal land seizures.

Success of the growth mantra, largely responsible for the excess of human population, arises from the natural inclination to procreate, exploitatively conjoined with mercantile, political and religionist interests. It is a convenient device for those who seek short-term advantage at the expense of impacts on future generations. However, there are ways to grow aside from numbers and consumption volumes. Societies can try to develop better human beings, and in the process learn to live more in tune with irrepressible and undeniable nature.

Wealthier countries have to continue serving as havens for the oppressed, but should otherwise determine immigration policies in the light of world conditions and their long-term impacts. Limiting access to the US, for example, may cause some governments to take more seriously the constraints of their own living environments when they determine their population policies (e.g., Mexico, where population growth is essentially out of control—a five-fold increase in the span of a single lifetime). Migration is a major factor in the global population problem. So long as countries with excessive population growths are permitted to dump them through the safety valve of the developed countries, there will be little incentive for these governments to deal seriously with their burgeoning populations. Former US president Richard Nixon actually commissioned a study on world population and planned to promulgate a US population policy, but church and industrial leaders undercut his idea to serve their own population agendas. At issue is not immigration, but rather massive human migration from lands with unsustainable rates of population growth. Ecological excesses engendered by human demands on Earth are the real threat, on the verge of straining an already overloaded system of natural resources to the breaking point.

Rather than tarring those who view loose immigration standards as a globally dangerous policy encouraging further growth in human numbers with the brush of racism or lack of compassion for the downtrodden, better to admonish political leaders to promote family planning efforts throughout the world as the surest path to avoiding global environmental catastrophe.

OPTIMAL WORLD POPULATION

One objective approach to determining the optimal world population is the "ecological footprint." The method estimates the amount of land area necessary to sustain the average lifestyle of an economy—to provide the resources consumed and to absorb the waste produced, as determined from its productivity—compared with the actual land available. The world apparently crossed over the sustainable threshold in the 1970s, when world population was about four billion. We now consume about 1.4 Planets Earth to sustain today's population level, and will need about two to sustain the projected population by mid-century (2050).[82]

Another similar objective approach is "carrying capacity," the largest population size of a species that can be supported in a specific area without reducing its ability to support the same species in the future, which is equivalent to the number that can be supported by the availability of renewable resources. Wilson (2003) points out that Earth's 3.5 billion acres of arable land would feed 10 billion vegetarians, but only 2.5 billion meat eaters by US standards. There are other constraints: atmospheric carbon concentration, mineral deposits (e.g., phosphorous required for cultivation).

Ultimately, availability of energy will determine Earth's carrying capacity. In a 2007 paper based upon the World Energy and Population Model, Paul Chefurka relates energy available at any point in time and average annual global per capita consumption, currently at about 1.7 tons oil equivalent (toe), to Earth's capacity to sustain its population.[83] In the model, consumption declines to a level of 1.0 toe by 2100. "To put that in perspective, the world average in 1965 was 1.2 toe, so the model is not predicting a huge decline below this level of consumption. An increase in the disparity between rich and poor nations is also likely, but that effect is masked by this approach."

According to the availability of non-renewable and renewable energy sources compared with average energy consumption to sustain a minimal lifestyle, world population will peak at under 7.5 billion by 2020 [perhaps a little later with advanced extraction techniques for fossil fuels] and then decline to under 2 billion by 2100. "If the model is correct, there will be no ongoing overpopulation problem at all, as natural processes intervene to bring our numbers back in line with our resource base." This is at odds with the UN Population Fund estimate of about 9 billion by mid 21st century, but Chefurka's energy constraint must not have been sufficiently taken into account.

The decline in human population predicted by this model is staggering: "It's safe to say it will be catastrophic far beyond anything humanity has experienced. The loss of life alone beggars belief. In the most serious part of the decline, during the two or three decades spanning the middle of this century, even with a net birth rate of zero we might expect death rates between 100 million and 150 million per year." In contrast, during World War II, from 1939 to 1945 (six years) there were 10 million excess deaths (above the normal death rate) per year, so the carnage resulting from the energy dearth could be 10-15 times worse, without taking into account the social upheavals that would result.

Even if Chefurka's energy peaks for various sources are postponed, or his rates of decline are overly precipitous, certainly within this or the next century his scenarios will play out. The "ace in the hole" seen by some analysts is nuclear power generation, but fission is a Faustian bargain at best, where the devil will eventually have his due, and fusion appears to be a pipe dream. The two thirds of humanity "made of oil" will most likely have to find an alternative basis for sustenance or disappear. The outlook for us and the rest of life on Earth would be well served if we would take our heads out of the sand, but our propensity for allowing myths to predominate in our calculations are overpowering, particularly when they serve short-term aspirations.

OVERPOPULATION DENIAL

Why is it so difficult to accept the idea of overpopulation?

In their calculations, economists tend to treat resources as if there are no limits. They create optimization models assuming that resources are infinitely available, and then prescribe policies accordingly. What's the difference if current sources of energy are finite? There is the sun, wind, tides, nuclear—we'll figure out a way. Why should we be concerned with the amount of arable land for food production? There is always a green revolution at hand, fish farming, hydroponics.

People are inclined by evolutionary imperative to covet offspring. From this perspective, humanity can't be criticized for being in a state of denial concerning its propensity to proliferate. We can't help ourselves, because our internal programming dictates the production of progeny as part of our survival strategy, a manifestation of the life force in every living thing. Even though our collective fecundity is a threat to life on Earth, as individuals the urge to procreate is overwhelming, often precluding rational analysis of its collective consequences.

Capitalists, who rule the roost, want multitudes of willing hands at the factory gate clamoring for employment, so that they can pick and choose according to their criteria and play one against the other in their quest for more services at lower cost. They also want hordes of devouring consumers, the better to amass surplus value out of the throughput of their production machinery.

Politicians want larger and larger constituencies, particularly within special interest groups—mainly ethnic and social classes—upon whom they can focus their appeal as a means of continuing to maintain their incumbencies, which by one means or another usually confer privilege, prestige and, most importantly, wealth.

Religionists want more parishioners to maintain and extend their influence and to support their exotic lifestyles.[84] They have the advantage of declaring practices that would tend to limit human numbers as immoral and even sinful, such as reproductive control mechanisms and abortion of fetuses, with everlasting consignment to hell as the penalty for transgression.

On the other hand, it's amazing that there appears to be so little concern about increasing numbers of humans presently inhabiting our planet. Although approximately 75-80 million new souls are added to the throng each year,[85] approximately another Egypt or France or Germany, crises of food supply, water, or clean air are almost never attributed to our growing numbers. Reticence among industrialists, politicians, religious leaders and the media to suggest that limiting population might be one way to address the global, national and regional ills to which they constantly call attention is comprehensible, if misguided. It appears as if they have purged from their consciousness the fact that there are limits to the numbers that our small planet can sustainably and adequately support, but they are surreptitiously driven by their own aspirations served by increasing numbers.

A visit to any major city, for example mingling with frenetic New Yorkers oblivious for the most part of the looming threat, as demonstrated by the equanimity with which they apparently accept nose-to-nose packing density on subways and at other public venues, and belied by the glamor and lights of tinsel town, is a reminder of how precarious is the existence of humankind. How can inveterate urbanites, insulated for their entire lives from natural exigencies by municipal services, theatre, subways and the like, be aware of their indispensible links to the natural world? Of course, even the trappings of urban society, as the handiwork of a class of its constituents, are part and parcel of nature, but would rarely be recognized as such. Even E.O. Wilson (2003), defined nature as "Everything that we see in the cosmos with the human impact extracted ... If all mankind were to disappear, the world would regenerate back to the rich state of equilibrium that existed ten thousand years ago. If insects were to vanish, the environment would collapse into chaos." The problem with this assertion is that nature is the only game in town; so isolating humans from nature is like assigning independent existence to a bodily organ.

With 7.2 billion of us occupying this space that was meant for no more than 2 billion or so and continuing the explosive increase, in addition to our fellow species on Planet Earth (who generally have enough "sense" to keep their numbers in check), no issue seems more daunting than the need to diminish our presence. This would most peaceably be achieved through attrition over extended periods of time, but our procreative proclivity does not make this a good bet.

Insensitivity to the consequences of our "choices," including procreation, has been attributed to duality, most decidedly expressed in childhood—the more dualistic, the more childlike we are. The most obvious manifestation of dualistic thinking is dividing people into "them" and "us," but many other apparent dualities—black and white, good and evil, man and nature, happiness and depression—continually reinforce its conceptual prevalence. It's quite satisfactory if benefits for "us" are at the expense of "them"; at root is the most fundamental ontogenetic human imperative. Unity in all things is only within the province of Bodhisattvas.

The human race seems be saddled with a very short planning horizon, ignoring long term trends for the most part. This syndrome is demonstrated repeatedly: industry typically plans for three years or less, ignoring socio-economic trends and cycles of much longer duration; politicians seek primarily to retain their incumbencies, trading short-term popularity for long term economic peril; individuals buy now and leave the issue of payment aside, in the hope that providence will intervene. Similarly, what is surely happening to the world's climate and its implications—the impending energy crunch that will have dramatic consequences for life styles, the state of the world's underprivileged at the root of our security threats, any major issue with long term consequences—is treated as an insignificant blip on the radar screen. We seem to respond meaningfully only when there are obvious signs of distress (e.g., bodies piling up in the streets).

TOO MANY OF US?

Virtually all segments of every society covet new additions to their populations. Parenting is a natural inclination, a most basic imperative of any organism. Productive elements of civilized society, e.g., commerce, industry and agriculture, seek abundant workers and consumers. Politicians and religionists thrive when there are minions to proselytize and bind. Economists neglect limits to resources in their models, thereby anesthetizing people to the possibility of over-exploitation from excessive demand. The result is ever-growing numbers of human beings, increasingly straining the carrying capacity of our planet. All of the interlinked problems threatening life are related to inordinate growth in human population—militarism, terrorism, climate change, environmental degradation, economic boom and bust, mal-distribution of wealth.

Excessive population is, in essence, part of the human condition. Even our consciousness of the problem does little to alleviate our overwhelming propensity to procreate. Even population exploiters, with their devious machinations for increasing population as a means of feathering their own nests, are hapless subjects of its ubiquitous influence. Behavioral transitions that may alleviate the condition are not out of the question. After all, we were once much simpler creatures with very different habits, which might still have been us, had an inadvertent stomp of a mastodon obliterated the deviant gene that ultimately gave us to the world.

PART II

PATTERNS OF BEHAVIOR

CHAPTER 3

SOCIETY'S JEWELS

As a derivative of their inherent inclination to grow intellectually, emotionally and physically, children are like fresh nutrients with the potential to restore and rebuild societies. No weakness is more debilitating to its health, nor is any issue of greater concern to a society seeking long-term survival and elevation, than that its youth are deprived of opportunities to develop and exercise their full capacities. And yet this fact is ignored in most corners of the world. Rather than being delicately and painstakingly groomed as society's future pillars, with all the care and resources that can possibly be brought to bear, children around the world are neglected, exploited, abused and even murdered to satisfy aspiration, convenience, whim and sadism of their elders. There does not appear to be a self-correcting mechanism that adjusts for what is tantamount to societal suicide, and in the process wreaking havoc on other forms of life by sending out into the world young people too stressed to think about the wider implications of their actions. This testifies to our corrosive presence within nature's domain.

In the United States, for example, school boards throughout the country typically are driven by the imperative of creating a competent workforce to serve industry and commerce. Children are looked upon as potential engines of prosperity. They need to "learn the basics" so that they can get good jobs and generate income for the community.

Rather than regard each child as a budding treasure to be cultivated to her highest potential, school systems typically filter children through sieves that segregate the promising from the also-rans. This is no less true in "higher" education than it is in the K-12 system. Misguided priorities and denigration of the needs of children in the minds of politicians and the general public in the US is reflected in its allocation of resources: of the president's proposed $3.9 trillion budget for 2015, only 1.7 percent is dedicated to education while 16.0 percent is allocated to the military. Other public agencies directly or indirectly impacting the lives of children garner another 2.8 percent of the budget (housing, health and human services, each 1.4 percent).

EARLY LIFE

Humans enter life in a state of immaturity or neoteny, with decidedly infantile traits such as relatively small brain size and physical weakness. Ours is the only species on Earth that enters life so ill prepared for it, with utter dependence on parents or other caregivers for survival. Were humans to come to full term in the manner of most other mammals, we would be born perhaps at eighteen months rather than nine. Our purported intelligence is somehow to blame for this condition: the birth canal could not enlarge evolutionarily so quickly to accommodate our rapidly increasing brain size as we transited from primordial form to modern human. As a consequence, post-natal nurturing is a more significant component of the life support system for humans than for any other species. This is something we have to live with, at least so long as our evolutionary path has not yet either sufficiently broadened the hips of females to accommodate a more mature brain case or more efficiently packed our neurons and synapses to allow for a smaller cranium.

Pulitzer Prize science writer Ronald Kotulak (1997) compiled much medical and psychological research information dealing with the effects on human biology of genetic makeup and environmental influences, and their behavioral consequences. Researchers have since amassed an enormous amount of information concerning the biological effects of pre-natal and early childhood experiences on behavior patterns, but are so enmeshed in the strictures of their professions that they are incapable of proposing the dramatic actions that are indicated to ameliorate or eliminate the deleterious effects of typically deficient rearing processes. The totality of human expectations, the complex of influences—nutrition, security, intellectual stimulation, social orientation, etc.—that determine character are wired into the brain very significantly from the womb to the age of three.[86] Lesser, but strongly significant impacts, occur up to the age of twelve, but continue at a reduced level indefinitely. Much of the misery that children currently endure, and its social consequences, are created by ignoring developmental needs and often subjecting children to abuse, which has lasting physical and psychological impacts that affect outlook and character.

In the United States, one of the dire consequences of excessive consumption at the cost of investing in children, and the resultant neglect of their developmental needs, is that children bear children. In 2012 approximately 40.7 percent of American births were to single parents, many of them teenagers (about 8 percent),[87] who are by and large incapable, under the social structure, of proper nurturing. This is creating a virtual nightmare for the children (and ultimately for society) of these child procreators, who understandably lack the wisdom and other capacities to serve the comprehensive needs of their offspring.

As an illustration of the effect of intellectual stimulation on the outlook for children, David Weikert[88], president of pre-school study in Ypsilanti, Michigan, conducted a study in late 1960s in which two groups of black children born in poverty were exposed to two different learning methodologies for two years starting from the age of three. One method involved what was termed "direct learning," which consisted of direct teaching of academic skills, enforced attention and reward for correct answers. The alternative was the "self-starting" method, where the group of children planned, executed and reviewed their own activities and engaged in active learning with people, materials, ideas and events. Although there were early signs of improvement in cognition in both groups, by age twenty-three there were large differences between the two groups (direct learning vs. self-starter) in treatment for emotional problems (about half vs. 6 percent), felony arrests (39 vs. 10 percent), plans for a college education (27 vs. 70 percent).

The study concluded that the brain has the capacity to rapidly reorganize in response to external stimuli during early life, as brain cells are being created and broken down at a rate much greater than in later life. "These windows of development occur in phases from birth to age twelve when the brain is most actively learning from its environment. It is during this period, and especially the first three years, that the foundations for thinking, language, vision, attitudes, aptitudes and other characteristics are laid down." After this early period when much of the brain architecture is completed, development opportunities presented in early life are markedly diminished, particularly after the age of twelve.

There is widespread (but by no means universal), agreement among neuroscientists, psychiatrists and behavioral scientists that imprints of experiences in early childhood have long-lasting and perhaps indelible consequences. Kotulak (1999) cites findings from a number of experts in the field:

> Felton Earls, professor of human behavior and development, Department of Society, Human Development, and Health at Harvard University: "A kind of irreversibility sets in. There is this shaping process that goes on early, and then at the end of this process, be that age two, three or four, you have essentially designed a brain that probably is not going to change very much more."
>
> Neurobiologist Martha Constantine-Paton, investigator, McGovern Institute; professor of biology and brain and cognitive sciences, Massachusetts Institute of Technology: "The aspects of brain development most closely tied to human behavior can be affected for better or worse by the care we give our children ... the actual structure of the brain can be adversely affected by neglect."

> Torsten N. Wiesel, Nobel Laureate in physiology or medicine 1981, formerly of the Harvard Medical School and President of Rockefeller University: "There is a very important time in a child's life, beginning at birth, when he should be living in an enriched environment—visual, auditory, language and so on—because that lays the foundation for development later in life."

Bruce McEwen, Alfred E. Mirsky Professor at the Harold and Margaret Milliken Hatch Laboratory of Neuroendocrinology of Rockefeller University,[89] identifies our behavior and misbehavior as the greatest problem for humanity in the future, alluding to their dependence on the social and physical environment on our bodies and brains. Genes are a significant influence on behavior, but the environment regulates how genes are expressed. This is confirmed by a Harvard University study[90] of early child development, which concluded that early stimulation, such as interaction with parents, caregivers and the environment, is required for brain development and that mere observation is not sufficient. Child abuse, neglect, maternal depression and substance abuse, family violence and malnutrition are also detrimental to proper brain development in children.

David A. Hamburg, professor of psychiatry and behavioral sciences and former president of the Carnegie Corporation of New York, emphasizes the adverse consequences of child abuse regarding fulfillment of developmental potential: "For all the *atrocities* (italics added) now being committed on our children, we are already paying a great deal ... in economic inefficiency, lost productivity, lack of skill, high health care costs, growing prison costs, and a badly ripped social fabric."[91]

Evidence that a child's environment is crucial to development is overwhelming.[92] The consensus is that the development of the individual in terms of personality and intelligence is greatly influenced by early experiences. A newborn child has twice as many synapses[93] as she will have as an adult, which are rapidly adjusting to environmental influences. "The human brain is fundamentally an adaptive organ, whose physical organization is shaped by the environment. In this sense, learning is the process by which the brain responds adaptively to the environment in which a child is reared." Anecdotal evidence supports the notion of a window of opportunity for young children. For example, their ability to learn properly accented language is well documented: typically children of expatriates learn local languages much faster, and with far less foreign accent than their parents. Many studies have confirmed that children have an advantage over adults in acquiring a second language, and that the ability diminishes starting from very early age, and even more sharply at the close of puberty.[94]

President-elect Barack Obama in 2008 indicated that early childhood education would be one of his top priorities, although he alluded primarily to the formal system of education rather than the complex of experiences that comprise proper nurturing. Some communities have instituted programs that address one or more nurturing issues. In Illinois, "Character Counts," a program promoted by the non-profit Josephson Institute, focuses on character-building in communities and school systems by inculcating social responsibility through promotion of its "six pillars of character": trustworthiness; respect and tolerance; responsibility and perseverance; fairness; caring and compassion; and citizenship. But as a rule, there has not yet been a serious attempt to develop a comprehensive program of adequate nurturing comprised of all of the elements that are necessary for the fulfillment of a child's potential (see "*The Essentials of Nurturing*" below), for even a small percentage of American youth, and much less for the children of the world. School boards at the local level, and politicians in state capitals, in Washington, and throughout the world, appear to have little cognizance of their most important responsibility.

How can it be that professionals in the field of child development are not demonstrating for comprehensive nurturing for every child in the United States and the rest of the world, intended to allow each to fulfill her potential, insisting that this must be the number one social priority, making enough noise so that political forces will sit up and take notice? Perhaps it is the unfortunate consequence of their own nurturing, during which their perceptions were stultified by deficiencies in the system in which they were raised and "educated." A serious impediment is the compartmental nature of our academic system, where "subjects" and "disciplines" are treated as separate and distinct components of knowledge: even the most gifted and perceptive teachers or mentors face great barriers to an holistic view of their professional involvement. These strictures hinder development of intelligence, as young minds are passed through the academic meat grinder, which produces only one kind of sausage at each turn of the wheel. Not only is knowledge segregated into distinct lines to conveniently conform to departmental structures defined by academics and educational administrators, but also individual interests and needs are usually ignored in the factory atmosphere (see Chapter 7).

FLAWED CHILDREN

As youths traverse the bewildering path from a state of dependency to self-awareness and identity, clearly something is going awry. Not only are children's needs widely neglected, but also in many instances their helplessness engenders abuse and exploitation by their elders. Influential political and community leaders woefully misunderstand them, and so have generally failed to provide the nurturing framework to serve children's developmental requirements. What most adults seem to forget is that children are the decision-makers of the future, so that their capacities and attitudes will determine a society's fate.

Awareness of a relationship between early childhood environment and subsequent social attitudes and behavior is not universally shared. Tom DeLay of Texas, once a powerful Republican member of Congress as house majority whip, in an article for the Washington Post attributed child crime to the "fact that we enter this world flawed and inclined to do the wrong thing, as the Judeo-Christian tradition has taught."[95] The flaw, according to Mr. DeLay, is a sinful nature, which can be held in check only by two forces: the restraint of conscience and the restraint of the sword. "Tolerance, as the guiding moral imperative (of misguided social engineers) forces acceptance and understanding of even appalling behavior as the product, not of our flawed (sinful) selves, but of flawed processes." Mr. DeLay makes clear his attribution of "conscience" to religious teachings: "Our Founders were right when they insisted that self-government is suitable only to people with a restraint of conscience that flows from accepting absolute standards grounded in religious conviction."

Atrocious behavior on the part of youth is, then, attributable solely to inherent sinfulness of humankind arising from the absence of conscience that might have been instilled only thorough inculcation of religious values. The "flawed processes" of a youth's environmental experience amount to misguided tolerance, a diversion from religious orientation, with adverse social consequences.

In one fell swoop Mr. DeLay has clarified a centuries-old controversy, the attribution of bad behavior to a sinful nature, with little or no influence of the environment in which a child is nurtured, or to her genetic endowment. If humans were inherently inclined to "do the wrong thing," it's unlikely that any of us would be here to tell the tale. In fact, the numerous kindred species within the hominid line doomed to extinction apparently *did* enter the world inclined to do the wrong thing, at least in relation to survival value. If it's wrong to survive then we humans are, indeed, inclined to do the wrong thing, as we have been the most successful survivors among the multitude of larger species that have inhabited this Earth through the ages. However, cultural developments that increasingly exploit rather than cherish youth as society's treasure trove have significantly diminished the odds on our survival.

Mr. DeLay and others of his persuasion find it convenient to ignore their own complicity in widespread failure of youth to attain their full potential as individuals and as responsible citizens of democracies. As global leader, the US is derelict in failing to seize its opportunity to set an adequate nurturing standard. Only by acknowledging, and acting upon, the links between the nurturing process and qualities of citizens will a future of world peace, justice and prosperity be possible.

THE ESSENTIALS OF NURTURING

Science doesn't have to tell us that the assertion about children having to overcome inherent "flaws" is chimerical. Nor do we have to be told about the ill effects of deprivation and other forms of abuse during a child's early years—this is all too obvious. Life experiences and good sense inform us about what children need to reach their full potential, not only good educational opportunity as promoted but misconstrued by members of school boards across the country,[96] but a chain of complementary support services whose weakest link determines its overall strength. It's all too apparent that failure to provide any component of a nurturing environment diminishes the effectiveness of other positive influences, perhaps to the least common denominator. This list of elements may not constitute the whole package, but none of them can be ignored if we are interested in rearing healthy, intelligent and socially responsible citizens:

- Adequate nourishment
- Comfortable shelter
- Freedom from violence, threats and other forms of abuse
- Protection from exposure to real or simulated (media) violence
- Emotional support
- Wholesome social interactions
- Intellectual stimulation—development of cognitive capacity
- Inculcation of democratic values
- Reinforcement of identity with nature

Most of these elements are probably indisputable, but the last two might elicit some skepticism. Regarding democratic values, first, it's axiomatic that a democracy can't function effectively with unprepared citizens. Even the US isn't an effective democracy, as amply demonstrated by widespread dismay concerning unilateral actions of federal officials after the economic meltdown of 2007. Had democracy functioned properly, public involvement would have precluded responses to the economic crisis that were so much at odds with the wishes of the general public. Furthermore, only a bare majority of eligible voters cast a ballot in national elections (invariably less than 50 percent in off-year Congressional elections).

Democracy isn't an inherent social propensity for humanity, as attested by the rarity of its institution, and far greater rarity of its success. The societal structure of primates, our nearest kin, and our own historical experience in social organization, indicate that hierarchy, autocracy and oligarchy have been much more the rule. The democratic experiments of ancient Greece and Rome reverted to autocracy and ultimate ruin when commitment to the challenging tenets of democracy slackened. The attainment of democracy has its price. Its values have to be worked at continuously to maintain its vitality, with inculcation of democratic values in youth the most significant part.

In any social organization invariably the dominant personalities are the decision-makers, but if democracy is functioning properly they will be strongly constrained by popular opinion. True democracy doesn't reign anywhere in the world, certainly not in the country that holds itself up as exemplar extraordinaire. In 2013 its Supreme Court struck down the heart of the Voting Rights Act of 1965, which was intended to redress impediments to voting by minorities, particularly in southern states with their history of slavery and racial discrimination. The Court also ruled in January 2010, in the case of Citizens United v. Federal Election Commission, that the first amendment of the US Constitution prohibits the government from restricting independent political contributions by corporations, unions or other associations. It struck down provisions of the Bipartisan Campaign Reform Act (McCain - Feingold) that had outlawed independent political campaign expenditures and financing of electioneering communications by corporations (including nonprofits) and unions. It allowed corporations and unions to spend as much as they want to convince people to vote for or against a candidate. In effect, it declares that in politics "money talks": it's legitimate for the wealthy and powerful to employ their leverage at the ballot box to define the (most often self-serving) agenda for the entire society.

Yet aspiration for democracy appears to be widespread. Beatriz Magaloni (2007) studied the issue of transitions between autocracies and democracy during the period 1950-2000 (monarchy, military, single party, hegemonic party, democracy), concluding that "the simulation yields good news for democrats, but not the dream of a democratic world." Only democratic and hegemonic party systems gained in frequency, with democracy transitions outpacing those of autocratic systems of all types. Democracies increased to slightly more than double the number at the beginning of the study period, many occurring at the time of the breakup of the former Soviet Union. Simulating the next 50 years using the transitions of the past decade (considering that the Cold War conditions that prevailed are no longer present), 77 percent of the regimes in the world would be democratic (this is probably wishful thinking in terms of prevalence, but even more questionable is the degree of democracy). The predominant form of authoritarianism would be party autocracies (in 18 percent of countries).

Children need to be oriented toward democracy because only informed self-governance inherently leads to a secure future for our planet—for them as individuals, for society and for the rest of life. Intelligent and emotionally mature citizens, a prerequisite for a properly functioning democracy, make collective decisions from a perspective that takes in all dimensions of the social and environmental panorama.

As nature is virtually synonymous with existence, humanity as a species apart from it is a dissonant concept that has somehow found its way into the rhetoric of politicians and religionists. Children need to be insulated from such destructive influences, or at least exposed to countermanding interactions and experiences that stress the identity of the individual with nature. One who so identifies will be unlikely to behave in ways that are disrespectful or destructive, thereby serving personal as well as societal interests.

The system of nurturing in the United States (and throughout the world) falls far short of what is required. Rather than create an environment for children that offers all of the essential elements indicated above, instead children are institutionalized each day in mind-addling classroom settings. Typically their natural inquisitiveness is stultified by the demand that they adhere to a lockstep force-feeding program and their identities are undermined by segregation from the daily societal rhythm. Is it any wonder that schools throughout the country are denizens of disoriented children and teachers? And yet, "educators," their associations, unwitting parents and the politicians who rely on their support, continually press for more of the same, demanding more edifices, higher compensation, and in general, more of a say in governance of the system to assure that it conforms to their distorted criteria—too deeply mired in the hole created to even recognize the possibilities that lie just over the crest.

What the school system in the United States and the rest of the world needs is revolutionary. Children will develop their capacities to a much fuller extent, and maintain their identity with nature and society, if they are fully integrated into the social fabric from day one and from day to day. Children must never be shunted off to remote holding pens, and treated as if they are economic fodder. Certainly we have it within us to devise a system of nurturing that provides each child in the country, and in the world, the full panoply of elements required for healthy and productive citizenship.

A child living in deprivation is very likely to become a problem for society. Does it make sense to leave a child's environment to chance, particularly when there is a likelihood of inadequate support or even abuse? The mere begetting of children is not a license to treat one's offspring according to whim or to exploit them to satisfy self-oriented criteria. The stakes for society are too large to leave nurturing to chance. Our jails are already filled to overflowing with the products of poor parenting, and children around the world suffer unconscionable deprivation and abuse, so that some more secure guarantee of universally adequate nurturing is essential.

CHILD CARE

Do people who bear children and then abuse them (they cannot be called "parents" in the true sense) have the right to control the lives of their offspring? Not only is it a miscarriage of justice to allow such people to willfully deprive any child of the necessities for solid upbringing, but an unwanted, maltreated and deprived child becomes a burden to society, with associated costs for the remainder of that young person's life.

Who is to be the nurturer of last resort? When individual caregivers fail, a society must be the default provider for the next generation. Standards are required that assure at least adequacy for each child in every area vital to her development and growth. People who are unable to provide for their children, or who are likely to raise them in substandard conditions have to forfeit their claim to direct the activities and fortunes of their offspring. On the other hand, procreation can no longer be considered a "right," and some means must be found to prevent pregnancy in women and siring by men who are unfit to serve as parents. Although interference in parenting decisions appears to be counter to the principles of freedom that prevail in the United States and many other countries, the severity of the problem of inadequate nurturing calls for draconian measures. Legislative bodies have to consider the balance between freedom and license regarding begetting of children.

At this writing 45 million Americans lack access to health care.[97] This is indicative of a mal-distribution of opportunity even in the country widely considered to be the wealthiest on Earth. It is reflective of the fact that many families, and particularly their children, are being deprived of adequate means to make the most of their lives.

Some attention has been paid to the plight of children by the United Nations. The Covenant on the Rights of the Child was promulgated by General Assembly resolution 44/25 in November 1989 and became international law on Sept. 2, 1990. The covenant outlaws exploitation and provides for their safety and well-being, specifically:

- growing up in safe and supportive conditions;
- access to high quality education and health care, and a good standard of living;
- governments agree to protect children from discrimination, sexual and commercial exploitation and violence;
- care provided for orphans and young refugees.

The rights of children are defined (inadequate, but a start):

- to express opinion, especially concerning decisions that affect their lives;
- freedom of thought, expression, conscience and religion;
- private life and the right to play;
- to form their own clubs and organizations;

- access to information, particularly from the state and the media;
- to make their own ideas and information known.

Another initiative was the formation of the Committee on the Rights of the Child, which began working in February 1991. There have been some positive developments: several countries have included articles in their constitutions that reflect the provisions of the Covenant. The World Health Organization (WHO) points to the need for data concerning the status of children around the world, but has not yet embarked upon a program of collection. However, WHO in 1999 acknowledged that child abuse had become a worldwide public health problem, and that about 40 million children suffer abuse each year. The organization asserts that they have evidence that it is possible to reduce the prevalence of child abuse when parents are provided training in parenting skills before and after birth in an environment supported by skilled personnel. Whether or not the impact of these initiatives has been significant is difficult to assess, but there is little evidence that the incidence of deprivation and abuse has improved worldwide.

CHILD ABUSE

At birth a human child is the most helpless offspring of any species on Earth. Without intensive protection and external management of virtually every area of its life support system, the child would certainly expire from lack of care, if not otherwise harmed or devoured by predators.

As previously noted, this extreme level of helplessness has been explained by retention of embryonic characteristics by juveniles (see "*Early Life*" above): because the human survival strategy is based upon intelligence and brain size, restrictions on the size of the pelvic opening in the birth canal required that human infants be born "ahead of their time."

For this reason, much of a child's brain development occurs

after birth. Jean Piaget[98] and other investigators of early childhood development have confirmed the significance of the immediate environment for youngsters, even during the prenatal stage. The conditions under which young persons are nurtured, the physical and social climate of the early years, are of greatest significance in the development of physical, intellectual and emotional characteristics. People whose interests are closely aligned with those of the child best provide a supportive environment for emotional health: caring parents, mentors and competent child care professionals. In the event of imminent or actual danger, these individuals' reactions would most likely serve the child's developmental needs.

Symptomatic of abuse are learning disorders, malnutrition, failure to thrive, conduct disorders, emotional retardation, and sexually transmitted diseases in very young children.[99] Andrea Sedlak and Diane Broadhurst (1966) explain abuse and neglect as a function of socio-economic status of the family, respectively 14 times and 44 times more common in poor families, findings that "cannot be plausibly explained on the basis of the higher visibility of lower income families to community professionals."[100]

In 2008, 772,000 children were victims of maltreatment in the US, 10.3 per 1,000 in the population. Children were subjected to neglect (71.1 percent), physical abuse (16.1 percent), sexual abuse (9.1 percent), psychological abuse (7.3 percent) and medical deprivation (2.2 percent).[101] An additional 9 percent of children were victims of abandonment, threats of harm or congenital drug addiction. Victimization rates by state varied from 1.5 to 29.1 per 1,000 children. Of all victims of maltreatment, 32.6 percent were younger than 4 years old.

At the beginning of the current century, almost two thousand children in the US die of abuse or neglect annually. About 20 percent of survivors of abuse suffer permanent injury. Children suffering from birth defects or other disorders are at higher risk. An estimated 1,356 children died from child abuse and neglect in 2000, *nearly four children every day.* Of these fatalities, 80 percent of children were under five years and 40 percent under one year, second only to congenital anomalies as the cause of death in children of ages one to four years.[102]

In some cases those responsible for a child's welfare may not even be aware of abuse: children are particularly vulnerable to air, land and water pollution, which have been linked in numerous studies with some of the abuse symptoms. Community, commercial and industrial leaders are often insensitive to the cumulative buildup of pollutants in children's bodies.

The obvious forms of child abuse are denounced in most cultures, but are all too common: beatings and other physical maltreatment, abusive language and psychological oppression, sexual and labor exploitation. However, children are being increasingly abused and exploited in ways that have become acceptable in the industrialized countries and, through a kind of cultural imperialism, throughout the developing world.

A child is abused whenever its actions are directed by adults toward an objective that does not respond to the child's needs for developmental support and protection. Abuse and deprivation among children takes many forms: they are physically and emotionally constrained to conform to the needs of their "guardians"; neglected and left to fend for themselves; pressed into work, often in hazardous and stressful conditions with little or no compensation; widely malnourished; conscripted for military service and often manipulated into committing atrocious acts by sadistic overlords, sexually exploited by a wide array of pedophiles—rapacious offenders, members of the clergy, often relatives who demonically betray the child's trust. For insensitive or exploitative people around the world, children's vulnerabilities present too easy a target.

Dorothy Lewis, M.D., in a paper published in 1993[103], explained the relationship between abuse of children and subsequent antisocial behavior. One factor rarely discussed in associating behavior and early experience is the intrauterine environment. For example, minor viral infections, maternal anxiety and psychological stress during the prenatal period, maternal alcoholism and other substances abuse by the mother affects fetal development and subsequent postnatal social and intellectual functioning. Other factors precipitating aggression and other antisocial behavior patterns, according to Dr. Lewis, include living under stress, isolation and neglect, exposure to aggressive adults, pain and physical abuse and the quality of early parenting—high rates of obesity, smoking, use of hallucinogens and other unhealthy practices leaves an inordinate number of child begetters in a state of health not conducive to proper child rearing.

But we do not need to be reminded by scientific investigators of the indelible effects on children of experiences of abuse. Think of a child locked up in a closet from birth for a number of years (there have been a number of instances of this kind) and deprived of most, if not all, of the elements required for development. Would it be any wonder that this child emerges from such maltreatment disoriented, angry, hostile and otherwise anti-social?

CHILD HUNGER

Even in the United States of America, purportedly the wealthiest country on the globe, children go hungry. Deprivation of opportunity for children in the United States is endemic[104]:

- Nationwide, 18 percent of children, more than 12 million, live in families that are officially considered poor (13 million children), ranging from 7 percent in New Hampshire to 27 percent in Mississippi.
- Among children of ethnic groups (percentages): black - 35, Latino - 28, American Indian - 29, Asian – 11, white children living in poor families - 10.
- 20 percent of children under age six and 16 percent of children age six or older live in poor families.

Hunger is one consequence of poverty. In 2012, 14.5 percent of households were food insecure at least some time during that year, an increase from 11.1 percent in 2007.[105] This is close to the highest recorded prevalence rate of food insecurity since 1995 when the first national food security survey was conducted.

In a study of childhood hunger in the United States, investigative journalist Loretta Schwartz-Nobel (2002) recounts horrific stories of areas in the United States where children forage for food in garbage cans. Deprivation of adequate nutrition in early childhood leaves an imprint that is virtually permanent: the impacts can only be reduced by extensive and long-term therapy.

"A young child's brain grows so rapidly that, by the age of two it has achieved 80 percent of its full development. If adequate nutrients are not available during this critical period, the brain's weight and size may be irreversibly compromised. The result may be a child who is mildly to moderately retarded for the rest of his or her life." Schwartz-Nobel reviews the consequences of advanced malnutrition: children's hands and feet lack warmth and color; muscles weaken and subcutaneous fat is depleted; in advanced cases the abdomen and extremities become swollen, the nervous system is stressed, mental faculties diminished, maintaining normal body temperature, blood pressure and pulse rate become difficult; injuries do not heal, intestinal bleeding occurs—the signs of advanced protein deficiency, or kwashiorkor.

The extent of childhood hunger in America was covered in a report by the *All Things Considered* newscast of National Public Radio on March 10, 1998, which asserted that "hunger in America had reached a point where one in ten Americans regularly use a neighborhood food bank or soup kitchen in order to eat ... More than a third were families where at least one adult was working and 38 percent of the hungry were children." Based on a 2012 federal survey of 44,000 households, "49 million Americans are "food insecure"—people who sometimes eat less, go hungry or eat less nutritious meals because they can't afford to eat better. Almost a third of them are children."[106] Emergency food from food banks and soup kitchens is no longer being used to meet temporary acute food needs; instead, for the majority of people seeking food assistance, these are now a part of households' regular sources to supplement food shortages.[107] Globally, the UN Population Fund report for 2013 indicates that about a third of the nearly billion people worldwide suffering from malnutrition are children.

ANTISOCIAL BEHAVIOR AND INCARCERATION OF YOUTH

Social ostracism and economic deprivation among minorities is reflected in the rates of incarceration of youth and adults.[108] In 2011 black males of ages 18-19 were imprisoned at more than 9 times the rate of white males, and in the 20-24 age group, at a rate of about 7 times (for all ages the ratio is about 6 to 1). More than 60 percent of prison inmates belong to racial or ethnic minorities. For males of all ages, imprisonment was higher for black males (16.6 percent) and Hispanic males (7.7 percent) than for white males (2.6 percent), and higher also for black females (1.7 percent) and Hispanic females (0.7 percent) than white females (0.3 percent). The rate of incarceration in the US is higher than any other industrialized country: although only 5 percent of the global population, 25 percent of global prisoners are in US detention facilities.

Is it any mystery that minority youths in the US suffer greater rates of incarceration than whites? Even with minority parents who have every intention of raising their offspring to be responsible citizens, children who are deprived of opportunity or who are otherwise singled out for discrimination of one sort or another, as minorities have typically experienced, are more likely to exhibit antisocial behavior patterns that often end in brushes with the law.

Children who are given adequate nurturing in the early years are far less likely to exhibit antisocial behavior as adolescents and adults: "Powerful evidence from one study after another proves that quality education child care in the first years of life can greatly reduce the risk that today's babies and toddlers will become tomorrow's violent teens and adults."[109] In one study, half of a group of at-risk three and four-year-olds were randomly assigned to a pre-kindergarten program. Twenty-two years later those who had been left out were five times more likely to have become chronic lawbreakers with five times more arrests. "[110] Children whose needs are neglected will inevitably vent their frustrations by resorting to dishonesty and violence against their peers, their caregivers and society in general.

CHILD HEALTH

Children suffer widespread abuse in another form, which leaves its lasting imprint on their bodies and mental states. The polluted environment to which all too many children are exposed is a significant factor in high rates of childhood physical and mental illness. In children's rapidly growing bodies, their rates of ingestion and respiration compared with body weight are much greater than for healthy adults, which leaves them exceptionally vulnerable to the contaminants that are now so prevalent in the air they breathe, the water they drink, and the food that they consume. To add to this assault on their health, when symptoms of illness arise, rather than provide quality parenting by seeking common sense solutions that change the children's unwholesome living conditions, they are usually quickly shuttled off to medical facilities that use them as guinea pigs (see below).

Childhood illnesses have increased dramatically over the past few decades.[111] The incidence of asthma has been growing steadily. Currently as many almost 14 percent of children in the US were, at some point in their lives, diagnosed with this disease. The incidence of cancer in children has been on a steady rise in past three decades, from about 120-175 cases per million children. Diagnosed mental retardation afflicts about 5-10 children per 1000, although the incidence of diagnosed childhood mental disorders of all types is much greater.

Diagnoses of bipolar disorder in children have increased 4,000 percent over the past decade.[112] Uncertainties within the medical establishment concerning diagnosis and treatment has led many practitioners to essentially experiment with medications because they have little knowledge about if, why and how they work. In recent years, there has been a dramatic increase in the number of children being diagnosed with serious psychiatric disorders, who are prescribed medications in the testing stage. Administered drugs can cause serious side effects, and virtually nothing is known about their long-term impact. "It's really to some extent an experiment, trying medications in these children of this age," according to child psychiatrist Dr. Patrick Bacon. "It's a gamble. And I tell parents there's no way to know what's going to work."[113] Child psychiatrist Dr. David Axelson states that "Very little is known about the effects of medications being used in the treatment of a complicated illness like bipolar ... So far, no antipsychotic drugs have been approved for treating children who have schizophrenia or bipolar illness. These drugs are used "off-label," for purposes others than for what they were tested or approved by the FDA." Nonetheless, they are being used on children. In the PBS report on the "medicated child," Dr. Kiki Chang explains how researchers are "at the forefront" in understanding how the medications work, but the field is not there yet.

Children are routinely exposed to a variety of harmful substances: PCBs, dioxins, furans or volatile organic substances (e.g., formaldehyde from insulation and carpeting). Data from the EPA study[114] suggest that childhood illness is attributable to the environment surrounding their growing bodies: About 65 percent of children are exposed to levels of ozone exceeding EPA standards, 15 percent to excessive particulate matter. Removal of lead as an anti-knock component in gasoline a few years ago, and improved emissions standards in many states have led to a significant decrease in childhood exposure to lead and carbon monoxide. About 11 percent of children are routinely exposed to cigarette smoke (2003 data). Fortunately, serum cotinine, a marker for nicotine exposure, has reduced from about 2 to 1 micrograms per ml in the past 2 decades or so, but this has not nearly corrected the problem. About 2 percent of children in the US drink water with contaminants exceeding EPA standards: nitrate/nitrite, coliforms, lead and copper, disinfection byproducts, chemical and radionuclides. Detectible residues of organophosphate pesticides are found in approximately 20 percent of foods (grains, fruits, vegetables, drinks). 1-2 percent of children live within 1 mile of a hazardous waste site.

One study performed over a period of twenty years on about a thousand people of Seveso, Italy exposed to dioxin during an industrial accident in 1976[115] revealed an increase in incidence of all cancers. An excess of lymphohemopoietic neoplasm (malignant or non-malignant tumor originating in bone cells) was found in men and women. Hodgkin's disease (cancer originating in the white blood cells) risk was elevated in the first 10-year observation period, whereas the highest increase for non-Hodgkin's lymphoma (a type of cancer involving cells of the immune system) and myeloid leukemia occurred after 15 years. An overall increase in diabetes was reported, notably among women. Chronic circulatory and respiratory diseases were moderately increased, suggesting a link with substances released during the accident. Results support the contention that dioxin is carcinogenic and is associated with other health issues, including cardiovascular and endocrine-related effects. This exposure is all the more significant for of children with low body weight compared with their levels of respiration and ingestion.

Americans engage widely in unhealthful activities. Of Americans 12 years of age or older, an estimated 20.1 million Americans were current substance abusers, including hallucinogens and non-medically-prescribed drugs.[116] Slightly more than half of Americans use alcohol, and more than one fifth, 58.1 million people (23.3 percent) participated in binge drinking at least once in the 30 days prior to the survey, and 17.3 million were reported as heavy drinkers. An estimated 70.9 million Americans (28.4 percent of the population) were current (past month) users of a tobacco product. Approximately 70 million Americans, about a quarter of the population, are obese.[117] When their role models engage in these self-destructive practices, they will be replicated in current and future behaviors of impressionable children.

From all indications, a number of conditions are adversely affecting the mental and physical health of children of the US and other industrialized countries:

- Exposure to harmful substances that pollute the environment, particularly significant for children with low body weight compared with adults;
- Control by parents who are, themselves, suffering ill effects of pollution and unhealthy life styles (drinking, smoking, poor dietary choices, obesity);
- Inclination of unhealthy parents (physical and mental) to routinely seek treatment for real and imagined illnesses of their children from the medical establishment, rather than taking responsibility for providing a healthy environment

(availability of publicly subsidized medical service plans such as Medicaid and Medicare provide cop-out solutions);
- Complicit medical practitioners, prone to treat symptoms that could easily be alleviated with proper parental care and involvement, and who prescribe drugs for children with little to no understanding of the impact mechanisms in the body or their consequences;
- A medical services system operated for profit and controlled largely by the insurance industry.

Hippocratic Oath notwithstanding, too many practitioners of the medical establishment appear to be uninterested in keeping people healthy, having invested huge amounts of time and money in gaining authorization to medicate people and to carry out surgical procedures. How often have you heard one of them tell you that you do not really need them, that if you go home and do the right things for your health, your body will take care of itself? After all, though there are useful analogies with machines, the body has a capacity that no automobile engine possesses: to heal itself. And yet, all too often medical practitioners act as if this capacity does not exist, and behave rather like auto mechanics, STP and wrench at the ready. This is a tragedy for everyone, but especially for children.

CHILD PERFORMERS

One form of flagrant child abuse that is scarcely recognizable is subjecting children to the rigid control and confusing direction demanded in media, theatre and other types of public exposure. Children's helplessness is exploited by directing them to assume roles and to utter scripted materials that are, if anything, antithetical to their developmental needs. The resulting confusion and sense of betrayal appears to be of little concern to the perpetrators. It's one thing for children to take part in the school play, dances or games, coached and directed by mentors and parents who presumably care for them and would not place them in frightening or tense situations, and quite another to be manipulated by commercially oriented media personnel, who generally regard the child actor as nothing more than an instrument of the trade.

Children have been exploited in this way for their obvious appeal in movies, plays, advertisements, and other forms of public display. If directed by one who is sensitive to the pitfalls, these experiences can be positive for children, but more often than not they are detrimental to the child performer's interests. Marketing and entertainment professionals have discovered the latent vicarious pleasure of their target audiences to identify with the powerful: viewing a child in simulated subjugation strikes a responsive chord. This is a potent mechanism for both titillating the passions and inspiring brand loyalty.

Media technology has progressed to the point where it should be possible in most cases to simulate the actions and utterances of children. In fact, many television and film presentations already have figured out how to do this, and the practice is already widespread. In some respects this is regrettable, as it does allow media to depict children in exploitative situations without employing real children. When the adult population has progressed socially to the point of being sufficiently repelled by such images, the practice will be curtailed either through legislative action or as market forces come to bear on the issue. There is no reason any longer, if ever there was, to directly involve children, or even images of children, in such productions.

The routine employment of children by media is of concern beyond the immediate consequences for the children involved. These public displays tend to condone acceptability of preying on the helpless. They reinforce a cultural tendency to justify the exercise of advantage, regardless of the consequences to others. So much for the Golden Rule.

In the US these unwholesome practices are defended by some under the provision of the First Amendment of the Constitution. The equal protection clause, however, has greater relevance, as the ability of children to cope with exploiters is inherently inferior to that of adults. Equal protection implies that defenses from exploitation must be statutorily strengthened for children. The issue goes far beyond abuses covered under child labor laws, other forms of physical molestation, or corrupting the morals of a minor. The emotional health of a child has to be protected under any circumstances. Until there is general recognition of these pernicious practices, statutes can be promulgated that would prevent adults from influencing a child to perform any action or to make any utterance that is not related directly to the child's well being: criminalizing these practices would tend to keep the child out of harm's way. Community activities in which the child's interests are the predominant theme would be encouraged. Harangues by autocratic and domineering sports directors and coaches would not. Certainly exploitation of children by media (and some misguided parental handmaidens) would be outlawed.

Some children led into performing or other public roles win lucrative contracts, awards or medals, usually shared with parents, guardians or agents. Others do not fare so well, and in addition to deprivation of their childhood, are forced to work excessively under physical and mental stress. The needs of the child performer are not always aligned with those of her directors, who may be interested in gaining access to the child's earnings or driven by ambition. Child performers are exposed to dimensions of adult life with which they lack experience to cope, e.g., sex, alcohol and drugs. Involvement as public figures reduces the amount of time and opportunities for learning and character development, which for children may be irredeemable.

Child athletes typically develop eating disorders from demands to maintain size and weight. Malnutrition is problematic for young girls who develop menstruation and other problems of puberty, leading to fractures and osteoporosis. Child performers of all types are subjected to pressures of exposure to audiences, which can be difficult even for seasoned adult performers

A case in point is the life of Judy Garland, child star of "*The Wizard of Oz*" and many other theatrical "successes." Garland was thrust into the theatre by her vaudevillian parents and the tender age of three, along with a sister. It was apparently the root of great antipathy that she eventually came to feel for her parents, from whom she became estranged, once characterizing her mother as "no good for anything except to create chaos and fear" and accusing her of treating Garland essentially as a cash cow from the earliest days of her career.[118]

To keep up with the frenetic pace of making one film after another, Garland, her frequent child costar Mickey Rooney, and other young performers were constantly given amphetamines and barbiturates to take before bed so that they could meet the demands of production schedules.[119] For Garland, this regular exposure to drugs led to addiction and a lifelong struggle, and contributed to her eventual death from an overdose of barbiturates, after reeling through five marriages. Despite her theatrical triumphs, Garland was plagued throughout her life with self-doubt and required constant reassurance that she was talented and attractive.[120] Garland's physical appearance was a source of consternation to the film moguls who sought to milk her talents to the utmost. During the filming of *The Wizard of Oz,* corseting and other devices were applied to alter her 16-year-old figure to the director's criteria. Her insecurity was exacerbated by insensitive treatment by her theatrical controllers, one of whom[121] referred to her as his "little hunchback."

REALITY TV

The latest fad promoted by avaricious media moguls is Reality television, which presents ostensibly ad-libbed situations with ordinary people performing rather than professionals. Children are frequent participants, placed in embarrassing and often dangerous situations that are a reflection of decreasing concern for children's welfare. It's clear that the quest for innovative programming runs wild as Reality television programming exploits children for the benefit of uncaring producers. Children's marketing appeal is too much of a lure for avaricious media functionaries, who will do anything to increase revenues and control costs. Children have great appeal, while at the same time not demanding much. They are malleable and vulnerable, qualities that endear them even more to money-grubbing producers.

Unthinking parents often sign away protections for their children, usually in violation of child labor laws, exposing them to danger. In one program a child reportedly burned her face and two children drank bleach from an unmarked bottle.[122]

Reality TV shows are "an opportunity for networks and producers to exploit kids' weaknesses, their frailties, their vulnerabilities, by putting them in unknown, shocking and often very embarrassing situations. They're making the mistake of assuming that children are adults in little bodies and that they can handle all these things. And it simply isn't true."[123] One former child actor, Paul Petersen, so concerned about the effects on children, formed the organization A Minor Consideration in 1990 to advocate legislation and other interventions to protect child actors, who are susceptible to great confusion in being directed to act according to script or circumstance rather than just being themselves. The American Academy of Child and Adolescent Psychiatry lobbied NBC to cancel the Reality show "Baby Borrowers" on the grounds that the program could cause distress and anxiety for the on-camera babies and toddlers. The creator defends it as "an educational tool designed to prevent teen pregnancy—one that borrows from reality TV to keep folks engaged while it makes its point: Parenting isn't for the faint of heart and is best left to grown-ups." *What better way to educate,* he says, *than to entertain* (italics added)? Entertainment as education? Many academics apparently think so. Rather than focus on opportunities for enlightenment, instead they treat the lecture room podium as a sound stage, essentially performing a stand up routine and mesmerizing their students to serve their inflated egos.

What is wrong with Reality TV, you ask. It is simply this: any time a child is placed in a situation where she is directed to do something outside the context of her intellectual and other developmental needs, particularly by people with whom she is neither familiar nor comfortable, she is confused and troubled, if not needlessly exposed to danger. In fact, children should never be directed to do anything, much less by outsiders. What a child needs is proper nurturing, part of which is careful, delicate and scrupulous illumination of the nature and possible consequences of the situation in which she finds herself. This is best accomplished by caring people, mainly enlightened parents and others totally committed to the child's interests and welfare.

Reality TV with children is a bad idea that should be scrapped, along with the avaricious producers who cravenly exploit children, without concern for the consequences for the most precious of segment of any society's population.

SLAVE LABOR AND PROSTITUTION

Employment of children in jobs that not only amount to slave labor but that also place children in situations where they suffer beatings, malnutrition, and sexual exploitation is rampant across the globe. Children make up a significant part of the industrial work force in many countries. They are often employed under stressful and otherwise dangerous conditions, and paid little to nothing. Many millions of children are producing furniture in Indonesia, soccer balls in Asia, and doing difficult and hazardous agricultural jobs throughout the world.

According to the United Nations Children's Fund (UNICEF), as many as 1.2 million children per year are caught up in trafficking. Aside from being denied the opportunity for a normal family environment, trafficked children are used as sources of cheap or even slave labor and suffer violence in addition to sexual exploitation. Over 30 percent of the sex workers in southeast Asia are between 12 and 17 years old.

In 2005 NBC News investigators from the Dateline television program found impoverished families in Cambodia selling their children, as young as 5 years old, for sex. In a country still reeling from the effects of the atrocities of the Khmer Rouge a few decades ago, sexual predators are able to gain control over these children for a pittance. Their exploiters, who operate sex-for-hire emporiums, sell virgins for premium prices because the demand is so great. A 14-year-old from a poor Vietnamese family while walking home from school one day was lured to work in a café that was really a brothel. The girl was forced to have sex with men, including many Americans. One pimp led stunned investigators to his "stable" of prostitutes, some of whom were as young 8 years old. The same sort of thing is happening in other trafficking centers such as Bangkok and Amsterdam.

The Cambodia Daily (newspaper published in Phnom Penh) in December 2000 exposed the case of 57-year-old American pedophile engaged in sexual encounters with a 14-year-old. The Cambodian prosecutor publicly exonerated the child molester because he claimed that the child was not a virgin and had previously operated as a prostitute. The fact that the child had been sucked out of the cesspool of grinding poverty, and manipulated by desperate or unfeeling family members or pimps, was of little significance to the prosecutor. The assertion of willing participation by a 14-year-old for this kind of activity is so patently absurd as to strangle the imagination.

Aside from direct sale of children, a typical ploy for operators is to set up an agency ostensibly for supplying domestic workers for the relatively affluent. In many cases, desperate but well-meaning parents release their children in hopes of giving them an opportunity for gainful employment, for education or for providing adequate shelter. Typically the reality is that these young children become slaves who are forced to provide household services without compensation and often sex. A case in point is Adiza, a 10-year-old Togolese girl sent to work as a domestic by her aunt, who raised her after her parents separated. Adiza was sent to the home of a woman in Lome, Togo's capitol, who was only marginally better off economically. She was forced to work long hours without pay, beaten and denied schooling and adequate nutrition. She finally ran away and found her way to a shelter run by a Swiss charity.[124]

POVERTY AMONG CHILDREN

In 2010, 15.1 percent of all US residents lived in poverty, over 45 million, defined as an individual earning $11,670 or less and $19,790 or less for a family of three.[125] This currently amounts to 10 percent of all families, 7.6 million. The poverty rate in 2010 was the highest since 1993. Children represent a disproportionate share of the poor in the United States, 24 percent of the total population, but 36 percent of the poor. Poverty is substantially greater among children of racial and ethnic minorities. The rate of child poverty in the United States is more than double that in most developed countries.[126] According to J. Lawrence Aber, director of the National Center for Children in Poverty

(NCCP), the current child poverty rate is about twice as high as it was in 1969. The poverty rate among African Americans and Latinos is almost three times that of Whites.[127]

What is even more ominous is that the disparity in incomes between rich and poor is accelerating. Jared Bernstein, a labor economist with the Economic Policy Institute: "in the last few decades, pay for wealthier Americans has risen dramatically—fueled by growth in salaries, bonuses, stock options and other compensation, but wages for millions of lower-wage workers have dwindled. Many have lost their jobs altogether."[128]

Emanuel Saez, economist at UC Berkeley, points to dramatic shifts in income distribution in the US since early 20th century.[129] The share of the bottom 90 percent of income earners looks like a roller coaster, 50.7 percent in 1928, up to 67.5 percent in 1944 and then plummeting to 49.6 percent in 2012 (less than 50 percent for the first time in history). For the top 1 percent the pattern reversed: for the corresponding years, 23.9 percent, down to 11.3 percent and then back up to 22.5 percent. Income was equalized during the war years as worker shortages and defense production allowed breadwinners to find high wage employment. Since the 1970s the top 1 percent has reaped benefits of globalization. Although suffering a setback during the Great Recession starting in 2007, their incomes not only recovered quickly, but also continue to accelerate.

Kent Hughes (2005), economist at the Woodrow Wilson Center in Washington DC, predicts that the wage gap in the US will most likely continue to increase. Hughes believes that competition from the foreign labor force, often willing to work for minimal compensation even in the skilled professions, will further pressure the collapse in wages for American workers. Competition in the labor market arises from outsourcing and also from importation of expatriate workers. Economic globalization is a potent factor in income disparity (see Chapter 10).

Economic growth does not necessarily translate into a better deal for children, even in the United States, purportedly the richest country in the world. Poverty among American youth has increased during the past three decades, while the average annual GDP increase was a bit less than 3 percent (major recessions occurred only in 2008 and 2009 and short and shallow recessions in 1990-91 and 2001). After the longest peacetime expansion in American history that ended in 2007, one in five American children still lived in poverty in 2012, up from about one in six in 2000. Poverty among children is endemic in the western world and catastrophic everywhere.[130] Sweden has the lowest rate of child poverty with 2.4 percent, but New York leads all states with 20.6 percent of its youngsters living below the poverty line.

Robert F. Drinan, S.J., a priest who was a member of the United States Congress, discussed the plight of children around the world in his study *Poverty in America, A Global Revolution for Children.*[131] Almost a billion people entered the 21st century unable to read a book or sign their names. Father Drinan predicted then that each year over 130 million children would grow up without access to basic education, currently almost 50 percent of children in the 47 least-developed countries. The United Nations Children's Fund (UNICEF) estimates that 101 million children of primary school age were not attending school in 2007. Girls constitute 73 percent of this number, which is linked to high rates of infant mortality. Drinan points to the state of Kerala in southern India, where universal literacy results in the lowest rate of infant mortality in any developing country. Progress in literacy rates continued up to the time that developing countries were confronted with payments on massive debt and were forced into restructuring by the International Monetary Fund in the 1980s.

Children living in poverty have a few more strikes against them, plagued with sickness and malnutrition. "There are still nearly 11 million children who die every year of preventable causes."[132] Almost always they are the poorest and most marginalized. A more recent menace in sub-Saharan Africa is the prevalence of HIV/AIDS, with young people between 12-24 years of age constituting about 60 percent of infected individuals. Impoverished children typically have greater rates of school failure, illness and premature death.

CHILD SOLDIERS

"Approximately 250,000 children under the age of eighteen are thought to be fighting in conflicts around the world, and hundreds of thousands more are members of armed forces who could be sent into combat at any time. Although most child soldiers are between 15-18 years old, significant recruitment starts at the age of ten and the use of even younger children has been recorded."[133] This has led to efforts of international bodies to prevent the recruitment of children as participants. In May 2000 the General Assembly of the United Nations adopted the *Optional Protocol to the Convention on the Rights of the Child*, which had been first promulgated in the 1980s. The Convention affirms that children around the world require special protections and calls for improvements in the status of children, stressing peace and security. The Rome Statute of the International Criminal Court identifies conscription or enlisting children under the age of fifteen or using them to participate actively in hostilities in both international and non-international armed conflict as a war crime. In June 1999, the International Labor Organization Convention No. 182 approved a provision to prohibit forced or compulsory recruitment of children for use in armed conflict.

Efforts to restrict or eliminate the use of children in armed conflict have not been particularly successful. "Armed groups in at least 24 countries located in every region of the world were known to have recruited children under 18 years of age, and many have used them in hostilities. Many have proved resistant to pressure and persuasion. Their widely diverse characters, aims and methods, and the varied environments in which they operate militate against generic solutions."[134] Myanmar is identified as the worst offender, with thousands of children used in the government's counter-insurgency campaign. Other countries that continue to press children into armed hostilities are Chad, D R Congo, Somalia, Sudan and Uganda. Children were used as human shields in some instances, for example by both Israeli forces[135] and the Palestinians[136] in their conflicts. In some instances children have been employed as spies, subjecting them to the risk of reprisal.[137]

Regrettably, the US military has apparently fought to prevent international agreement on a minimum of 18 years of age for conscription or recruitment[138] by inducements aimed at younger children, leaving high school students within their target population.

No aspect of human behavior is more irrational than the treatment of children around the world. That such a small proportion are being nurtured with all of the elements necessary to grow up mentally and physically healthy, and socially responsible, is a recipe for continued degradation in the quality of life on Earth. If universal peace, prosperity and justice are ever to reign, or even become the norm, and if the future of life is to be secured as our natural heritage is preserved, nurturing children will have to become the first priority of society, above economics, military prowess, adult health care or any other activity or program for which society budgets resources. The reason is that each child deprived of the opportunity to reach her highest potential intelligence and mental and physical health becomes to that extent a drag on society. Only when children are nurtured so that they identify with nature, of which they are indelibly a part, and with holistic societal goals, will humanity reach a sustainable mode of existence. This is the surest path to lasting security.

CHAPTER 4

RIGHTS ARE WRONG IN DEMOCRACY

Societies that consider themselves enlightened and progressive take great pride in having granted their citizens "rights"—legal guarantees concerning respect and support for citizens' aspirations, so long as they conform to social norms. While primitive societies tend to be autocratic, with little protection from arbitrary decisions of elites concerning the welfare of ordinary members, civilized societies usually promulgate rules of behavior and legal standards that provide a greater degree of security for life, limb and property.

The second section of the Declaration of Independence of the United States of America, adopted by the Second Continental Congress on July 4, 1776, contains these words: "We hold these truths self-evident, that all men are created equal, that they are endowed by their Creator with certain inalienable *rights* (italics added), that among these are life, liberty and the pursuit of happiness"

Inalienable rights? What is inalienable is absolute, immutable, undeniable. As used in the Declaration of Independence, rights are fundamental perquisites that may not be abrogated. There are at least two problems with this statement: First, even if there is an interventionist creator, it's not likely that she, he or it would be concerned with rights. Overwhelming evidence indicates that such a creator would have to be considered anything but benevolent—too much bloodshed, other forms of violence and injustice inflicted even on its most devout followers (see Chapter 7). Even if a creator does grant rights, there is little evidence that it carries much weight. Life, liberty and the pursuit of happiness are far from universally secure. In their earthly manifestations, rights granted to citizens of any state have proved to be anything but inalienable.[139]

Life? Citizens are routinely put to death by the state (with or without due process according to the particular system for doling out this type of punishment), either as retaliation for certain acts considered to be of capital offense or as a deterrent. *Liberty?* Millions of people are incarcerated and deprived of liberty, some for committing acts with only themselves as victims. *Pursuit of happiness?* In early 2010 there were officially approximately 15 million unemployed persons in the United States alone, many desperate to find a source of income. Millions more have abandoned the quest and are in a virtually permanent state of unhappiness. About 45 million people live in poverty: feeding themselves is a constant challenge.

No, if there are any rights granted, it is by consent either of the governor or governed, depending on political structure. Obsequious politicians seeking the good graces of their "creator" may claim a theological origin for rights, but only designated authorities in the political hierarchy can effectively grant them, and can as easily take them away or otherwise deny them on the grounds of expediency or security.

Granting "rights" to subjects of political authority is a rather new social invention, probably derived initially from the Magna Carta, negotiated with King John in 1215 by English barons who were interested in protecting some of their privileges. The document was amended from time to time, and the version of 1297 is still in effect in England and Wales. One of the main clauses is that of "due process," whereby citizens are guaranteed a hearing by their peers for offenses charged by state authorities.

A "Bill of Rights" was a condition for conferring the crown of England to William of Orange by the Westminster Convention of 1689, an "Act Declaring the Rights and Liberties of the Subject, and Settling the Succession of the Crown." By virtue of this act, William and his wife, Mary, were enjoined from enacting or suspending laws or levying taxes for their personal benefit without the consent of Parliament. Similarly, in an "Act of Settlement" of 1701 the Hanoverian Princess Sophia accepted the crown along with a Bill of Rights containing a proviso that she and her heirs would be powerless to enact laws without the consent of Parliament.[140]

So, historically, the concept of rights derives from reaction to what were considered unjust laws and levying of taxes by royal prerogative. The mechanism of redress was to assign powers to a representative body of peers or citizens for approving royal initiatives.

In the US the founding fathers in 1791 proposed and sent to the states during the First Congress the first ten amendments to the US Constitution, a Bill of Rights that enunciated a series of liberties for individuals vis-à-vis constitutional authority. James Madison proposed the Bill of Rights as a concession to anti-Federalists, who threatened ratification of the Constitution, fearing the strong central government advocated by the Federalists. One early proponent was George Mason, a southern planter and delegate to the Federal Convention in 1787 charged with drafting the Constitution, who had previously proposed something similar for his home state of Virginia. Mason refused to sign the constitutional draft because it lacked a clear statement of individual rights.

The concept of officially specified rights resonated with libertarian national leaders based upon the prospect of virtually limitless opportunities for resource exploitation, which carried more weight than its functions as a constraint on authority or on the practice of selective granting of privileges, as in the Magna Carta.

The ninth amendment asserts that the enumeration of certain (individual) rights in the Constitution "shall not be construed to deny or disparage others retained by the people." However, enthusiasm for the Constitution's "inalienable rights" was tempered by caution even of Federalists. who championed individual rights during the Constitutional Convention of 1789, but who, according to Morrison (1965) "had learned from experience that the natural rights philosophy, taken straight, would go to the nation's head and make it totter, or fall." There appeared to be at least a sense that rights granted to citizens, or even those "retained by the people," might be a polarizing influence, turning citizens inward to seek their own advantage even, if need be, at society's expense.

As these individual rights have been so firmly entrenched in the American ethos, the concept has been extended accordingly, far beyond the original intent. The notion has surfaced in many contexts, such as human rights, civil rights, property rights, and ultimately to what makes the society essentially the provider of last resort. Local governments in the United States and elsewhere, corporations and individual citizens, who have exceeded their ability to support their desired levels of expenditure or consumption, now routinely appeal to the federal government to bail them out.

Within the past century or so, and particularly since the publication of *Origin of Species* by Charles Darwin in 1859, it has become clear that humans descended from primitive organisms such as bacteria and archaea that formed initially during the Archeozoic Eon of 3.9 to 2.5 billion years ago. Only about five to seven million years ago, *H. sapiens* shared a common ancestor with the apes. During the past 4-5 million years several species of hominids (bipedal, large-brained primates), evolved and became extinct. *Homo sapiens* alone among these hominids stood the test of exposure to the changing environmental challenges. If the creator was to invest humans with inalienable rights, it had to be a fairly complex endeavor, as the first human genes were propagating and replacing the then extant hominid stock. During the transition, the creator would have had difficulty deciding if a particular individual or generation had been sufficiently transformed to qualify for inalienable rights (however, see comments of Pope John Paul II, Chapter 6, in which he reconciles the existence of soul in humans, while denying it for our primate ancestors and cousins, implicitly identifying the precise point at which his deity produced the genetic alteration separating humans from beasts).

It appears doubtful that rights are writ large in the sky. This does not restrain massive numbers of Americans from assertions about their rights, whether or not constitutionally sanctioned. For example, many individuals proclaim their right to do with their property as they wish, regardless of consequences to their neighbors. The right of control over one's offspring in a manner of one's choosing, regardless of the possibility of engendering—through negligence, incompetence or other deficiencies—insensitivity, abuse or (even worse) menaces to society, is stoutly defended. The right to vitriolic, hate-mongering, or abusive speech is asserted to be under the protection of the First Amendment. The right to drive an automobile in any condition of repair and at any level of control, particularly in the US, is widely thought to be inviolate (although about one third of states do conduct annual safety inspections).

The right of access to firearms is so firmly entrenched that efforts merely to keep guns out of the hands of incompetents and children are strenuously opposed by powerful lobbies, despite, in the US during 2010, 31,672 Americans losing their lives in homicides, suicides and unintentional shootings, and another 73,505 treated for gunshot wounds. Firearms were the third-leading cause of injury-related deaths, after poisoning and motor vehicle accidents.[141] However, gun deaths are expected to exceed motor vehicle deaths by 2015. "While motor vehicle deaths dropped 22 percent from 2005 to 2010, gun fatalities are rising again after a low point in 2000, according to the Center for Disease Control. Shooting deaths in 2015 will probably rise to almost 33,000, and those related to autos will decline to about 32,000, based on the 10-year average trend."[142]

Is there any serious doubt about the connection between homicide and gun availability? Although the number of juvenile homicides has decreased from a peak in 1993 (about 2,840), still in 2011 almost 1,500 juveniles were murdered (about 10 percent of all victims). Of these, 47 percent were killed with a firearm.[143]

In early twenty first century United States, exercise of some rights has been catastrophic for the nation's youth. The mass media exercise their right (if not obligation) to court the attention of children (and the legions of adults who are similarly vulnerable), adapting them through clever psychological devices to revel in violent solutions to every sort of problem. Couple this with the inviolable right of citizens to bear arms, and you have a situation in which young people have taken to dealing with their "enemies" in one of the prominent modes of their socialization—to blow them away in a hail of gunfire in simulated, and sometimes all too real, assaults. Access of youth to firearms, coupled with the culture of violence embedded in video games and Internet web sites (e.g., those that provide instructions on how to construct pipe bombs) is an explosive mixture. There is little doubt that these media devices provide powerful influences for vulnerable youth, inciting them to violent responses to conflict, and heightening their anger from ordinary frustrations.

The inclination to resort to violence is reinforced as children emulate their role models, adults who most influence their behavior. For large segments of the US population, gun ownership is considered a sacred right, protected by the Second Amendment to the Constitution. In its last decision in the case of McDonald v. City of Chicago in 2010, the Supreme Court struck down the city's handgun ban, which prohibited possession by most private citizens, on the grounds of the incorporation doctrine (that the Bill of Rights applies to the states). This was consistent with other judicial decisions concerning the amendment, attesting to the success of the main lobby group promoting individual access to firearms, the National Rifle Association (NRA). In his recent book former US Supreme Court Justice John Paul Stevens (2014) proposes a modification to the amendment that would better reflect the intention of the founding fathers to provide for the common defense, rather than protection of the individual: "A well regulated Militia, being necessary to the security of a free State, the right of the people to keep and bear Arms *when serving in the Militia* (italics added) shall not be infringed." He notes that Chief Justice Warren Burger, who served from 1969 to 1986, stated on a news broadcast in 1991 (The MacNeil/Lehrer NewsHour on PBS) that the amendment "has been the subject of one of the greatest pieces of fraud, I repeat the word "fraud," on the American public by special interest groups that I have ever seen in my lifetime." That fraud is the contention that the amendment was intended to guarantee unrestricted access to firearms for all citizens for any purpose.

RIGHTS—FOUNDATION OF THE "TRAGEDY OF THE COMMONS"

Every privilege protected by rights sows the seeds of social disharmony, as so cogently explained by Garrett Hardin's analysis of the use of the commons. Hardin explained the phenomenon as the "tragedy of the commons": "Ruin is the destination toward which all men rush, each pursuing his own best interest in a society that believes in the freedom (right to access) of the commons. Freedom in a commons brings ruin to all."[144] Hardin alludes to psychological denial that evolution has created through natural selection, allowing the individual to ignore the deleterious consequences of misuse of the commons. He suggests education as a way of avoiding this catastrophe, but that it must be applied relentlessly to have any significant effect.

Rights set the individual against society. Citizens who are imbued with a sense of rights have to be inclined to think of themselves as aliens, outside the social structure and conditioned to seek to extract perquisites that tend to enhance personal wealth, prestige and social advancement. Consequences for the society are far down on the list of concerns.

Whence cometh rights but the commons, the socio-political structure shared by all citizens? And yes, the sense of responsibility required for circumventing the menace to which Hardin alludes, requires virtually constant reinforcement. Rather than being indoctrinated with a sense of rights, if instead a sense of responsibility is stressed, the individual is drawn to society. One's status would be dependent upon the degree of social contribution. Societies need more cohesive elements, not less, if they are to function successfully. Even though humans are, by nature, a socially oriented species, in the raw state it is a marriage of convenience, with individual goals and aspirations predominating.

CIVIC RESPONSIBILITY

The rights enumerated in the Constitution by the founding fathers were promulgated in an era when fear of autocratic rule predominated as a consequence of their experience with English monarchs. However, a very functional system of social organization and governance can more effectively be predicated on the concept of individual responsibility. Think what the consequences might be if all citizens are encouraged from the early years to internalize the virtues of social responsibility. Laws and regulations would admonish citizens to carry out their responsibilities rather than to exercise their rights. Most importantly, youngsters would be universally inculcated with the responsibilities of citizenship. If penalty, retribution or castigation were needed, they would result from failure to adhere to standards of responsibility rather than from violating others' "rights."

Given the hierarchical nature of primate social organization and its obvious implications for human society, acceptance of civic responsibility by the individual citizen, the fundamental and essential characteristic of democracy, does not arise spontaneously. It requires that citizens throughout their life span be nurtured in an environment functionally democratic in every dimension, and thereby inculcating responsibility, so that each citizen is thoroughly imbued with its principles and tenets.

Under the judicial system individuals would be held accountable for violations of their social responsibilities. Laws and regulations would be constructed so that the social implications of an illegal act or activity would be emphasized. Rather than defining robbery as "the felonious taking of property of another from his person, or in his immediate presence, against his will, by violence or intimidation" (Webster's Dictionary) it would be defined as an act in which the perpetrator irresponsibly deprived a fellow citizen of the possession and enjoyment of property to which he/she is entitled.

The Bill of Rights instead would be a Bill of Responsibilities. The following is one rewriting of the first ten amendments to the United States Constitution that reflect responsibilities, rather than rights, of citizens and governmental authorities (original and proposed modification):

Article I: Congress shall make no law respecting an establishment of religion, or prohibiting the free exercise thereof; or abridging the freedom of speech, or of the press; or the right of the people peaceably to assemble, and to petition the government for a redress of grievances.

Mod: The Congress shall be empowered to make laws that foster understanding on the part of citizens of their *responsibility* to respect the exercise of religion, the free expression of ideas by individuals and the media, the peaceable assembly of the people, and of their *responsibility* to petition the government to redress grievances of their fellow citizens.

Article II: A well-regulated militia, being necessary to the security of a free State, the right of the people to bear arms shall not be infringed.

Mod: The people shall be apprised of their *responsibility* to provide for the security of a free State, by participating, when called upon, in the activities of a well-regulated militia.

Article III: No soldier shall, in time of peace be quartered in any house, without the consent of the owner, nor in time of war, but in a manner prescribed by law.

Mod: It shall be the *responsibility* of the people, in time of peace and war, to provide for the quartering of soldiers, as prescribed by law.

Article IV: The right of the people to be secure in their persons, houses, papers, and effects, against unreasonable searches and seizures, shall not be violated, and no warrants shall issue, but upon probable cause, supported by oath or affirmation, and particularly describing the place to be searched, and the persons or things to be seized.

Mod: All citizens and governmental bodies shall be *responsible* for assuring that the people are secure in their persons, houses, papers, and effects, against unreasonable searches and seizures, and warrants shall be issued only upon probable cause, supported by oath or affirmation, and particularly describing the place to be searched, and the persons or things to be seized.

Article V: No person shall be held to answer for a capital, or otherwise infamous crime, unless on a presentment or indictment of a grand jury, except in cases arising in the land or naval forces, or in the militia, when in actual service in time of war or public danger; nor shall any person be subject for the same offense to be twice put in jeopardy of life or limb; nor shall be compelled in any criminal case to be a witness against himself, nor be deprived of life, liberty, or property, without due process of law; nor shall private property be taken for public use, without just compensation.

Mod: Citizens and government bodies shall have the *responsibility* to assure that no person be held to answer for a capital, or otherwise infamous crime, except on a presentment or indictment of a grand jury, unless such crimes arise while in the service of land or naval forces, or in the militia during time of war or public danger; and furthermore, to assure that no person for the same offense be twice put in jeopardy of life or limb; nor compelled in any criminal case to be a witness against himself, nor be deprived of life, liberty, or property, without due process of law; nor have private property taken for public use, without just compensation.

Article VI: In all criminal prosecutions, the accused shall enjoy the right to a speedy and public trial, by an impartial jury of the state and district wherein the crime shall have been committed, which district shall have been previously ascertained by law, and to be informed of the nature and cause of the accusation; to be confronted with the witnesses against him; to have compulsory process for obtaining witnesses in his favor, and to have the assistance of counsel for his defense.

Mod: In all criminal prosecutions, citizens and government bodies shall have the *responsibility* to assure a speedy and public trial for the accused, by an impartial jury of the state and district wherein the crime shall have been committed, which district shall have been previously ascertained by law, and to be informed of the nature and cause of the accusation; to be confronted with the witnesses against him; to have compulsory process for obtaining witnesses in his favor, and to have the assistance of counsel for his defense.

Article VII: In suits at common law, where the value in controversy shall exceed twenty dollars, the right of trial by jury shall be preserved, and no fact tried by a jury, shall be otherwise reexamined in any court of the United States, than according to the rules of the common law.

Mod: In suits at common law, where the value in controversy shall exceed twenty dollars, citizens and governing bodies shall have the *responsibility* to assure that the accused be tried by jury, and no fact tried by a jury, shall be otherwise reexamined in any court of the United States, than according to the rules of the common law.

Article VIII: Excessive bail shall not be required, nor excessive fines imposed, nor cruel and unusual punishments inflicted.

Mod: Citizens and governing bodies shall be *responsible* to assure that excessive bail not be required, nor excessive fines imposed, nor cruel and unusual punishments inflicted.

Article IX: The enumeration in the Constitution, of certain rights, shall not be construed to deny or disparage others retained by the people.

Mod: The enumeration in the Constitution, of certain *responsibilities*, shall not be construed to deny or disparage other *responsibilities* of the people.

Article X: The powers not delegated to the United States by the Constitution, nor prohibited by it to the states, are reserved to the states respectively, or to the people.

Mod: The *responsibilities* not delegated specifically to the United States by the Constitution, nor unassigned by it to the states, are reserved to the states respectively, or to the people.

The effect of these changes would be to encourage cooperation rather than alienation of citizens, who would no longer be set in opposition to society by their fundamental structural relationships. This would tend to preclude situations in which individual citizens or groups press claims against society primarily to satisfy their own special interests at public expense. Stressing responsibilities brings people closer together, encouraging them to adopt social goals and aspirations, without sacrificing individual identity.

The extent to which civilized society grants rights to its citizens, rather than inculcating a sense of civic responsibility (rights' antithesis), is the measure of how far it is from achieving the salubrious environment and concomitant peace, justice and prosperity that are common aspirations of people everywhere. Society's granting of rights is a threat to the future of life, as it promotes excessive demands on Earth's sustainable capacity and hastens the day of reckoning.

CHAPTER 5

SEXUAL REPRESSION AND THE PEEPING TOM

Humanity's transition from social organization based upon hunting and gathering to what is now known as civilization has greatly enhanced our potency as a cosmic threat. Acceptance of a more extensive and intrusive hierarchy, and repression arising from frustration with a greater range of mores, strictures and laws that are alien to our nature, is conducive to aggressive behavior.

Marcus Hamilton, et. al. (2007) describes how hunter-gatherer societies were, and are, essentially egalitarian, and yet organized in a hierarchy of sorts, comprised of a nested series of discrete, yet flexible social units that occupy demarcated areas and interact with exchanges of materials and information as a means of dissipating social tension.

During our formative stages of development, our large and active brain detected some ontogenetic advantage in more complex associations, but to our lasting misfortune, did not see the entire picture. Why not sow crops instead of wasting a lot of time looking for them? Why not domesticate beasts instead of risking one's neck in a mad, coordinated dash through the brush as hunger pangs dictated? Why not assemble in communities rather than the rude and dispersed accommodations of our developmental experience? Why not accept a leader and a few underlings to manage things so that subsistence would be better assured?

Each new acquiescence to the gradual encroachment of civilization was accompanied by commensurate acceptance of concessions on limits to individual liberty. In its most intrusive form, civilization is hierarchical, with defined social classes (potentates, nobles, chiefs, aristocrats, freemen, serfs, slaves), institutions, and rules embodied in mores, laws and statutes that constrain behavioral instincts derived from our evolutionary past. The price of security gained under civilization is usually the acceptance of a ruling class, accompanied by their bureaucratic underlings—generally urbanites who are largely detached from the messy business of finding or producing what is needed for sustenance and beyond.

Sigmund Freud (2005), in a compact but potent essay, analyzes the impacts of civilization on the human psyche and how the repressive elements of social organization promote aggression. Freud explains that impulses of the libido, creative energy directed toward personal (including sexual) objectives, are conflicted by civilization: "love thy neighbor" and the Golden Rule are inimical to its fundamental aspirations.

Civilization upset the applecart. The social safety net provided in many of them relieves (in some cases, eliminates) for the parents, particularly the male, the natural demands of parenthood—investing time and energy in survival of offspring—thus allowing these impulses to be diverted to other (aggressive?) purposes. One of them might involve free expression of libidinal impulses. However, this would be disruptive: the monogamous love bond, one of civilization's pillars, is a libidinal constraint deeply rooted in the process of human developmental. Paleoanthropologists generally agree that it derives from neoteny of human infants (inordinate retention of infantile characteristics)—the gestation period is insufficient to bring fetuses to anywhere near a state of self-sufficiency at birth, as is the case with most other animals. Nature then created devices that would ensure sufficient support for a period that would allow the faculties of the newborn to reach a state of readiness for survival in the environment.

The mother and father became an "item," primarily through the device of making the female sexually active, not only during estrus, but continually. In codifying the sanctity of the love bond, civilization has added to libidinal frustration.

Civilization then becomes antagonistic to sexuality. The libido, and particularly sexual expression, has to be repressed to avoid its potential for dissolving civilization's cement—cooperative, if not friendly, associations and collaborations among its citizens. Unfettered expression of the libido is antithetical to maintenance of friendships, particularly dangerous with the potent instruments available to the individual to redress real or imagined slights or offenses.

Although sex has become virtually a public sport in modern industrial societies, it is nevertheless repressed, with bizarre consequences. Rape, for example, is endemic in the United States, although the rate of victimization has apparently declined in the period from 1995 to 2010.[145] . Somewhere in the country, according to one estimate, more than two women are raped or sexually assaulted every minute, although apparently only a small percentage of rapes are reported to police.[146]. About one in six women and one in thirty-three men were raped at some time in their lives,

Civilization, at least the American brand, has not been very successful, it seems, in repressing libidinal urges. While perpetrators fall into at least two categories, "criminal" and "psychiatric," the common theme seems to be one of releasing aggression rather than merely satisfying sexual appetite. Research on the psychology of rape indicates that the criminal perpetrator is viewed as a poorly educated male from lower socioeconomic levels, with a criminal record of offenses such as exhibitionism and fetishism, generally antisocial and subject to manipulation. The psychiatric rapist is of a higher socio-economic stratum, suffering from feelings of inadequacy or other personal problems. A more general analysis places the root at a subculture of violence "whose values may be different from those of the dominant culture ... these adolescents and young men may be demonstrating their toughness and masculinity in a more violent and antisocial manner."[147]

In some other societies, sexual taboos are taken so seriously that offenders risk being ostracized, incarcerated, maimed or even killed for offenses. Islamic law prescribes corporal and capital punishment for offenses such as rape and adultery. Women's honor and modesty are to be protected, so immodest clothing is proscribed. Young men and women are encouraged to marry early, and many other restrictions are intended to avoid rape and other crimes. The punishment for rape in Islam is the same as the punishment for *zina* (adultery or fornication), which is stoning if the perpetrator is married, and one hundred lashes and banishment for one year if not married.

Although not specifically mandated by religious tenets, cultural tradition often dictates isolation for Islamic women in the home, who are relegated to special areas forbidden to males. In many societies a woman may not leave the home unless accompanied by a male. Women are often permitted to be in public only when attired in the *burqa*, a form of dress that conceals everything but the eyes, and even they are covered with a mesh screen.

In some Islamic societies, females are subjected to genital mutilation and circumcision, although the practice is also prevalent in other religious and cultural environments, mainly in Africa and the Middle East. In its most extreme form the clitoris and both *labia minora* and *majora* are excised, with two sides of the vulva sewn across the vagina leaving only a small opening for passage of urine and menstrual blood.

When societies were still mainly rural and agricultural, the packing density of people allowed for sexual inclinations to be expressed privately and clandestinely in a variety of ways. Humans have probably always engaged in the same variety of sexual acts, whether through encounters with the same or opposite sex or through other outlets for sexual expression available in the pastoral setting.

With the onset of urbanization and spatial density of humans much compressed, outlets for sexual expression in a natural and unhurried manner were reduced to the point of inducing sexual stresses that demanded relief. Sexually suggestive music, attire and behavior are very likely protests against the disappearance of trysting places that were so easily found in forest, field and farm. All of the hysterical mayhem of the "entertainment" industry that has since followed is a phenomenon of sympathetic resonance, in which the pendulum has swung ever higher with increasing population density and other constraints on sexual expression imposed by civilization. Sexual repression in modern society is another wrong turn for humanity, with potentially devastating consequences.

There was a time when across the United States on any given day, a few articles could be found in the local press dealing with cases of the "peeping Tom." These were primarily males who sought to indulge in vicarious sensual pleasures by peering in on the unknowing while they were either in states of undress or engaged in some kind of sexual endeavor. The voyeur was not only considered immoral, but was often subject to arrest and prosecution by virtue of having violated an ordinance or statute.

In that bygone era, voyeurs, if they were sufficiently discreet, would find plenty of opportunity for their lascivious satisfaction. With little concern for security, most Americans rarely took pains to secure their lodgings either from entry or observation. Humans are probably the sexiest creatures on Earth: lesser species generally engage in sexual activity, whether for pure procreation or for recreational, dominance or bonding purposes, only when conditions are ripe—when the female is in estrus; human females, on the other hand, are sexually receptive almost always, even during lactation and menstruation. There is certainly no lack of sexual interest or constraint on human males outside of emotional or physical impediments, many of which, incidentally, are related to their preoccupation with sex. So, the voyeur would have a better than even chance of success picking his targets at random.

Voyeurism is considered a psychosis, or serious mental disorder, in particular *paraphilia*, which involves sexual interest other than normal copulation. A characteristic of the disorder is that the perpetrator is motivated by an urge to surreptitiously observe others who are either naked, in a state of undress or engaged in sexual activity. In the voyeur, this is the primary mode of sexual arousal and expression. The voyeur is different from a person who simply enjoys nakedness or watching people have sex, since the arousal comes from the fact the other person is unaware they are being watched. Sigmund Freud

(*"Instincts and Their Vicissitudes,"* 1915) and other psychoanalysts have identified the condition as an obsession to see other's genitals while hiding one's own, but with a desire to be noticed as observer. Other disorders are responsible for related antisocial behaviors.

It's very unusual at the turn of the 21st century to encounter any public notice of the "peeping Tom," or voyeur, and interesting to speculate why this is true.

The public media, up to the 1960s, had to be content with occasional tentative forays into the forbidden land of sexual explicitness. Prior to the advent of television and its rapid acceptance as an entertainment and information medium after World War II, the local cinema was the primary source of family entertainment, supplemented by feature articles and comics in the local paper.

In films, sexual encounters were not so subtly hidden behind restrained physical contact and timely cuts. Sometimes sexual symbols were employed, such as the gushing fire hydrant. In this way, even films that were laden with sexual innuendo were rendered acceptable for even the most sensitive eyes and ears. All members of the family could attend without embarrassment or concern for moral corruption of the young.

When describing adulterous trysts, the print media alluded to "indiscretions." Sexually aggressive behavior was seldom identified explicitly. Rape was described as assault, violation, despoilment, or some other oblique terminology was employed.

A voyeur with the price of admission to a burlesque show, a kind of bawdy theatrical presentation featuring risqué skits and provocative choreographies, could somewhat satisfy his lustful proclivities, but usually liberties that could be publicly exhibited during such performances were constrained by local religious and civic authorities. Under these conditions, the serious voyeur had no choice but to scuttle among the bushes on a moonless night.

As television began to capture the attention of the masses during the 1950s, diminishing the market for traditional entertainment and information, the industry sought to differentiate its product as a means of survival. Dismantling inhibitions and proscriptions on sexually explicit exposition was a process of acclimatization.

Legitimating public sex was easily, albeit programmatically, absorbed by viewers chafing at Victorian constraints, but generally reluctant to be the "first one in the water."

Media moguls who suddenly found a use for the US constitution that was certainly not envisioned by the founding fathers systematically demolished social and legal barriers to what was previously considered anathema to the social warp and weft. Incremental escalations in the degree of explicitness were skillfully orchestrated. Whenever challenged, producers claimed to be merely following the evolving mores of an enlightened social transformation. Their role was not to overturn cultural norms but they certainly had a responsibility to respond to what their audiences demanded.

It's safe to assume that large numbers of people have some voyeuristic tendencies, even if they are usually below the clinical threshold. The primary clinical factor is the requirement that the subject be unaware—that viewing of nakedness or sex be surreptitious—, but commercial media operators have cashed in on the widely incipient affliction by cleverly simulating the condition in darkened theatres or dimmed dens in the modern home. The presentation is designed specifically to exploit widespread voyeuristic inclinations, as the object of observation in a film or TV show is inherently unaware.

There appears to be a direct correlation between penetration of these new players in the entertainment and information market and the ostensible disappearance of the voyeur. The reason is very simple. Opportunities for sexual titillation have been so successfully disseminated that voyeurism has replaced baseball as the national pastime, and is now no longer noteworthy. In other words, we have become virtually a nation of voyeurs, with little distinction between the average upstanding citizen and one who, short decades ago, would have been locked up and prosecuted for criminal behavior.

An observer from Mars, unaware of the sexual potency in the dominant species on Earth, would attribute our ubiquitous preoccupation as observers of sex—in provocative street dress of both males and females, in posters and advertisements for everything from soda pop to military aircraft, in "entertainment" media directed toward all age segments including young children, in both amateur and professional sports activities—to a vital element of the social fabric conferring great benefits.

SEX IN ITS PROPER TIME AND PLACE

The truth is something quite different. Our obsession with sex in vicarious forms that make up such a large part of our daily intercourse is symptomatic of mass psychosis. But should we be chastised for our illness? Oh, that it were otherwise! Its existence is certainly not a cause for optimism. Untreated, it will surely be a contributor to the ultimate catastrophe. Why? Rational thinking, oriented to the welfare of future generations, is necessary to change behavioral patterns that might avert a disastrous outcome for life on Earth. The powerful force of the sex drive, as many human traits, if continued along its current bizarre trajectory, is adverse to this possibility.

CHAPTER 6

POLITICS AND RELIGION: A MARRIAGE MADE IN HEAVEN

The Hubble space telescope has provided a powerful source for insight into the significance of life on this tiny planet relegated to a remote corner of the vast Milky Way, just another one of billions of galaxies floating in space. It would be a boon if every human being would not only view the images produced by this impressive instrument, but would also contemplate their significance. We might then humbly ask if our existence, from the cosmic perspective, is something special, designed and fabricated by a celestial superpower, perhaps even in its image. If so, why do we find ourselves on such a remote speck of terrestrial matter? If we were really wonders on a cosmic scale, why would we not have a more prominent place in the heavens, perhaps beings acclimated to thriving on a supernova or quasar?

These questions arise, not only because we are sentient beings, but also because we have taken a step beyond to be aware of self. We humans suffer this incurable malady of self-consciousnesses, a blessing that's really a curse in disguise, and which may be our undoing. It may also be a precursor of our dark and mysterious unconscious, although the order of development may never be known. Consciousness of self leads to questions that are unanswerable, with attendant frustration and self-flagellation, one form of which is religion. It has been said that god did not invent man, but rather that man invented god, many times over if its ubiquitous presence among human societies is any indication.

Henri Bergson, French philosopher, proposed the concept of *élan vital* in early 20th century, referring to the propensity of matter to auto-organize and to move toward increased complexity. The inexorable élan of sentient beings (as well as other life forms) derives directly from this life force,[148] a characteristic of nature underlying the evolutionary process that brought us from specks in the primordial sea to our current state of existence. Élan[149] beats in the breast of every human, as well as every other living thing

In humans, and perhaps some of the more intelligent animals with varying degrees of SC, élan intrinsically engenders identity with nature, but this sense of cosmic connection can easily be undermined through manipulation of the vulnerable psyche. Aggressive opportunists, seeking advantage in control over others, conjure up self-serving concepts and images purporting to answer questions that arise in the inquisitive and impressionable mind concerning the unobservable or logically imponderable. One of the more common forms of this subterfuge is assertion of authority to intervene with a supernatural force, and the capacity to negotiate favorable terms for proselytes in conditions of life on Earth as well as a life beyond conventional existence. There are both psychological and physical perquisites for interveners: successful perpetrators of this chimera undoubtedly feel fulfilled emotionally, physically protected by a cohort of loyal acolytes, and uplifted by extended spheres of influence. In more extreme circumstances, these allegiances are exploited to the point of gaining or expanding political and/or territorial hegemony.

Gaining control over élan by these middlemen—or women—(hereinafter, religious operative or RO) is what we call "religion," one of the more corrosive influences on human behavior. To achieve their ends, élan is corralled with at least two lassos: first, shepherding the flock to collective acquiescence to the dominion of one or more ROs, abetted by the natural tendency of sheep to run with the herd; and second, for the sake of improving their effectiveness at proselytizing and maintaining subordination of their subjects, organization into some sort of hierarchy with the ROs at the top of the heap, a structure so effectual that it has been successfully emulated by commercial and industrial enterprises throughout the world.

In the primeval state human hunter-gatherers had little need for hierarchical organization, which likely first rose to prominence in a "religious" context, as shamans and other types of pioneering ROs introduced a structure that would serve as the pattern for diffusion throughout the world. It's likely that religious hierarchy was the model for what we now call "politics," the art of gaining allegiance of the multitudes in the earthly ambit. The main difference, then, between politics and religion is the manner of gathering and retaining the flock: religion's appeal relating primarily to supernatural phenomena and politics to what earthly life has in store. For religion, personal salvation is usually the carrot (rarely is there a collective appeal) and condemnation to eternal hell the stick, whereas in politics collective appeal gains some traction from social instincts that were part of the fabric of our ancient cooperative lifestyle. In both cases, benefits and costs are linked to the magnitude of acquiescence to, or rejection of, the intervener's dominion.

Generally, the political operative (PO, counterpart of the RO) ostensibly centers the appeal on something outside herself, a cause, objective or goal selected for its acceptability by sufficient numbers of the target population who can be convinced of its prospects for security and prosperity to make it worthwhile. The subliminal appeal is to the indispensability of the PO to shepherd the flock to the verdant pasture. The efficacy of hierarchy obtains, so that populations are organized into wards, towns and cities, provinces and nation states, which are mutually compatible with, and reinforced by, parallel organization of commerce and industry.

The unholy connection between religion and politics has a long history (Diamond 1999). By the late medieval and renaissance periods of the 13th century and beyond, feudal and tribal organizations that previously predominated in most of Europe and Asia came under the control of nation states and empires, which sponsored "official religions that contributed to state cohesion, being invoked to legitimize the political leadership and to sanction wars against other people." Their RO collaborators amply provided divine inspiration for the territorial ambitions of medieval POs, truly a marriage made in heaven.

While élan directs the unfettered individual, ROs foster belief in a superhuman power to be obeyed and worshipped as the creator and ruler of the universe, in accordance with rules promulgated through divine edict, or at least guidance. The dogma, canons and hierarchies of ROs constitute a system of worship and obeisance. Their counterparts are the system of rules, statutes and laws, and political organizations of civil society, set up to be appropriated by POs through a variety of mechanisms such as heredity, coups d'état, conquest, election.

Now that it's clear that politics is indistinguishable in essence from religion, we might just as well concentrate on one or the other. Religion is the more interesting domain.

SELF-CONSCIOUSNESS (SC)

As a *sine qua non* of religion, examination of the origins and characteristics of self-consciousness will shed some light on the RO phenomenon and what is behind their successful endeavors to co-opt the minds and bodies[150] of potential adherents. In this context, "consciousness" is generally assumed to mean not only a state of wakefulness, but also awareness (or consciousness) of self.

The descent of humans from much more primitive forms of life is well established, so there seems little reason to suppose that one of humanity's essential qualities, consciousness, arose in any way other than the process of human evolution. Consciousness is apparently non-existent to shadowy in the simplest life forms from which all more complex forms derive (including humans), so it must be an acquired characteristic that evolved by natural selection, in a manner similar to the somewhat earlier acquisition of the ear, nose, finger or toe. In early stages of the hominid line, certainly the level of consciousness that we currently experience did not exist. At some phase in the evolution of modern humans it developed gradually as a consequence of its selective advantage.

This assertion is not universally shared. Some paleontologists, for example Dr. Ian Tattersall[151], are uncomfortable with the idea that human consciousness arose through the process of natural selection. He does not invoke divine intervention, but rails against "strict Darwinians" who explain all phenomena in natural terms. Does rational analysis suggest any other mechanism that we can even speculate about? Is it possible, for example, that a creator implanted consciousness in latent form in a more primitive human ancestor? This would deny the entire premise upon which the foundation of evolution is constructed, accumulation of (what we now know to be) random genetic mutations that confer selective advantage in a particular environment.

We apparently experience instantaneous sensations, for example, banging one's head against a pole, but is this consciousness? Any organism needs a survival strategy, some instinctive way of dealing with crises. An amoeba must "sense" that it's corpus is being crushed or otherwise harmed, and automatically deploys whatever defense mechanisms it can muster.

How can consciousness be defined? It is a subject contemplated by philosophers over millennia, but inevitably involves displacement of sensory impressions over time and space:

Robin Allott (2000): "evolutionary epistemology (study of the basis of knowledge) proposes that the natural selection of brain processes has provided us with practical concepts of time and space to allow us to manage reality. The momentariness of everything and thus of ourselves means that we are in constant changing patterns, changing aggregations of material." The continuous process of metabolizing and being impacted by external stimuli means that we are not the same person from one instant to the next. The present moment is fleeing—it has "melted in our grasp."[152]

Consciousness, then, might be defined as the displacement of awareness of the individual in time and space, the translation of observation from the here-and-now to the there-and-then. Does consciousness have meaning at an instant? As many philosophers who have pondered the question have concluded, change is inherent in animate beings. Strip away the time domain and change is necessarily precluded as well. Limited only to the present, awareness seems to be divorced from consciousness, as it cannot relate to change, to *what was* compared with *what is* or what *will be*. According to Immanuel Kant (1996): "Time and space are necessary forms under which sensation and perception are accommodated in our minds, in our brains; we can have no knowledge of the ding(en) an sich (the thing itself)."

Popper (1998) alludes to change as an inherent characteristic of being: "Human experience does not perceive real life as simply a uniform progression along some imaginary line extended in space, but rather a continuous flow. The real world is one of continuous becoming or process. This discreteness is not real. So-called discrete elements are only apparent when we have a need to pluck them from our continuing experience. We may appear to ourselves as things but we find that we are processes." James (1890) describes the continuous alteration in conformation of the brain as differential elements of experience are processed: "Whilst we think, our brain changes, and, like the aurora borealis, its whole internal equilibrium shifts with every pulse of change ... from one relative state of equilibrium to another, like the gyrations of a kaleidoscope."

Some philosophical schools, e.g., the Sautrantika of Buddhism (also known as the Holders of Discourse), assert that all events and phenomena exist only at the present moment, that past and future are mental constructs.[153] But even if this is true, the notion of consciousness is virtually impossible to conceive in a timeless framework.

With the river as his model, Siddhartha[154] concludes that the flow of time does not exist, that all of past, present and future are indistinguishable: "the river is everywhere at the same time, at the source and at the mouth, at the waterfall, at the ferry, at the current, in the ocean and in the mountains, everywhere, and that the present only exists for it, not the shadow of the past, nor the shadow of the future."

On the other hand, some Buddhist schools explain time in relative terms: "it (the Madhyamika-Prasangika school) generally explains time in terms of relativity, as an abstract entity developed by the mind on the basis of an imputation, the continuity of an event or phenomenon. This philosophical view ascribes, therefore, an abstract concept whose function is dependent on the continuum of phenomena. From this point on, to try to explain time as an autonomous entity, independent from an existing object, proves impossible. That time is a relative phenomenon and can claim no independent status is quite clear."[155]

Anyone who has ever been lost in the woods, with no obvious references for direction and time, can begin to comprehend how consciousness arose in our distant forebears. The senses scan the environment for information: visual clues from the type and condition of grass and foliage, sounds and smells emanating from the presence and movement of other creatures. It is one thing to know that a predator or prey is about, and quite another to project, on the basis of sensory information, its past or future. It's only a small step from this kind of consciousness to self-awareness, as the observer takes her place in the array of physical entities that comprise one's environment.

Consciousness is not unique to *H. sapiens*. It is a characteristic that we share at least with some of our primate cousins, the chimpanzees and apes.[156] Studies of language capabilities of primates have indicated a high degree of self-awareness by our nearest relatives. As there was a stage in our evolutionary tree when consciousness was absent, that we are presently aware of self indicates that this characteristic evolved much as any physical attribute. There is nothing very special about its origins, except its profound influence on the environment of Earth and its consequences for our fellow inhabitants of the planet.

The acute level of human consciousness must have arisen during the transition from our primate ancestor to sapient *homo:* exactly at which state its first stirrings appeared is uncertain, but it almost certainly arose as an evolutionary response to a selective opportunity.

Acknowledgement of the evolutionary origins of consciousness could have salubrious impacts on the future of life. Greater awareness of self as an outgrowth of natural forces can only serve as social cement, a unifying and binding link for all of humanity. A sense in the individual of a closer relationship with fellow humans promotes altruism and cooperation, which are essential ingredients for a new approach to our relationship to the commons—the planet that we share.

WHENCE RELIGION?

Familiar questions have rattled about in the mind since the dawn of self-consciousness:

Who are we? Is humanity unique as an intelligent being?

Consciousness inevitably leads to the issue of identity—what is the significance of being human. Clearly humanity has dominion over all of life on Earth, on the strength of intelligence more than any other characteristic. The individual may be, and usually is, in awe and bewilderment of the vastness, order and beauty of the heavens, the creation of life from seed, the power and occasional fury of nature, the cycle of life and death. There is also unease about the future after death, and the disposition of élan that apparently resides in every living thing.

As we humans progressed toward greater comprehension of our surroundings, we observed that we could do some things—fabricate tools, hunt and domesticate other animals, find alternative foods, then cultivate crops. But there remained many things that we could not do or create, leading to the conclusion that some superior force was necessary to explain what was beyond our capacity or control (there are also many things that we *can* do that *shouldn't* be done). Even today, in an era of global communications, intricate knowledge of cosmic events and phenomena, fabrication and replacement of body parts, speculations about our origins and uniqueness continue: are we a select form of life, commissioned to this role by a higher power, the creator of the cosmos? Are there other, more intelligent forms of life, as yet unidentified either because we have not found them or are incapable of understanding what they have to say?

Our uniqueness as an intelligent form of life has been the subject of speculative scientific investigations. One organization, SETI (Search for Extraterrestrial Intelligence), based in California, conducts a program to find other intelligent life in the cosmos. They search for electromagnetic signals from outer space, justified, according to their mission statement, by expanding knowledge about the natural origin of life on Earth and discovery of planets with environments conducive to originating life, even though its form may differ from the carbon/oxygen base found on Earth.

Among the general population, rather than anticipating interactions with alien life forms through orderly exploration, it's more common that our propensity for mysticism elicits imagined observations of unidentified flying objects (UFOs), with expectations that they carry alien creatures seeking opportune conditions to invade the planet.

What are we? Made in the image of a god or a flawed creation?

According to the Old Testament of the Bible, Genesis 1:27 KJV, "So God created man in his own image, in the image of God he created him; male and female he created them." To what extent the likeness prevails is unstated. Moses (if he was indeed, the conveyor to humanity of the word of god) may have understood the likeness to apply only to physical attributes, but there are other possibilities. In fact, the assertion gains some credibility when other attributes of humanity are taken into account. Rather than ethical and moral behavior—universal brotherhood, truthfulness, kindness, generosity, compassion—instead humanity often displays characteristics of Jehovah as described in scriptures: jealousy, venality, violence, deception.

There's little doubt that serious flaws exists in our constitution, if for no reason other than our propensity to despoil our home planet and to consign to extinction so many of our fellow travelers on Earth, cousin species that have shared with us eons of evolutionary history. No other species is so heedless, if not overtly contemptuous, of its own living environment. If humans were purposefully created, it would appear that either we were the product of the creator's sadistic streak or, left to our own devices, we gravitated toward depravity.

Another indication of our fall from grace is our inclination for violence (Chapter 9). For example, according to data of the World Health Organization, more than 1.6 million people worldwide lose their lives from suicide, homicide and armed conflict, one of the leading causes of death for people aged 15-44 years worldwide, accounting for 14 percent of deaths among males and 7 percent among females. In addition to death by violence, many more are injured from violent acts, and thereby suffer from a range of physical and mental health problems. In the United States alone there are about 50,000 deaths annually attributable to violence. About 1 million annual fatalities globally are attributable to another type of aggressiveness—motor vehicle collisions.

Aside from fatalities, aggressiveness of humans toward their fellow men, and particularly women, (see Chapter 5 for more thorough discussion) is rampant. Rape is an all too familiar form of aggression against women, with about one in six experiencing this kind of outrage at some point in their lives.

Why are we? Is there a purpose, or end, to life? Does it have any meaning?

ROs make a lot of hay promoting the idea that life has purpose, which, they generally propose, is to serve their particular gods. In some cases alternatives are proscribed, with severe penalties for transgressors.[157] In the more benign versions, service to a god takes on a number of earthly forms: individual and collective worship in which the benevolent deity is extolled (often in cadence); prayer for one's self, one's soul and for one's fellow men, even occasionally for other life forms; following prescriptions for acceptable behavior, often merging with cultural norms such as marital constraints, dietary choices, times for work and play. ROs have parlayed fealty of their "subjects" to gain political hegemony, sometimes to the point of inciting them to commit mayhem and even murder. Islamic jihadists, at the instigation of Muslim clerics, and backed by the government of

Sudan, declared holy war against the largely non-Muslim south in 1989, although conflict had erupted over a decade earlier.[158] An estimated 2 million people died, in what then Sec. of State Colin Powell identified in September 2004 as genocide and "the worst humanitarian crisis of the 21st century." The real issue is control of oil deposits of the south.

If there is a purpose to life, it is rooted in the life force, the inexorable quest for survival and propagation that seems to be embedded in every living thing, which ROs have been able to commandeer by conflating ordinary life with an afterlife—treating them as if the latter is an hyperbolic extension of the former. An eternity of either pleasure or pain, intensified by orders of magnitude as compared with ordinary experience, depends on assessment of one's fealty to the deity, as evaluated by its mortal subalterns. The life force transcends its earthly constraint and seeks expression in the exotic domain of the afterlife. For example, Islamic suicide bombers carry out their missions in the expectation that extraordinary perquisites, including unlimited access to a harem of virgins, will be at their beck and call for eternity.

How did we get here? Was there a creator or first cause that initiated a process that made us what we are? Or, is there no "isn't?"

A recent poll revealed that 40 percent of American citizens believe that heaven and earth, humans and all other forms of life were created in their present state within the last 10,000 years, in accordance with the six-day program specified in Genesis, the first book of the Old Testament. Creationists, as these literal interpreters are currently identified, propose the existence of a Grand Designer, who decided to utilize its powers to give us the planets, the heavens and all other forms of matter, animate and inanimate. They often attack the principle of evolution on what they see as purposeful design embedded in biological organisms, asking rhetorically, for example, if there is any use for half an eye.[159]

The cycle of birth and death of living things is a convenient framework for ROs to postulate a creator of heaven and earth. But if this inherent bias, derived from ordinary human experience, can somehow be put aside, it is possible to speculate that the cosmos is eternal, that is, there was no beginning, nor will there be an end. Even though cosmologists estimate that the universe appeared in a "Big Bang" about 15 billion years ago, this is not inconsistent with the idea that matter and energy exist eternally, that it was merely the onset of another cycle in a progression without a creative event in past or future. It is, in fact, axiomatic in the domain of science that matter/energy can neither be created nor destroyed.

The billiard ball concept of cause and effect has been shown to be a macroscopic illusion. At the level of atomic sub-particles of which billiard balls, and all of matter, are comprised, events are unpredictable. A property of nature is that a physical system cannot be described completely, the result of quantum indeterminacy[160], but rather can only be described in terms of probability. Physical systems, such as the human brain, can be affected by quantum indeterminacy.

Physicist Richard Feynman developed the idea of the Feynman Diagram which illustrates the relationship of two subatomic particles over time as the exchange of a third particle. These diagrams show particles traversing time and space in both the forward and backward direction. As antimatter, particles are "allowed" to travel backward in time, so cause and effect as commonly conceived are called into question. Whether or not this applies to the everyday world has been debated, most analysts concluding that departures from our common conception of time sequence are precluded. For example, it should not be possible, and a violation of quantum mechanical principles, for you to travel back in time and murder you grandmother.

Many people who identify as "scientists"[161] see no inconsistency between what "science" has revealed about the cosmos and the existence of a superior creative force, some to the extent that they profess membership in one or another organized religious denomination. Others dismiss the idea of religion while maintaining their spirituality, inspired and enhanced by their greater knowledge of the intricate workings of nature, and profoundly awed by proportions of the cosmos, its majesty and its fascinating rules of behavior. However, there is not complete agreement concerning the extent to which the superior force, once having lain down the rules, either stood back to observe the results or engaged in their enforcement.

The efforts of scientists are mainly concerned with discovering these rules of nature and how they are expressed in interactions between matter and energy (physical sciences), or between individuals and societies (social sciences)[162]. These studies reveal increasingly greater detail and complexity of natural processes, but at the end of the day they are still left with the imponderable question of how the apparently immutable rules of nature were framed and set into motion. When they encounter the unanswerable, they are inclined, as are most human beings, to attribute what is intellectually inaccessible to a superpower operating beyond the realm of ordinary life. This leads many of them to a kind of deist or spiritualist philosophy. It leads others to more traditional forms of religious belief. For example, 40 percent of US scientists believe in a God with whom they can interact through prayer.[163]

Victor Stenger (2008), who identifies as a physicist, has studied the attributes typically associated with the existence of a god from the scientific point of view. If a god exists, it should be reflected in characteristics of the natural universe: if they are absent, then it's difficult to postulate the existence of a god. The author concludes that the facts do not support the existence of the kind of god commonly perceived, and that all attributes of the universe derive from natural forces.

Few scientists have not embraced the principles of evolution, as expounded by Charles Darwin in "*Origin of Species*," published in 1859, but according to a Gallup poll in 2001, 45 percent of Americans failed to accept evolution as the process leading to the existence of modern humans. Scientists, who generally look upon biblical accounts as allegorical, almost universally reject a literal interpretation of Genesis, in which God is purported to have created the universe and all of its life forms in six days.

Einstein asserted that "Science without religion is lame, religion without science is blind."[164] For him there are at least two "religious" tiers, one reserved for the scientifically minded, for whom a god exists, which does not intervene in the ordinary affairs of humankind, but who set the clockwork in motion. Another is the spiritual vehicle for the ordinary human, a god who not only lays out the rules, but engages in shepherding adherents, meting out rewards and punishments depending on one's compliance with its guidelines: "You will hardly find one among the profounder sort of scientific minds without a peculiar religious feeling of his own. But it is different from the religion of the naive man ... For the latter God is a being from whose care one hopes to benefit and whose punishment one fears; a sublimation of a feeling similar to that of a child for its father, a being to whom one stands to some extent in a personal relation, however deeply it may be tinged with awe."[165]

Einstein firmly believed in the principle of universal causation, which put him at odds with many members of the scientific community. Morality he considered a human affair, having nothing to do with divinity. Scientists, he suggested, were religious in the sense of awe at the harmony and order in the universe, a revelation of superior intelligence of which ordinary affairs are an insignificant reflection. So long as the scientist can maintain a distance from "the shackles of selfish desire," religiosity is the guiding principle of his life's work.

When did we appear? Four thousand years ago as envisioned by some biblical scholars, or are we of ancient origin?

Fundamentalist Christians and Jews have calculated the origin of the cosmos at about 4,000 years, based upon generational chronology as described in the holy Bible. Genesis contains a detailed description of the sequence of events during Creation Week, the seven days in which heaven and earth came into being. According to one account[166], 1,656 years elapsed between Creation Week and the great flood, in which Noah preserved all life forms by bringing a mating pair of each species onto his ark. Literal interpreters calculate their time line from Creation Week to the present based upon the chronology of biblical figures. However, other analysts take the position that the chronology is correct, but incomplete, either only a skeleton of the actual sequence of begetting or perhaps a biblical year is a compression of an eon or so. The chronology described, in this view ignores generations, which if included, would exactly conform to the scientifically determined progression of life on Earth.

According to Hebrew scholar William Henry Green (1890), "The result of our investigations thus far is sufficient to show that it is precarious to assume that any biblical genealogy is designed to be strictly continuous, unless it can be subjected to some external tests which prove it to be so. And it is to be observed that the scriptures furnish no collateral information whatever respecting the period covered by the genealogies now in question."[167]

The writer laments the absence of a continuous genealogical record between creation and the Great Flood (during which the master mariner Noah preserved posterity), and from the flood to Abraham, and the absence of other data that might have provided a basis for testing completeness of the genealogies described in Genesis.

The general scientific consensus is a universe of an age in the order of 13-14 billion years. Radiometric dating indicate that Earth has existed for 4.54 billion years, the first life forms appear at about 3.5 billion years, the split with our primate cousins about 5-7 million years, about 2.5 million years for the *homo* line, and modern humans approximately 200 thousand years, only about 4 thousandths percent—a minute fraction of Earth's life span.

It's fairly clear that our planet got along quite well without us for almost its entire existence. And yet in this blink of an eye humans have managed to create havoc on this once beautiful orb, with excessive presence and all of its consequences—war and mayhem, disfiguration, contamination, and destruction of countless species that shared our evolutionary experience.

Why are the just often punished and evildoers rewarded?

Innocent children, who have not yet had the opportunity to commit what might be considered "evil deeds," incomprehensibly have been injured, abused and murdered. In Iraq, for example, during and after the invasion of US military forces in 2003, many young children were maimed and killed while attending school. There are countless examples of children, clearly too young to be held accountable for moral transgressions, meeting agony and horrible death. As one example,[168] in 1998 a five-year-old child fell into a well while out with his mother. The child cried for several hours and then nothing more was heard. The boy's body was recovered after thirty hours of rescue operations.

On the other hand, many individuals who committed heinous crimes against humanity lived out their lives in comfort. Many Nazi war criminals of WWII, which ended in 1945, continued to enjoy the good life over 60 years after their incredibly horrible deeds were committed.

It seems incongruous that an omniscient deity, of the interventionist type that is usually the object of worship and adoration, would create humans to make them miserable, or to leave innocents to the mercy of predators, such as pedophiles who occasionally stalk children on the streets or who abuse them in the sanctity of their houses of worship.

President John Kennedy once reiterated what is virtually an adage, the observation that "life isn't fair. It's very hard to assure equality [justice] ... Some men are killed in war, others are wounded, and some never leave the country."

That performers of altruistic deeds are punished, and perpetrators of acts of destruction and mayhem rewarded, is well established. Under these circumstances, isn't it a virtual certainty that if a creator exists, it is either detached from earthly phenomena, or downright sadistic? Is it unfair to suggest that if there were a creator who promoted justice, that justice would prevail on Earth?

Guidelines prescribed by the deity, delivered through transcription by ROs, are sometimes conducive to peaceful relations among men and respect for all forms of life. In other cases gods have been known to sow the seeds of hatred, particularly against those who fail to heed its strictures. The Old Testament is replete with sadistic acts of Jehovah, the god of the Israelites. For starters, God creates Adam and Eve in the Garden of Eden, along with the tree of knowledge. They are enjoined from eating its fruits, and yet are imbued with traits that cause their expulsion. Cain and Abel experience god-created sibling rivalry, resulting in the murder of one by the other. In Exodus 20:5 and 4:7, KJV God decrees that children must pay for the sins of their fathers (contrary to the principles of the US constitution concerning cruel and unjust punishment, a feature purportedly inspired by this very god).

God informs Moses about the dire fate of the Egyptians if Pharaoh does not release the Israelites from slavery, then diabolically tells Moses that he will cause Pharaoh to refuse to free the Israelites, virtually assuring a bad ending (Exodus 12:29 KJV). As punishment for his own induced imprisonment of the Israelites by the Egyptians, God decides to kill all of their first-born, a model for genocide to be perpetrated by his earthly creations. Neither is Jehovah above condoning murder by his followers against those who stand in the way of their hegemony. Although one of the Ten Commandments collected by Moses on Mt. Sinai proscribes murder, he is directed to "save alive nothing that breatheth: but thou shalt utterly destroy them; namely the Hittites and the Amorites, the Canaanites and the Perrizites, the Hivites and the Jebusites, as the Lord, thy God, hath commanded thee" (Deuteronomy 20:16-17, KJV),

In the New Testament slavery and oppression is condoned by Jesus and his apostles in the gospels and in the letters of St. Paul: Jesus (Luke 12:45-48, KJV): "The lord [owner] of that servant will come in a day when he looketh not for him, and at an hour when he is not aware, and will cut him in sunder [in pieces], and will appoint him his portion with the unbelievers. And that servant, which knew his lord's will, and prepared not himself, neither did according to his will, shall be beaten with many stripes. But he that knew not, and did commit things worthy of stripes, shall be beaten with few stripes. For unto whomsoever much is given, of him shall be much required: and to whom men have committed much, of him they will ask the more."

While in Prison, the apostle Paul met a runaway slave, Onesimus, the property of a Christian. Rather than providing sanctuary, in a letter he agrees to return Onesimus to his master, Philemon: "Therefore though I have all boldness in Christ to command you that which is appropriate, yet for love's sake I rather beg, being such a one as Paul, the aged, but also a prisoner of Jesus Christ. I beg you for my child, whom I have become the father of in my chains, Onesimus, who once was useless to you, but now is useful to you and to me. I am sending him back. Therefore receive him, that is, my own heart, whom

I desired to keep with me, that on your behalf he might serve me in my chains for the Good News. But I was willing to do nothing without your consent, that your goodness would not be as of necessity, but of free will. For perhaps he was therefore separated from you for a while, that you would have him forever, no longer as a slave, but more than a slave, a beloved brother, especially to me, but how much rather to you, both in the flesh and in the Lord." (Philemon 1.8, KJV)

Although there are mitigating sentiments concerning the fate of Onesimus, the act perpetrated by Paul is proscribed in Deuteronomy 23:15-16, KJV: "Thou shalt not deliver unto his master the servant which is escaped from his master unto thee ... He shall dwell with thee, even among you, in that place which he shall choose in one of thy gates, where it liketh him best: thou shalt not oppress him." Apologists have ascribed Paul's action to other motives suggested in the letter, one that Onesimus remain with him as a disciple, no longer a slave to Philemon; another is that Paul is returning Onesimus to Philemon after he (Philemon) had proffered his slave as a servant in Paul's mission.

Judeo-Christian scriptures allude to god's creation of evil. Isaiah 45:7, KJV: "I form the light, and create darkness: I make peace, and create evil: I the Lord do all these things." Amos 3:6, KJV confirms this contribution to the spice of life: "Shall a trumpet be blown in the city, and the people not be afraid? shall there be evil in a city, and the LORD hath not done it?" The Hebrew "rah" has been interpreted in a number of ways in the Bible, so the KJV interpretation as "evil" is not necessarily accurate. Some claim that evil is not a thing to be created in any case, on grounds that one can neither "see, touch, feel, smell or hear" it. However, neither can intelligence—a characteristic attributed by believers to the creativeness of the superpower—be detected from any of these sensory impressions. But there is really no controversy: if evil exists (say, extreme anti-social behavior), it was surely created by god, who created everything. Skeptics have good reason to reject the existence of a benevolent creator, since such a god would neither create evil, so prevalent on Earth, nor a universe in which evil exists.

Need more be said? ROs sometimes cleverly fabricate their gods with characteristics that are imponderable in the context of civil society, the better to confuse and, thereby, conquer and bind souls to their nefarious objectives.

What is religion, anyway?

Many people around the world have conceived relationships between humans and supernatural forces, perhaps since the dawn of human history. Even Neanderthals, whose final days on Earth occurred about 20 thousand years ago, appear to have embraced the concept of afterlife, a central feature of most religious systems. Artifacts found at the earliest burial sites yet discovered, of our now extinct cousins, indicate a concern for the fate of the deceased. Some sites contain remains of groups, perhaps with the intention of keeping families united even after death. Gravesites also contained tools, food and other items, which suggest that they may have considered death as a kind of extended sleep or perhaps a period of transition to the next life. Bodies were adorned with plants and pigments, and carefully arranged in the fetal state, as if they were being prepared for rebirth. One in Shanidar, Iraq, contained a number of plants currently used for medicinal purposes.

Before trying to set down the essential features of religion, it's useful to understand what it is not. Individuals and groups have devised frameworks for evincing social harmony, for producing and dispensing goods and services required for sustenance, and for assuring justice based on respect and support for the aspirations of others, without the need for a supernatural force to set the rules and mete out rewards and punishments proportioned on the basis of the degree of compliance with its tenets. Secular humanism, for example, predicated on a kind of operational, ethical morality from a naturalistic perspective, lacks some of the main features of what might be identified as religion.

So, what might be essential features of religion, indispensable elements in the relationship of its adherents to the supernatural?

- First, the existence of a superpower, who:
    - Creates heaven and earth, and all animate and inanimate components;

    - Sets immutable laws of nature;
    - Defines the relationship between humanity and nature (e.g., dominion over other creatures of Earth);
    - Defines rules governing acceptable human interactions, a set of principles, guidelines or commandments;
    - Dispenses perquisites for adherence to the above, and exacts penalties for transgressions.
- Acceptance on *faith*, rather than reason, of the superpower's existence, edicts and powers of intervention;
- A collective endeavor of humans;
- An ecclesiastical hierarchy of ROs, who intervene in the relationship between the individual and the superpower.

The superpower, god, or divine being, is evoked to justify existence of what is perceived by the senses. In the context of human experience, anything that exists must at some point not have existed. Since there is no ready explanation for all that sensory impressions tell us is out there, postulation of a supernatural creator is rather easily accepted.

That nature operates under rules or laws is confirmed by everyday natural phenomena: apples always fall from trees; water seeks a level; lightning only strikes from heavy cloud cover; the moon incessantly goes through its twenty-eight day cycle; the sun always rises in the east. Those who investigate the rules of nature in great detail are usually even more greatly impressed with order in the universe, even though some of the rules are obscure and seemingly undecipherable. Does Heisenberg's uncertainty principle mean that there is fundamental unpredictability in natural phenomena, at least at the subatomic level, or is this just a matter of our incapacity to penetrate to deeper levels of understanding, as Einstein suggested? Alluding to the vast difference in behavior of subatomic phenomena as compared with everyday experience, Neils Bohr, a leading quantum theorist of the early 20th century, stated "Those who are not shocked when they first come across quantum mechanics cannot possibly have understood it."[169]

How does humankind relate to other creatures and material substances? Judeo-Christian scripture assigns to man dominion over all other forms of life. However, a Buddhist precept unifies all things, as elaborated in the Four Noble Truths and the Eightfold Path, guidelines for relating to the everyday world, leading to liberation from attachments and delusions, and prescriptions for attaining cessation of suffering.

The Judeo-Christian Bible, the Islamic Qur'an (Koran), the Analects of Confucius and the Mahayana (Buddhist) Sutras are now widely accepted as scriptures prescribing behavioral relationships between humans and their deity, and in some cases defining the benefits of adherence and penalties for transgression. Although the Bible and Qur'an are overtly in the religious tradition, the Analects and the Sutras are essentially philosophical treatises dealing with life on Earth that were co-opted by ROs who were followers or disciples of Confucius and the Buddha, and gradually converted over millennia into essentially religious dogma functioning similarly to theological canon in the Western religious tradition.[170]

For example, the sutras of the Mahayana, which have a decidedly religious connotation, are claimed to be original teachings, while Theravadas assert that these are later compositions not taught by the Buddha. Perceptions of Siddhartha Gautama, the Buddha, more akin to philosophy than religion, contain no reference to intervention of a divine being. As his teachings spread throughout India and then China and much of the rest of the world, ROs, apparently with a variety of motivations, attributed divine qualities to the Buddha, forming the Mahayana and Theravada schools. Mahayana, the Great Vehicle, stresses inclusiveness and a devotional structure that is antithetical to Theravada's doctrinal approach. Mahayana Buddhists universally reject personal salvation, an effort reserved only for Theravada elite. Theravadas tend to seek salvation individually, whereas a Mahayana congregation often has responsibility to inculcate spiritual values in its members. Mahayana adheres to the principle of the Buddha-nature, with innate potential in every individual, whereas Theravadas look upon the human state as an obstacle in the way of enlightenment. These divisions are analogous to the dichotomy that prevails in most political arenas, one segment more populist and liberal, the other more conservative, traditional and elitist.

ENSOULMENT

One of the major selling points of ROs is that they have the power to affect the disposition of the immortal soul, a non-material entity that purportedly lives on after the physical body in which it resides in life is no longer around. The idea of the soul or eternal spirit apart from the body has ancient Greek origins,[171] and was likely invented many times in the course of human history, but Hebrew and Christian theologians considerably modified the original conception. By promoting the idea that the soul can find an eternal haven through their intervention, ROs have discovered a potent mechanism for binding adherents to their doctrines and purposes.

Strange as it may seem, considering the general acceptance among Christians and Jews that the immortal soul lives on after death, there is little in theological scripture to support it. The Old Testament Hebrew uses the term *nephesh*, which is translated into the Greek *psuche* in the New Testament. In almost all instances, there is little reason to believe that the writers of the old and new testaments connected these terms with immortality.

Soul has various shades of meaning in the Old Testament[172], which may be summarized as follows[173]: living being, life, self, person, desire, appetite, emotion and passion. *Nephesh,* a euphemism for soul, can only denote the individual life with a material organization or body. The terms are mentioned numerous times in the Old and New Testaments, with few allusions to immortality, although one is contained in Matthew 10:28, KJV: "fear not them which kill the body but are not able to kill the soul: but rather fear Him which is able to *destroy* (italic added) both soul and body in Gehenna [the equivalent of hell]."

Only the deity can kill the soul in this view, a quite different interpretation of its vulnerability than what is contained in most of the rest of Christian and Jewish scripture in which the *psuche* is killed or otherwise destroyed as a result of human intervention. As a general rule, biblical scholars admit that *soul* is throughout a great part of the Bible simply the equivalent of "life" embodied in a living creature. "In the earlier usage of the Old Testament it has no reference to the later philosophical meaning—the animating principle, still less to the idea of an "immaterial nature" which will survive the body."[174]

Another reference to the immortal soul, according to Luke 23:42, KJV: a thief crucified along with Jesus asks to be allowed into the kingdom of heaven. "Jesus, Lord, remember me when Thou comest into Thy kingdom." The dying Jesus answers: "Today shalt thou be with me in Paradise." Although his body would die, his soul would follow Jesus immediately into the domain of eternal peace and security.

Aside from the few biblical references, one of the principle exponents of immortality is St. Augustine[175], who infused Christian theology with the soul's immaterial and spiritual qualities: "For if the mind dies wholly when life abandons it, that very life which deserts it is understood much better as mind, as now mind is not something deserted by life, but the very life itself which deserted. For whatever dead thing is said to be abandoned by life, is understood to be deserted by the soul. Moreover, this life which deserts the things which die is itself the mind, and it does not abandon itself; hence the mind does not die." Who could dispute this impeccable logic?

In the Homeric epic poetry of the 9th century BCE, *psuche* denotes the entity that lives on in the underworld after death. However, its continued existence had to be linked to the "owner," along with personality traits and other characteristic activities and behaviors. Homer does not attribute any activity of the *living* person to its soul, so the soul represents more the life essence rather than the controller of ethical character. Moreover, the existence of the soul is restricted to human beings, and not to animate life in general, so that in the underworld there is no vestige of non-human animal life.

In Greek literature of the sixth and fifth centuries BCE the concept of soul was extended to all living things. Soul became the distinguishing feature between life and death, the soul departing after demise of the corpus, and, in the later part of this period, associated with emotional feelings. Ajax explains his imminent suicide in an ancient Greek tragedy of unknown authorship: "Nothing bites the soul of a man more than dishonor."[176] Oedipus' soul, the font of boldness and courage, laments the misery of his city and its inhabitants (Sophocles, 5th century BCE). Ignorant as they were of modern understanding of origins of the universe and evolutionary history of humankind, we can't blame early Greek philosophers and Christian theologians for postulating the existence of soul in their speculative flights into the unknown.

The traverse of life across the span from pre-Cambrian forms, through the Paleozoic era, when proto-mammals made their appearance, through the Mesozoic, when higher forms of proto-mammals were prey to the dinosaurs, and into the Cenozoic in which hominids and finally *H. sapiens* made an appearance, begs the question concerning the precise stage in which the soul was acquired. Only five to seven million years ago *H. sapiens* and other present-day primates shared common ancestry. If soul exists as a presence associated with the individual, may it be assumed that once having been granted by the Grand Designer to a species (presumably to all of its members), the bequest would never thereafter be rescinded, and therefore is passed along from one generation to the next, even as speciation occurs? If so, unless present-day apes have souls also, at some time during this span, from the split to the present, the hominid line acquired a soul, being blessed (or cursed) by the phenomenon of ensoulment (infusion of a body with soul). Several species of hominids that existed in the interval since the ape-hominid split have been identified from the fossil record, from *Ardipithicus ramidus* to the *Australopithecines* and the various species of homo including *H. habilus*, *H. erectus*, *H. neanderthalensis*, and *H. sapiens*.

What characteristics would qualify a species for "souldom" (it is assumed that soul is granted at the level of species)? It's beyond the human ken to contemplate the soul as a perquisite to be dispensed discriminately—, that is, for some members but not others. Presumably the soul is present from infancy, if not conception, perhaps waiting in the wings to suffuse the body as it exits from the womb. Fairness dictates that no helpless and unworldly fledgling, which is as yet incapable of contemplating consequences, should be denied a soul for the sins of its parents or for disqualifying thoughts or acts.

Matt Ridley (1999) describes the Papal version of the ensoulment process: "Pope John Paul II, in his message to the Pontifical Academy of Sciences on October 22, 1996, argued that between ancestral apes and modern human beings there was an "ontological discontinuity"—a point at which God injected a human soul into an animal lineage. Thus can the Church be reconciled to evolutionary theory. Perhaps the ontological leap came at the moment when two ape chromosomes were fused, and the genes for the soul lie near the middle of chromosome 2." [Humans have 23 pairs of chromosomes and apes have 24 pairs. It's postulated that two large ape chromosomes fused at the transition from the common ancestor to humans].

The Pope's neat reconciliation notwithstanding, does *H. sapiens* qualify?

From our narrow perspective as only one of millions of extant species, and dwelling (for the moment) on this side of the Great Divide between earthly and heavenly existence, we might venture to identify the behavioral repertoire of qualifying species: *altruism*; *fairness*; *compassion*, *loyalty*; to these would be added *monogamy*, or at least *family values* (in deference to the superior vision of the Moral Majority), *belief in an afterlife*, and indubitably, *belief in god*. One troubling aspect of this list of qualifying characteristics is that they are not universally shared among all humans, so it seems that some may be infused with souls and others devoid of that moral uplift. To circumvent this inconsistency, ROs differentiate between conformers and transgressors: at the end of life compliant souls will purportedly enjoy the rewards of heaven and transgressors the scourges of hell.

Although pre-Neanderthal and Cro Magnon cultural patterns are difficult to discern from archeological and fossil evidence, there is some indication that Neanderthals, and certainly Cro-Magnons, were concerned for their fellows and even believed in an afterlife, as evidenced by survival of individuals with what appear to be disabling injuries and by burial arrangements that indicate a concern for future perambulations of the deceased.

Carl Sagan (1997), astronomer and author, who popularized astronomy in a public television series during the 1980s, puzzled over the possibility of destroying the soul by aborting a human fetus: "The attempt to find an ethically sound and unambiguous judgment on when, if ever, abortion is permissible has deep historical roots. Often, especially in Christian tradition, such attempts were connected with the question of when the soul enters the body—a matter not readily amenable to scientific investigation and an issue of controversy even among learned theologians. Ensoulment has been asserted to occur in the sperm before conception, at conception, at the time of "quickening" (when the mother is first able to feel the fetus stirring within her), and at birth. Or even later."

Resolution of this question may differ for other species if ensoulment is available to them, particularly the many hominids that have gone extinct during the past 5-7 million years, and our current primate cousins, the monkeys and apes. If so, it may well be that other primate fetuses, which mature much more rapidly than their human counterparts, acquire their souls at an earlier stage of their development.

INCONSISTENCIES AND LIES

What may shake the faith of believers in Judeo-Christian theological precepts are inconsistencies, some bordering on outright deception, in Hebrew and Christian texts. Bart D. Ehrman (2010), professor of religious studies at University of North Carolina, has extensively analyzed inconsistencies in the Christian gospels and related texts. He laments the fact that there is such a gulf between public perceptions of scriptures and what has been learned from historical-critical analysis, even though there are thousands of scholars engaged in this type of biblical study. "Yet such views of the bible are virtually unknown by the population at large ... Many pastors who have learned this material in seminary have, for a variety of reasons, not shared it with their parishioners once they take up positions in the church ... before long, as students see more and more of the evidence, many of them find that the inerrancy and truthfulness of the Bible begins to waver. There is simply too much evidence, and to reconcile all of the hundreds of differences among the biblical sources requires so much speculation and fancy speculative footwork that eventually it gets to be too much for them."

Ehrman shows that New Testament writers have differing views on Jesus' origins, philosophy and actions. Parts of the New Testament that were attributed to apostles were actually written by others who may not even have been contemporaries—only 8 of the 27 books were attributed to the actual authors. Many fundamental doctrines of Christianity do not have their origins in the gospels, but are much later additions, e.g., Jesus' divinity, his messianic role, and the concepts of heaven and hell; the Trinity of Father, Son and Holy Ghost is nowhere found in the Bible; the popular story of Jesus' birth, death and resurrection is actually a composite of four different descriptions in the gospels. The gospel of Matthew and the letters of the apostle Paul are diametrically opposed regarding early Christian observance of Jewish law.

Theological scholars generally agree that the four gospels of the New Testament (Christian Bible) were written in the first century CE, although there are disputes among them concerning their timing and authorship. Whether or not any of the gospel writers were witnesses to the events surrounding the life and death of Jesus is uncertain. Matthew was possibly a disciple, but almost certainly Mark and Luke were not, and learned of the events from others. Mark was a disciple of Peter, who undoubtedly was the source of his information. The gospel of John is written from the perspective of one who actually witnessed the events of Jesus' life.

Although there are significant differences in the gospels, it is likely that information available to each of the writers differed. Some scholars believe that early Greek versions were, in some cases, translations from even earlier documents written in Hebrew and/or Aramaic, particularly the Gospel of Matthew. Some passages are identical in two or more of the gospels, for example, Matthew 10:26-33 and Luke 12:2-9, even though they were ostensibly independently written, leading some scholars to believe that both of these writers used Mark as their source, or perhaps some other as yet undiscovered source document identified as Q for "quelle" ("source" in German).

Another reason for differences in the gospels is that the authors had differing agendas. For example, Matthew sought to proselytize his Jewish brethren, while Luke, almost certainly a gentile, moved the tenets of Christianity further from the traditional Jewish law that prevailed as the code of conduct for transitional Jewish Christians.

The point is that differences in the gospels are to be expected, considering their variegated authorship and their differing perspectives and purposes. However, evangelical Christians take the word of the Bible literally, and it is they who need to be apprised of these inconsistencies. It's one thing to view an incident from differing perspectives, but this would not ordinarily lead to the kinds of contradictions in accounts of the same incident, particularly if a god was guiding the hands and pens of the writers.

Stephan Huller (2009) makes the case that the standard bearer of Christianity, Jesus, may not be the Jewish Messiah after all. He extensively supports the notion that the true Messiah was Saint Mark, who was designated Messiah as a young boy and who was the author of much of the canonical texts that comprises the present day New Testament. He bases his analysis on the existence of the throne of St. Mark, a miniature seat that could accommodate only a small person, and which is replete with symbols that have been analyzed by scholars to reveal that it was constructed for Mark, who allegedly was designated Messiah as a young boy by his Jewish contemporaries.

According to recent evidence, the first five books of the Old Testament, the Hebrew Torah, were written in the period after the life of Solomon, perhaps around 600 BCE, certainly not during the life of Moses, who lived many centuries earlier. The Dead Sea Scrolls, which contain fragments of the Torah, date from no earlier than 1 or 2 centuries BCE. Writings of the ancient prophets were apparently preserved over centuries and compiled by unknown authors. To claim that the Torah is the word of Jehovah does not appear supportable.

As confirmation of the earthly origins of the Torah (five books of Moses, or Pentateuch), researchers have found many inconsistencies, indicating that its origins are anything but godly. Only a few are listed below, just to provide the flavor (all based on KJV)[177]:

Man was created after the plants. Gen.1:12, 26.
Man was created before the plants. Gen.2:5-9.

The birds were created out of the water. Gen.1:20.
The birds were created out of the land. Gen.2:19.

The animals were created before man. Gen.1:24-26.
The animals were created after man. Gen.2:19.

SO, WHAT'S WRONG WITH RELIGION?

Let me count the ways[178]:

- Prescribes faith, rather than inquiry and reason, as the primary means of problem-solving (thrives on ignorance);
- Answerable to no system of earthly laws, but rather a law unto itself;
- Justifies unequal distribution of life's perquisites, on the grounds that accounts will be squared in an afterlife—misery, servitude and even slavery have been condoned;
- Promotes human population increase in the face of a global glut and unsustainable growth;
- Acquiesces, and is often complicit, in unequal administration of justice (castigates non-believers and sanctifies miscreant behavior of adherents, regardless of their contributions to society)
- Subverts the exercise of functional ethics (e.g., the Golden Rule) in relations between people; distracts people from doing the right things on Earth;
- Injects an intermediary between élan and nature; thereby diminishing spirituality;
- Promises what it can't deliver (eternal salvation) and threatens what it cannot impose (eternal damnation);
- Sets up competition among adherents of alternative deities, sometimes with violent or otherwise tragic consequences;
- Promises everlasting blessings for deeds in god's name, while justifying harming and maiming others with allegiance to another god or no god.

ROs thrive on human numbers. Without souls as subjects, for whom they serve as intermediaries with the superpower, they would have to find other, less profitable opportunities for satisfying their own objectives. The Catholic Church, for example, promotes population growth in the face of vastly excessive human numbers. A papal encyclical, Humanae Vitae of 1968, lays out the Church's position on birth control: The sexual act must "retain its intrinsic relationship to the procreation of human life." Direct interruption of the "generative process already begun" is proscribed. Abortion of a fetus, for any reason whatsoever, is forbidden, as is any means of contraception other than natural family planning methods, e.g., abstaining from intercourse during the fertile part of the woman's menstrual cycle, as this is "a faculty provided by nature."

One of the unfortunate consequences of this doctrine on the use of contraception as a means of birth control is the spread of HIV/AIDS, especially in Africa. As church influence spreads, so does the stricture on the use of condoms, which currently is the only way to safely protect transmission of the virus from one sex partner to the other. The church position that abstinence is the way to prevent pregnancy and HIV/AIDS is a chimera, as sexual encounter is a phenomenon whose ubiquitous occurrence will not be diminished by papal edict.

To assert that religion underpinned the founding of the United States is a misreading of American history. The founding fathers primarily identified as deists, believers in a supreme being, but disdainful of organized religion. In a letter to Benjamin Rush, after being vilified as an infidel by the clergy of Philadelphia, Thomas Jefferson (2009) voiced his attitude toward the church: "It is by the exercise of our reason that we are enabled to contemplate God in His works, and imitate Him in His ways. When we see His care and goodness extended over all His creatures, it teaches us our duty toward each other, while it calls forth our gratitude to Him. It is by forgetting God in His works, *and running after the books of pretended revelation, that man has wandered from the straight path of duty and happiness, and become by turns the victim of doubt and the dupe of delusion* (italics added)."

Thomas Paine, journalist and publisher in 1776 of "*Common Sense*," which was highly influential in coalescing opposition to British dominance and promoting independence of the American colonies from England, similarly had nothing but contempt for organized religion: "Except in the first article in the Christian creed, that of believing in God, there is not an article in it but fills the mind with doubt as to the truth of it, the instant man begins to think. Now every article in a creed that is necessary to the happiness and salvation of man, ought to be as evident to the reason and comprehension of man as the first article is, for God has not given us reason for the purpose of confounding us, but that we should use it for our own happiness and His glory."[179]

Paine identified a litany of appalling acts of the deity worshipped by Christians and Jews as described in the holy Bible: "Whenever we read the obscene stories, the voluptuous debaucheries, the cruel and tortuous executions, the unrelenting vindictiveness with which more than half the Bible is filled, it would be more consistent that we call it the word of a demon than the word of God. It is a history of wickedness that has served to corrupt and brutalize mankind; and, for my part, I sincerely detest it, as I detest everything that is cruel ... Priests and conjurors" he asserted, "are of the same trade ... All national institutions of churches, whether Jewish, Christian or Turkish, appear to me no other than human inventions, set up to terrify and enslave mankind, and monopolize power and profit. Of all the tyrannies that affect mankind, tyranny in religion is the worst; every other species of tyranny is limited to the world we live in; but this attempts to stride beyond the grave, and seeks to pursue us into eternity."[180]

Most adherents to one religion or another would be shocked, upon examining its scriptures, to learn that their gods are deceitful, vengeful and violent. "It was only when I undertook to read the Bible through from the beginning to end that I perceived that its depiction of the Lord God—whom I had always viewed as the very embodiment of perfection—was actually that of a monstrous, vengeful tyrant, far exceeding in bloodthirstiness and insane savagery the depredations of Hitler, Stalin, Pol Pot, Attila the Hun or any other mass murderer or ancient or modern history."[181]

John Adams, second president of the United States, similarly had little use for organized religion. Although he identified as a Unitarian, his writings demonstrate clearly that he did not believe in an interventionist god. He agreed that conventional religion was needed by some people as a means of stimulating ethical behavior, but his views are probably closer to Jefferson and Paine as deists, rather than consistent with tenets of any organized religious denomination. He castigates the Catholic church more than any other, but his primary objective, one that he adamantly propounded, was to keep the affairs of state free of religion. His essential views on religion, and particularly the relationship of religion and state, is summed up as follows (John Adams, 1980): "The United States of America have exhibited, perhaps, the first example of governments erected on the simple principles of nature; and if men are now sufficiently enlightened to disabuse themselves of artifice, imposture, hypocrisy, and superstition, they will consider this event as an era in their history. It will never be pretended that any persons employed in that service had interviews with the gods, or were in any degree under the influence of Heaven, more than those at work upon ships or houses, or laboring in merchandise or agriculture; it will forever be acknowledged that these governments were contrived merely by the use of reason and the senses."

In his searing condemnation of religion, Christopher Hitchens (2009) points out the failure of an omniscient and benevolent god to bring to humanity what it most covets—health, peace and prosperity: "If Jesus could heal a blind person he happened to meet, why not heal the blind? ... With all this continual prayer, why no result?" His objections to religious faith: "that it wholly misrepresents the origin of man and the cosmos, that because of this error it manages to combine the maximum of servility with the maximum of solipsism[182], that it is both the cause and the result of dangerous sexual repression, and that it is ultimately grounded on wishful thinking."

Scottish biologist Richard Dawkins (2008), a fervent critic of creationism, who has written extensively on natural origins of all animate and inanimate matter in the universe, similarly regards religion as a dangerous invention: "Had my chaplain (who was awed by the majesty of nature) been aware of Darwin's "*Origin of Species*" he would certainly have identified with it and, instead of the priesthood, might have been led to Darwin's view that all was produced by laws acting around us."[183] In a more recent work[184] Dawkins takes on the creationists in an exhaustive review of the evidence for evolution. He cites the extensive hominid fossil record with many "missing links" that clearly show the transition to modern humans from primitive primate ancestors dating from up to four million years ago. He also reviews genetic confirmation of evolution, and examples of evolution taking place virtually before the eyes of experimenters using organisms such as bacteria and fish species with relatively short life cycles. In his painstaking expositions on evolutionary processes, Dawkins is reminiscent Darwin, his great mentor as the originator of our modern concept of natural selection.

Charles Kimball (2003), professor of comparative religion in the Department of Religion and the Divinity School at Wake Forest University, discusses five warning signs of religious corruption: blind obedience, establishing the "ideal" time, the end justifies any means, and declaring holy war, and claims to absolute truth.

Is truth derived by any means absolute? Study of the laws controlling phenomena in the physical universe indicates that no concept is irrevocable, and certainly not in the domain of religion, which is a human invention. However, ROs convince their indoctrinated acolytes to believe that their version of truth supersedes that of all others, and that holders of opposing views are not only wrong, but often deserve condemnation or even persecution.

Believers are often led to obey the strictures and canons promulgated by their ROs without question, leaving their rational faculties behind in the process. Fundamentalist ROs exploit devotion of their followers to the point of provoking suicide in the process of doing violence to non-believers, in exchange for eternal rewards and other perquisites of blind obedience.

Extremist ROs often lead their followers to believe that a supernatural phenomenon, such as the second coming of Christ, Armageddon, the end of times, are imminent, sometimes with bizarre consequences. According to the Contender Ministries [185]: "It is increasingly obvious that the time of our Lord's coming is drawing near. Prophecy is being fulfilled daily, and at a faster pace than ever before. Whether you believe in a pre-tribulation rapture, or believe

Christians will be witness to the full tribulation, wrath, and final judgments, matters not." Imminence of the end of times, or the establishment of god's kingdom on Earth, has been used as a pretext for political action to impose religious law, e.g., the Taliban takeover of the government in Afghanistan in 1996.

Religious fervor is often the basis for justifying any means to achieve an end. Fanatical Jewish and Islamic ROs in the Middle East successfully exhort their followers to commit acts of violence and murder, including suicide bombings, to further their agendas. Since the Crusades of the 11th to 13th centuries CE, intended to restore Christianity to the Holy Land, mass killings of Muslims and other non-Christians were the rule. It was common practice to behead captive enemies and impale them on pikes as gory testament to the sanctity of the Crusaders' mission. According to the Gesta Francorum (anonymous chronicle of the capture of Jerusalem), "[our men] were killing and slaying even to the Temple of Solomon, where the slaughter was so great that our men waded in blood up to their ankles." Raymond of Aguilers, a chronicler of the First Crusade (1096-1099): "It was a just and marvelous judgment of God, that this place [the temple of Solomon] should be filled with the blood of the unbelievers." On the Second Crusade (1147-1149), St. Bernard of Clairvaux, a Cistercian monk who was canonized by Alexander III in 1174, pronounced: "The Christian glories in the death of a pagan, because thereby Christ himself is glorified."[186]

The Taliban, mainly militant Pashtun who comprise about 40 percent of Afghanistan's population and who are the predominant ethnic group in southern provinces bordering Pakistan, have attacked many girls' schools in both countries. For example, in Feb 2010 Taliban militants used explosives to destroy a girls' school in northwest Pakistan. In May 2009, 90 schoolgirls were hospitalized as a result of a gas attack on a school in Kapisa province, northeast of the Afghan capital. Other disciples spread god's word by throwing acid in the faces of schoolgirls. The Taliban's justification is that education for girls violates Islamic principles and that strict isolation of women is a Pashtun cultural tradition. In an incident similarly motivated, on April 14, 2014 a group of Nigerian Islamic extremists, Boko Haram, kidnapped over 270 schoolgirls. In a video sent to news media the leader stated, "Women are slaves. I want to reassure my Muslim brothers that Allah says slaves are permitted in Islam" in consonance with the ancient tradition of enslaving women captured during jihad, or holy war.[187]

On September 11th, 2001 disciples of al Qaeda, an extremist organization of Islamic fundamentalists, hijacked four commercial jetliners and crashed them into the World Trade Center (WTC) in New York City and the Pentagon in Washington, D.C. killing over 3,000 workers and service personnel. Justification for the attack is contained in a statement of the leaders of al Qaeda, in part a *quid pro quo* for the Crusades of 8 or 9 centuries ago. A rambling al Queda document provides further rationale for the attack, admonishing followers to struggle against non-believers in the "religion of truth." "Prayers and peace be upon the unique leader of the warriors (mujahedeen), Muhammad ibn Abdullah who said to unbelievers, 'I have come to you with slaughter.' May the most excellent prayers and perfect greetings be upon him, his family, and his friends."[188]

The document lauds the motivations and performance of the perpetrators of the WTC attack, attributing their martyrdom to sacrifice for the religion of Allah and for "defending Muslims whom American hands had mistreated by various types of torture and forms of domination and subjugation in every place." In 2004 information began to emerge about mistreatment of detainees (alleged terrorists) in prisons maintained by US military forces at Bagram in Afghanistan, Abu Ghraib in Iraq and at the detention facility at Guantanamo, Cuba.

Holy war is the instrument of scoundrels, some of whom are extremist ROs seeking to mobilize vulnerable segments of their co-religionists in pursuit of essentially political ends. The appeal is ostensibly predicated on carrying out theological mandates, but the prescribed actions intended to gain hegemony in the earthly domain.

"Just" wars, inspired by RO/PO cabals, have been undertaken on similarly shaky pretexts. One of George W. Bush's principle constituencies in his successful bid for the US presidency in 2000 was the religious right, evangelical Christians in the tradition of politically conservative preachers such as Pat Robertson and Jerry Falwell.

"Eighty-four percent of them voted for Bush, providing nearly one-third of his total."[189] After the September 11, 2001 attacks on the World Trade Center and Pentagon, Bush, with British cooperation under Prime Minister Tony Blair, launched the invasion of Afghanistan, Operation Enduring Freedom, purportedly as a struggle against the Taliban, which had taken control of the country, and their al Qaeda (self-pronounced perpetrators of the attacks) supporters, who were reportedly operating training camps for terrorists to launch further assaults in North America and Europe. The intervention eventually evolved into a counterinsurgency, whose target remains cloudy as the military intervention continues—the longest war in US history.[190]

In his State of the Union message of January, 2002 President G. W. Bush identified the world *center of depravity*, the "axis of evil"—Iraq and Iran, with North Korea thrown in to demonstrate equanimity. Subsequently, on March 20, 2003, Bush and Blair ignited the incendiary mixture of oil and religion by heading a multinational force in "Operation Iraqi Freedom." From the time of the invasion, justification metamorphosed according to political expediency: first the intent was to deny the government of Saddam Hussein non-existent weapons of mass destruction; subsequently, Iraqi insurgents became terrorists who posed a threat of further attacks on the US; by 2006 military leaders began to identify the conflict as a civil war between Sunni and Shia Islamic factions. In 2007 Iran became the culprit, a fomenter of terrorism.

As a result of Bush's pursuit of the unified agenda of the religious and political right, in the US presidential election of 2004, evangelical Christians were highly aggressive and organized: "The White House struggled to stay abreast of the Christian right and consulted with the movement's leaders in weekly conference calls. But in many respects, Christian activists led the charge that GOP operatives followed and capitalized upon."[191] These actions resonate with evangelical Christians, whose aim has been to dominate and even to convert Islamic people, including Afghanis, to Christianity.[192]

Not to be outdone, President Barack Obama, apparently in an attempt to wrest allegiance of the Christian right—now respected for their political clout—from his Republican adversaries, after his election in 2008 expanded military intervention in Afghanistan by calling for the insertion of more troops, in effect continuing the misguided policies of the Bush administration (in fact, this was a central feature of his campaign platform).

Exuberance for one's god extends even to protecting its name, as something owned by adherents of a particular faith. To many Muslims the name of the one god Allah belongs exclusively to them. They believe that liturgical use of the name by Christian clerics could confuse Muslim worshipers, even while Arabic and Malaysian language Bibles describe Jesus as the "son of Allah." Continuation of this practice by Malaysian Christians set off an uproar in Kuala Lampur, during which a number of churches and convents were firebombed and defaced. The attacks were in response to a Malaysian court ruling voiding a government ban on the use of the name Allah as the Christian God. According to news reports[193], Muslims were concerned that by invoking the name that Islam had assigned to the one god, who by Abrahamic tradition must be shared by Christians, Jews and Muslims, Christians sought to pave the way for conversion of Islamists to Christianity. This begs a question: what was the motive of the unique deity in creating monotheistic rivals? Was it merely mischief or downright pandemonium that *it*[194] intended?

Simply stated, this is the problem: once invented, god can promise things that the rational intellect knows are not possible from nature, so people succumb to mystical predilections and are thus distracted from doing the right things. Religious practices, taken in conjunction, constitute one of the most dangerous behaviors of the human repertoire, responsible for inordinate expansion of the human population, far beyond the capacity of Earth's sustainable, renewable resources and thus exploitative of natural capital. They are like placebos, which allow the "disease" to continue exacting its toll—empty promises of eternal salvation in exchange for following the agendas of religious operatives rather than focusing on fostering a decent life on Earth for all its inhabitants.

TO BELIEVE OR NOT TO BELIEVE—THAT IS THE QUESTION

What are the risks in believing or disbelieving in one god or another? Assume an interventionist god whose existence or non-existence is equally probable, and who will wreak vengeance on those who have the temerity to deny its existence. Aside from the problem of selecting the right god of the rather significant array of possibilities, four scenarios have to be considered: god does or does not exist, coupled either with one's belief or disbelief:

God exists, and one either
  believes, with eternal bliss visited upon one's soul, or
  doesn't believe, in which case eternal damnation, or
God doesn't exist, and one either
  believes, with neutral consequences, or
  doesn't believe, with neutral consequences.

Earthly cost of belief is small, perhaps some disdain on the part of those familiars who consider any sort of religiosity to be gauche, but there is always the possibility to have public and private faces that differ in this regard. Similarly, earthly cost of disbelief is usually small, except if one considers a public career, in which case the result could be political suicide, or if a malevolent god takes offense and imposes catastrophe on the offender in the earthly realm. However, earthly effects are transitory (nobody lives forever), while approbation or condemnation by a deity carries eternal consequences. So it seems that the wisest choice is to believe, as the result can only be neutral to highly advantageous, while to disbelieve carries the chance of consignment to everlasting hell.

Even so, some simply cannot bring themselves to the point of belief in organized religion, regardless of the consequences, Sam Harris (2008), for example[195]: "The fact that my public and continuous rejection of Christianity does not worry me in the least should suggest to you just how inadequate I believe your reasons for being a Christian are."

In the course of the 200 millennia human history, and perhaps in earlier ancestral populations, growing consciousness stimulated wonder at the majesty of the cosmos, leading to questions concerning the meaning of life—how and why we are here. For Descartes "Cogito, ergo sum" (I think, therefore, I am): consciousness (thinking) evokes a sense of self and introspection, but doesn't explain the origin of being. Some are merely awed by the majesty of the cosmos and inspired to a kind of spirituality, an identity with all that is observable or contemplated, and elevated to an even more profound reverence with the proliferation of information concerning the magnitude and order of the universe. For others, with no answer in sight, the agile human brain invokes a super-force as creator of the heavens, earth and its inhabitants. Still others, alert to the life force that drives all organisms to seek survival and growth, see opportunity in using their capacities to influence others by conjuring up versions of the superpower and preying on the vulnerable with carrot and stick to join a movement.

Evangelicals of every stripe have mesmerized their flocks with flowing oratory, preying on those who are particularly trusting by confiscating real property for their own accounts. Evangelism not only is good for business, it is good business. Evangelicals have amassed great wealth by exploiting human vulnerabilities, often leading private lives that are antithetical to their professed standards of spiritualism and purity. One TV evangelist profits handsomely from her long-standing ministry, consisting of TV and radio programs that reach millions of people in about 70 countries[196]. The evangelist and her husband receive millions in compensation, and perquisites befitting pop stars, whose ranks they have joined.

In one religion-centered irony, a member of the Catholic clergy accused the Disney entertainment enterprise of exploiting children by encouraging them to consume products marketed by the company. Christopher Jamison, Abbot of Worth in West Sussex, UK, condemns the corporation for "exploiting spirituality" to sell its products and of turning Disneyland into a modern day pilgrimage site.[197] He cites some films produced by Disney, e.g., *Sleeping Beauty* and *101 Dalmatians,* which he claims encourage consumerism among young children. While outwardly presenting a moral message, the underlying purpose is to implant materialistic sentiments in children, thereby enhancing commercial opportunities. The Abbot credits Disney films with showing good triumphing over evil, but explains that it is only a ruse to influence children to demand Disney products from their families. He laments the practices of Disney as a classic example of how consumerism is promoted as a route to happiness, an alternative to traditional moral behavior.

RELIGION'S THREAT TO POSTERITY

The negative side of religion resides in the propensity of vulnerable people to accept and to become devotees and mindless acolytes of purveyors of mythical supernatural concepts about superpowers, who promise eternal perquisites in the life after death and threaten eternal damnation if their dictates, with supernatural overtones, are not followed. Religion has been a corrosive and even cancerous force, a form of tyranny that is antithetical to development and use of rational faculties needed to solve the multitude of problems facing humankind. There are functional justifications for ethical and even moral behavior that are more productively evoked by appeal to the intellect. Religion is unnecessary in a species with cooperation as an essential component of its inherent operational strategy. The myths and superstitions promoted by ROs will fade into history, and the transition to a healthful environment and social climate of peace, justice and prosperity will occur if and when our intrinsic spirituality and rationality are predominant characteristics of the human ethos.

CHAPTER 7

THE DIVORCE OF SCIENCE FROM PHILOSOPHY

Although there are severe penalties for attempting to take down a sacred cow, one human activity that should evoke displeasure, if not condemnation, for its consequences is the manner in which knowledge is pursued under the aegis of *science*[198]. The transition over the past two millennia, from its foundation in natural philosophy to what we now know as the scientific method, has not been constructive for the continuation of life on Earth. A "road not taken" is the one that would have retained a philosophical underpinning.

Yes, there have been incredible strides in understanding nature—extending the human life span by a few decades is one example of the achievements of medical science. In the 1950's medical researchers Jonas Salk and Albert Sabin developed vaccines for polio, eliminating a scourge that particularly targeted young children. But in general the cost of scientific innovation has been horrendous for our planet. One only has to figuratively stand in outer space and regard our once magnificent orb crumbling under the onslaught of human "progress."

Advances in technology, and the pursuit and acquisition of scientific knowledge, upon which they are largely dependent, are considered widely to be defining characteristics of modern humanity. The word "science" has been adopted in most languages, even if a word for 'knowledge' already existed. "Scientific" has emerged to mean a special kind of knowledge, derived from application of a particular approach to its acquisition.

The march of science cannot be arrested—it's too indelibly ingrained in the culture of most extant societies—but something is amiss, and needs a course correction. The leading edge in the pursuit of knowledge would more assuredly be advantageous to the future of life in the hands of people whose perspective encompasses the broad consequences of their investigations. A more philosophical foundation is required for a reversal of the trend that has resulted in a virtual barrier between philosophy and science, even though they are, in some respects, mother and daughter. Scientists would be unlikely to engage in research on more effective poison gases, for example, were the framework of their inquiries fundamentally philosophical.

PHILOSOPHY AND SCIENCE

All living species, including humans, acquire and apply information. Charles Darwin shed much light on the impetus for the pursuit of knowledge in humans and all other species as an indispensible element in evolutionary development. A quest for a successful strategy, a plan for survival and replication, which needs information for its successful application, responds to the life force, or élan vital (see Chapter 6). Characteristics of species are adaptations to the exigencies of nature— a chameleon's color adjustment, a cheetah's fleetness, the human's cerebral cortex. Nature, in turn, provides austere feedback to inevitable modifications brought about by genetic mutation and sexual reproduction, vital elements in the process of natural selection. Our propensity and capacity to use information to alter the environment to suit our aspirations is the distinguishing feature of human existence acquired in this process, part of our fundamental strategic conformation—the most cerebral of all—that has proved to be one of the most successful, along with the strategies of cockroaches and rats.

Prior to the onset of civilization, humanity was too close to the brink of disaster to consider epistemology—the nature of knowledge, and *how and why* it is acquired. As agricultural and industrial revolutions changed the landscape so that resources could be managed rather than simply mined or gathered, knowledge about the manner of collecting information, and its consequences, took on a new level of significance.

In its earliest form, the pursuit of knowledge focused on the heavens and earthly matters, as there were utilitarian consequences. Celestial cycles and positioning were linked over time with seasons and climatic variations that were determinants of the food supply. The mystical side of human nature extended the relevance of celestial alignments to the social domain, inspiring the search for meaning in the heavens.

What grew out of this inquisitiveness came to be known as philosophy (from Greek *philosophos*),[199] the open-ended quest for (and love of) wisdom or knowledge: inquiry into the nature of the universe and analysis of principles for the conduct of life; comprised of the study of physical and social phenomena, in areas such as metaphysics, epistemology, logic, ethics, aesthetics. Definitions of the term "philosophy" often focus on its intellectual and speculative nature, but observation or empiricism has to be a part of any pursuit of knowledge. For one thing, mind-matter duality may be only an illusion (see Chapter 1): even thought itself, the cybernetic process of ideation, has a material quality. But of even broader significance is the inescapable connection of any organism, such as a human, to its internal and external material environment.

How does the pursuit of knowledge differ in the philosophical vs. scientific context? *Science* is derived from the Latin word *scientia*: knowledge, discernment. *Philosophy*, as noted above, has a very similar meaning. Historically, two forces were responsible for the birth of philosophy's child, science. Proliferation of knowledge, not only about the nature of matter but extending into the social domain, resulted in a trend toward specialization. Secondly, complexities of civilization demanded a more utilitarian approach to knowledge, attuned to the needs of increasingly organized, politicized, militarized and forward-looking (planning) society. While philosophy allowed for flights of intellect, science demanded more rigorous empiricism—acquisition of systematized knowledge derived from observation, study and experimentation.

In the West most notably during the two millennia from the age of ancient Greece to Galileo, but in the East thousands of years earlier, momentous advances in knowledge and its applications were achieved as an outgrowth of human inquisitiveness. Gradually, knowledge under the banner of science took on the aspect of a commodity, to be exploited in the mercantile arena, by intellectual monopolists in universities, and by governments, largely to support their military adventures.

What is the contemporary relationship between science and philosophy? It is simply this: aside from its insistence on more stringent empiricism and mathematical rigor as compared with philosophical inquiry, science has narrowed its field of view and has come to mean learning about some aspect of nature without implicitly referencing its wider social, political and ecological implications, something like knowledge in a partial vacuum—partial only because there is the unavoidable umbilical to a society that science feeds upon. For example, while sociology is now considered a legitimate science, behavioral phenomena and relationships, and not necessarily their wider socio-economic implications, are usually in focus. Some subdivisions of social science are inherently tied to the human environment, but tend toward a narrow, utilitarian orientation, e.g., political science (study of government and political processes, institutions, and behavior). Philosophy, in contrast, as open-ended inquiry, implicitly takes in the existential panorama.

Most scientific inquiry is like climbing Everest, not only because it's there, but also because it's a fundable challenge. But there is something wrong with this—climbers leave behind residues—tracks and trash and other detritus that mark the mountain and change it forever, usually not considered when knowledge is pursued in the scientific mode. The broader vista of philosophy evokes concern about these things.

THE UNFORTUNATE BIFURCATION

As human consciousness evolved in the transition from ancestral forms, the heavens and the nature of matter became the focus of intellectual scrutiny. Knowledge was undoubtedly pursued inevitably for utilitarian reasons,[200] as virtually endless cycles of stars, sun, moon and planets traversing the skies were progressively linked empirically to fundamental issues essential to food security and survival—drought, inundation, extremes of heat and cold. The pace and content of acquired knowledge was part and parcel of cultural development, among humans a powerful adjunct to genetic evolution.

Until the 1840s, what we now call science was natural philosophy, so that even Isaac Newton's great book on motion and gravity, published in 1687, was titled *Philosophiæ Naturalis Principia Mathematica* (The Mathematical Principles of Natural Philosophy). Newton was, to himself and his contemporaries, a philosopher. In fact, "although Newton may have provided physics with its paradigm [his laws of physics], he himself worked largely within its pre-paradigmatic context, and the latter, according to Thomas Kuhn (1996),[201] is typically characterized by extensive epistemological debates and controversies over the foundations or first principles of the science."[202]

The transition from philosophy, or natural philosophy, to science was certainly not an orderly process. The methods of some who identified as natural philosophers differed from those of later investigators such as Robert Boyle (known mainly for his work on temperature, pressure and volume relationships in gases), Francis Bacon (experimental and inductive scientific truth), and Galileo (kinematics and observational astronomy), who based assertions about their discoveries on experimentation and replication. Most natural philosophers instead employed a speculative, intellectual approach in developing their concepts about the natural world. Eventually science became largely divorced from epistemology, and natural philosophy in general, relying more on observation and experimentation to authenticate speculations.

The history of western civilization is commonly divided into periods predicated on advancement of culture, measured by the level, reliability and application of knowledge. Although intellectual innovation occurred in many parts of the world prior to the ancient Greeks, philosophical history usually begins from that era. None of the pillars of Greek philosophy, while engaging in the quest for knowledge and recording their ideas for posterity, very likely thought of themselves as scientists, and in fact probably never heard of science as it is currently understood. The term *scientist*, as epithet for a seeker of knowledge via the scientific method, was not in common use until the 19th century (attributed to William Whewell, 1794-1866, Anglican priest, philosopher, theologian and historian). Through prior centuries intellectual supermen sought knowledge without the benefit of modern scientific methodology, discovering ideas and principles, some of which involved empirical information, mainly through the intellect, without benefit of the instruments and mathematical tools available to modern day science.

How did the unfortunate split from a philosophic to a scientific foundation for the pursuit of knowledge come to pass? Let us touch on a few of the salient elements in the process of transition from open-ended inquiry into the secrets of nature, to what has turned out to be a decidedly utilitarian approach:

Socrates (4-5th century BCE) never wrote anything, and is known only through his student, Plato. His path to understanding focused on pursuit of truth rather than acquisition of knowledge *per se*. Plato, through dialogues with his master, gazed intently on human society, identifying reality in ideas and forms examined through the intellect. Plato's student, Aristotle saw reality more in physical terms, understood through observation. In the 3rd century BCE, Aristotle conceived a model in which celestial bodies were attached to 55 concentric spheres that rotated at different velocities, with angular velocity constant for a given sphere, to explain motions of the sun, moon and planets relative to the centrally positioned Earth. Aristotle was much concerned with the nature of physical reality, but wrote also on topics that we now identify as biology, morals and politics. Although a brilliant student, when his master died he was not appointed to head Plato's academy, probably because their philosophical outlooks differed so significantly. Even then, the knowledge arena was a battleground—a tradition that has mushroomed into open warfare in the laboratories of academia and industry.

Ptolemy (Claudius Ptolemaeus) was a Roman citizen of Greek ancestry, who in the second century CE produced several works based upon his celestial studies. Most significant was the *Almagest*, a treatise that explained celestial motions in geometric terms. In its preface he expressed his motivation and approach: "We shall try to note down everything which we think we have discovered up to the present time; we shall do this as concisely as possible and in a manner which can be followed by those who have already made some progress in the field. For the sake of completeness in our treatment we shall set out everything useful for the theory of the heavens in the proper order, but to avoid undue length we shall merely recount what has been adequately established by the ancients. However, those topics which have not been dealt with by our predecessors at all, or not as usefully as they might have been, will be discussed at length to the best of our ability."

He presented his astronomical models in convenient tables, which could be used to compute the future or past position of the planets. Through the Middle Ages it was regarded as the authoritative text on the motions of heavenly bodies. In his planetary hypothesis, Ptolemy improved on the Aristotelian model predicated on Earth not only at rest, but also at the center of the universe, with a concept that explained planetary motions in terms of epicycles (circles rotating on the circumference of a circle). Ptolemy's observations were systematic and extensive, but would hardly qualify for contemporary scientific approbation. In fact, Ptolemy also wrote on astrology, more or less confirming his speculative and philosophical dimensions. He asserted that astrology was a companion to his astronomical investigations, as it explained the effects of heavenly bodies on people's lives. In Book 1 of the *Almagest*, Ptolemy confirms the purity of his quest for understanding the heavens:

"Well do I know that I am mortal, a creature of one day.
But *if my mind follows the winding paths of the stars*
Then my feet no longer rest on earth (italics added), but standing by
Zeus himself I take my fill of ambrosia, the divine dish."[203]

Religious factions were drawn to astronomy to support theological concepts. For example, the timing of Ramadan, the Islamic period of reflection and fasting, is linked to the lunar cycle. The Qur'an, counterpart of the Judeo-Christian Bible as the principle guide for the practice of Islam, alludes to celestial significance: "And it is He who ordained the stars for you that you may be guided thereby in the darkness of the land and the sea."[204] From the 7th century CE Arabic astronomers assimilated and expanded upon the work of the ancient Greeks. Many navigational stars have Arabic names, from *Acamar* (end of the river) to *Zubeneschamali* (the northern claw) and *Zubenelgenubi* (the southern claw).

The Ptolemaic view of the cosmos reigned until the 16th century CE, when Nicolai *Copernicus* developed his heliocentric view of the universe, upending the idea that Earth was the center of the solar system. His model provided an explanation of obvious deficiencies in the Ptolemaic model, such as varying brightness of the planets and the fact that some planets exhibited inconsistent retrograde motions. Copernicus retained the idea of circular obits for the planets (now known to be elliptical) so there were still some anomalies that could not be explained by his model. He was motivated to undertake his study because "(he) began to grow disgusted that no more consistent scheme of the movements of the mechanism of the universe, set up for our benefit by that best and most law abiding Architect of all things, was agreed upon by philosophers who otherwise investigate so carefully the most minute details of this world."[205]

Copernicus was a reluctant revolutionary, fearful of retribution from ecclesiastical authorities, who clung to the geocentric model apparently to avoid upsetting their smoothly running applecart, so his ideas were not published until his death and were not widely disseminated until a century later. In his preface he expressed the wish to "contribute something to the ecclesiastical state whose chief office Your Holiness (Pope Paul III) now occupies."[206]

If the scientific revolution as a point in epistemological history is to be defined, perhaps it is with Copernicus, whose work encompassed—even if in rudimentary form—the essentials of the classical scientific method: observation and description of phenomena; formulation of an explanatory (and falsifiable) hypothesis; prediction of other phenomena based on the hypothesis; experimentation to test predictions of the hypothesis, and if eminently successful, elevation to the status of a theory or law of nature. On the other hand, designating astronomy as a scientific discipline at that point in time is somewhat misleading, as is considering Copernicus a scientist rather than philosopher—for an inquisitive mind there were not very many games in town, few alternatives to astronomy. The utilitarian character of science that emerged after the industrial revolution was, as yet, nowhere in sight.

During the thousand years from about 500 BCE, intellectual pillars of the ancient Roman empire were mainly concerned with war, expansion and political intrigue, so little attention was paid to philosophical matters other than essentially absorbing and building on the learning of the Greeks, although there were instances of literary brilliance in the works of Cicero, Marcus Aurelius, Plutarch and Seneca, among others. Religion followed the pattern of the Greek pantheon, although monotheistic Christianity arose as an outgrowth of ancient theologies, most proximately that of the Hebrews.

The Middle Ages (including the Dark Ages of the early centuries CE when invading tribal groups swarmed over much of Europe) are widely considered a period of cultural stagnation lasting until the mid 15th century, when Johannes Gutenberg's invention of the printing press with movable type served as the catalyst for the European Renaissance—a period of renewed interest in classical knowledge of the ancient Greeks and Romans, artistic advances (aesthetics and perspective of Michaelangelo, Rafael, da Vinci) and educational reform (classics, philosophy, humanities).

Study of astronomical phenomena and characteristics of matter has undergone an operational metamorphosis since the 17th century, when science began to be applied to secure information about anything (e.g., social phenomena such as John Locke's "*Two Treatises on Government*"), not only what was considered nature. In the early part of the century Johannes Kepler advanced on the Copernican model of planetary motions, doing away with the need for epicycles by formulating mathematical expressions to explain the positions of the planets in terms of elliptical orbits. Although astronomy and physics were already recognized as distinct scientific disciplines, what ignorance had torn asunder, Kepler unified by dealing with astronomy as a form of celestial physics.[207] Just as it was clear that a more thorough understanding of cosmic phenomena demanded integration of what were formerly distinct disciplines, so it is with modern-day science, where proliferation of disciplines and compartmentalization of knowledge are impediments to systematic analysis of natural phenomena, a situation that does not bode well for the future of life on Earth.

It can be argued that modern science originated with Galileo Galilei (1564-1642), since he added mathematical refinement to the astronomy of Kepler and applied mathematical rigor to other areas of knowledge. For example, by rolling balls down an incline, he was able to show that, contrary to Aristotelian observation, all objects fell essentially at the same rate, not dependent on the weight of each. In fact, he determined the value of gravitational acceleration (change in velocity over time), and explained why movement at constant velocity is not sensed, but only acceleration. His employment of optics developed in the Netherlands provided views of the heavens previously unknown, with planets as disks rather than points and moons of Jupiter. All of this was upsetting to church authorities, but validated the ideas of Copernicus. Galileo eventually fell into ecclesiastical displeasure and was compelled to recant by the Inquisition. But in his last moments he is reported to have said, "and yet it (Earth) moves" (religious dogma placed Earth at the center of the universe).

Isaac Newton, a giant in the pantheon of intellectual superstars, was born in the year Galileo died, 1642. Newton's laws of motion were fundamental principles of physics until Einstein's relativity superseded his concept of absolute space and time. In July 1687 Newton published *Principia*, in which he revealed his three laws of motion: a body with no applied force continues its motion; acceleration related to the force applied to a mass, action and reaction between two bodies in contact. He also developed the law of universal gravitation, and through his new models, explained Kepler's laws of planetary motion. Despite Einstein's refinements, Newton's laws of motion still constitute the foundation of much of modern engineering and technology.

Did Newton consider himself a scientist? The title of his major work indicates otherwise, that he was merely pursuing truth in nature. Furthermore, he states rather forcefully his philosophical approach in a letter to Robert Hooke (15 February 1676)[208]: "Hitherto I have not been able to discover the cause of those properties of gravity from the phenomena, and I frame no hypothesis; for whatever is not deduced from the phenomena is to be called an hypothesis; and hypotheses, whether metaphysical or physical, whether of occult qualities or mechanical, have no place in experimental philosophy. *In this philosophy particular propositions are inferred from the phenomena, and afterward rendered general by deduction* [italics added]." A statement attributed to him by Sir David Brewster[209] provides further confirmation that he was of a philosophical, rather than a scientific bent: "I do not know what I may appear to the world, but to myself I seem to have been only like a boy playing on the sea-shore, and diverting myself in now and then finding a smoother pebble or a prettier shell than ordinary, whilst the great ocean of truth lay all undiscovered before me."

However, even in Newton's time the pursuit of secure knowledge about anything, not only the natural world, began to be identified as science. By the 18th century the Enlightenment, characterized in the Western world by advancements in cultural life, set the stage for the industrial revolution, with technology feeding on the proliferation in scientific knowledge. In the 19th century, *philosophy* began to distance itself from *natural philosophy*, which in some quarters was transposed into a form of inquiry relying on empiricism with well-defined mathematical precision: increasingly the term *natural science* was applied.

Science up to the 19th century focused mainly on natural science. Gradually during this timeframe, researchers in various areas or disciplines took up places in the universities of Europe and later

North America, forming departments specializing in narrow areas of interest. Barriers between the disciplines were further fortified with the practice of conferring degrees within disciplines, and then filling the ranks of academic posts only with members of a particular "club."

During the 19th and early 20th centuries improved measuring instruments allowed researchers—Lavoisier, Rutherford, De Broglie, Faraday, Boltzmann, Kirchhoff, Planck, Bohr and many others—to probe more deeply into the structure of matter, at the atomic and then subatomic levels. Large telescopes allowed the study of astronomical phenomena with greater precision.

By the 20th century science had come into its own, the respectable way to pursue knowledge via the scientific method. In fact, it has become commonplace for knowledge gained by any other means to be attacked by both scientists and lay people alike as "unscientific" and unworthy of consideration. Legislative bodies, regulatory agencies and the press have similarly denigrated any conclusions, predictions or forecasts not scientifically supported.

Social sciences were not recognized as disciplines until the 20th century. The study of social phenomena began to employ techniques that mimicked the physical and biological sciences, leading to specializations in sociology, psychology and economics.

The result finally was a virtual compartmentalization of acquisition and application of knowledge, which has been the cause of much degradation of Earth and adverse consequences for inhabitants (See "Compartmentalization and division" below). Scientific knowledge and its offshoot, technology, have revolutionized culture, leading to unprecedented accumulation of wealth by a minority, subordination of the interests of vast numbers of humans by an industrial and commercial behemoth, and hazards to life on Earth in the form of environmental pollution, grinding poverty and ignorance among the masses. These developments have led to hostility among social classes, ethnic groups and nations, with attendant rise of terrorism, proliferation of weapons of mass destruction and the propensity to use them. In the hands of humanity, applications of scientific knowledge and technology, as awesome as they may be, have managed to vastly increase insecurity rather than serve to uplift the quality of life on Earth.

Despite the predominant transition toward compartmentalization and application of the scientific method from ancient Greece to the Enlightenment[210], two post Enlightenment intellectual luminaries illustrate the uplifting effects for humanity of a more wholesome approach to the accumulation and applications of knowledge:

DARWIN

Although the idea of evolution was not new at the time, Charles Darwin (1809-1882) revolutionized the entire framework for the existence of life on Earth with his explanation of speciation, with natural selection as the essential mechanism.[211]

Darwin attended Cambridge University, not a particularly good student, His passionate interest in insects attracted the attention of one of his respected teachers of botany, John Stevens Henslow, who arranged for him to serve as naturalist on a five-year round-the-world voyage of the Beagle, under the command of Vice-Admiral Robert FitzRoy, a noted meteorologist. Darwin spent most of these years investigating and amassing voluminous data about the geology and zoology of South America, the Galapagos Islands and the Pacific islands.

After his return to England, he learned that many of the species studied in the Galapagos were unique to the islands, but similar to species found on the mainland of South America, about 600 miles away. This led to speculations about the origin of species—anathema to ecclesiastical authorities, which clung to the biblical explanation of creation. Also weighing on him were his own religious upbringing and his devout and devoted wife.

He was not the first to suggest that species could be transmuted. In fact, he was familiar with the evolutionary speculations of his own grandfather Erasmus Darwin, a physician and also a respected naturalist, poet and philosopher, and by the French zoologist Jean-Baptiste Lamarck. After his return from the Beagle voyage, over many years he conducted exhaustive experiments in horticulture and animal husbandry. To supplement his own experiments, he communicated with many other naturalists and geologists, and with horticulturalists and animal breeders who were modifying domesticated species by successively selecting for desirable traits.

From Thomas Malthus' *Essay on the Principle of Population* (1798), which explained how unrestrained growth in human population would overextend the capacity for food production, Darwin realized that a large proportion of organisms do not reach reproductive age. Otherwise, population of every species would expand indefinitely, which was obviously at odds with experience: species populations eventually reach a stable level in a given area. He extended this idea to speculation that favorable variations within species would provide the wherewithal for some to survive to reproductive age and others to perish before they were able to beget offspring. This process he called "natural selection," as compared with selective breeding in domesticated animals and plants, which ultimately leads to new breeds (even to the point of speciation) over a number of generations.

Darwin's monumental work, *Origin of Species,* was finally published in 1859, over two decades after completing the Beagle voyage and after having first prepared the outline in 1842. He was prompted finally to introduce his ideas into the public arena because he learned that Alfred Russell Wallace, working independently in the Amazon River basin and in the Malay archipelago, had arrived at an almost identical explanation for evolution of species.

Darwin deliberately and painstakingly explained that species are not immutable, using examples from nature and from horticulture and animal husbandry. Then he showed how differential survival rates in isolated populations would favor propagation of some traits and extinction of others, leading to speciation, such that viable sexual reproduction with parallel populations would no longer be possible. He provided a view of the panorama of life with all species related through branching over the eons since life first appeared on Earth.

Although Darwin, on occasion, connected his efforts with the scientific milieu of his day, he would not pass scientific muster according to today's standards. First and foremost, Darwin was drawn to what we might now identify as zoology, as a moth to candlelight. He considered himself a naturalist, one interested in probing into the nature of nature, and focused on characteristics of species inhabiting Earth. Most significantly, his major contribution to human understanding, The *Origin*, which profoundly altered the conception of man's relation to nature, was written in a style that any layperson could read cover to cover without flinching. *He communicated with anyone who happened to be interested in his findings*—not just a select group of scientific specialists for whom a barrier existed between knowledge and its consequences. In the last paragraph of his monumental work on speciation Darwin illuminates the temporal panorama of life's natural origins: "Thus, from the war of nature, from famine and death, the most exalted object which we are capable of conceiving, namely, the production of the higher animals, follows. There is grandeur in this view of life, with its several powers, having been originally breathed into a few forms or into one; and that, whilst this planet has gone cycling on according to the fixed law of gravity, from so simple a beginning endless forms most beautiful and most wonderful have been, and are being, evolved."

Although he tantalized readers by alluding to human origins, it was only in a later work, *The Descent of Man,* that he proposed evolution of human life from simpler forms and a common ancestor with living species, in particular the other primates. "Man with all his noble qualities, with sympathy which feels for the most debased, with benevolence which extends not only to other men but to the humblest living creature, with his god-like intellect which has penetrated into the movements and constitution of the solar system—with all these exalted powers—man still bears in his bodily frame the indelible stamp of his lowly origin."[212]

EINSTEIN

Albert Einstein, who was born in the latter part of this period, and whose intellectual acuity was one of the greatest (arguably *the* greatest) in human history, continually alluded to the essential philosophical framework of scientific inquiry, which could not be ignored without diminishing the quality of scientific endeavor.[213]

That the breadth of his vista extended far beyond what is knowable about the physical universe is revealed in his response to assertions about the absence of causality in subatomic phenomena as described by quantum mechanics, which his own work on photons (packets of light energy) helped to advance: "Quantum mechanics is certainly imposing. But an inner voice tells me that it is not yet the real thing. The theory says a lot, but does not really bring us any closer to the secret of the "old one." I, at any rate, am convinced that He does not throw dice."[214]

As a young man Einstein had found it difficult to breach the barriers to academia within the university system of his native Germany, spending years as a patent investigator in Switzerland before finally landing an academic post. While at the patent office he wrote four papers, on the structure of light (which eventually earned a Nobel Prize), on Brownian motion, and two related to his later proposal on special relativity.

That this work involved little contact with the scientific community illustrates that Einstein was by no means a traditional scientist. His method of inquiry involved mainly intellectual exercises (thought experiments) in which he posed questions about physical phenomena and then tried to answer them by building explanations upon existing knowledge and mathematical structures.

Although it's clear that Einstein *identified* as scientist, he insists that a philosophical underpinning is essential for a secure path to understanding. However, in the midst of the tempest of intellectual ferment that prevailed during his most creative years concerning the nature of matter and energy, he was reluctant to deny to those at the leading edge the opportunity to choose its direction. In an article published in 1936, he acknowledges that the scientist, although perhaps a "poor philosopher," nevertheless might more appropriately identify questions about the implications and direction of the pursuit of knowledge, particularly at a time when the very foundations of physics were being shaken: "the physicist cannot simply surrender to the philosopher the critical contemplation of the theoretical foundations; for, he himself knows best, and feels more surely where the shoe pinches. In looking for a new foundation, he must try to make clear in his own mind just how far the concepts which he uses are justified, and are necessities."[215]

However, in a 1916 memorial note for Ernst Mach, physicist and philosopher with whom Einstein maintained a close correspondence, he expressed concern for the lack of interest on the part of many of his colleagues in epistemology (the nature, sources and limits of knowledge or truth), pointing out that those students whom he considered most able had a "vigorous interest" in the subject, who "happily began discussions about the goals and methods of science, and ... showed unequivocally, through their tenacity in defending their views, that the subject seemed important to them. Indeed, one should not be surprised at this."[216]

Only those concerned with the methods and larger consequences of their investigations and acquisition of knowledge gained Einstein's respect. Even though they follow the rites that characterize scientific research, nevertheless they must think as philosophers, always conscious of the wider implications of knowledge. The purely scientific variety, with such a profound impact on qualities of life, has to be treated with great caution. In this case, there is no such thing as "knowledge for its own sake": its repercussions spread like ripples from a stone dropped into a pond.

In a letter of 1944 to Einstein, young physicist Robert Thornton, who was beginning his tenure at the University of Puerto Rico, asked for his thoughts on introducing "as much of the philosophy of science as possible" into the modern physics course that he was to teach the following spring. Einstein replied: "I fully agree with you about the significance and educational value of methodology as well as history and philosophy of science. So many people today—and *even professional scientists—seem to me like somebody who has seen thousands of trees but has never seen a forest.* A knowledge of the historic and philosophical background gives that kind of independence from *prejudices of his generation* from which *most scientists are suffering. This independence created by philosophical insight is—in my opinion—the mark of distinction between a mere artisan or specialist and a real seeker after truth* [italics added]"[217].

To Einstein, knowledge outside the philosophical context

is dangerous. Professional scientists see the trees within their disciplines, but fail to see the forest of which the trees are both a part and a consequence. What are these "prejudices of his generation" from which most scientists suffer? They are the pressures exerted on them as a consequence of the strategic human plan, as manifested in this narrow context: (1) attain status and recognition; (2) accommodate to peer review of research papers and grant applications with "conformity, cronyism and plagiarism"; (3) select research topics following interests of those who pay the bills; (4) adopt the politically correct or advantageous point of view; (5) present a (deceptively) iconoclastic and skeptical image to the outside world.[218]

Yet, Einstein reveals the tension that he senses between philosophy and science, centering on epistemology, a fundamental feature of philosophy. The scientist, if isolated from the philosophical domain in which inquiry would have a sounder foundation and more universal relevance, employs an epistemological system only to the extent that it satisfies the need for structure in the line of investigation. "The reciprocal relationship of epistemology and science is of noteworthy kind. They are dependent upon each other. Epistemology without contact with science becomes an empty scheme. *Science without epistemology is—insofar as it is thinkable at all—primitive and muddled* (italics added)."[219] The tension erupts into rebellion, as the scientist ignores constraints that might be imposed when conducting investigations in the broader epistemological context: "However, no sooner has the epistemologist, who is seeking a clear system, fought his way through to such a system, than he is inclined to interpret the thought-content of science in the sense of his system and to reject whatever does not fit into his system. The scientist, however, cannot afford to carry his striving for epistemological systematic that far. He accepts gratefully the epistemological conceptual analysis; but the external conditions, which are set for him by the facts of experience, do not permit him to let himself be too much restricted in the construction of his conceptual world by the adherence to an epistemological system [thus ignoring its relevance to a higher order of knowledge]. He therefore must appear to the systematic epistemologist as a type of unscrupulous opportunist [using whatever aspects of epistemology seem to be useful in a particular circumstance]"[220]

However, in this way the scientist constructs a world in a kind of vacuum, maintaining the philosophical connection only to the extent that is convenient. The deleterious consequences of this isolation from the wider domain of knowledge have become all too apparent in devastation of the environment of Planet Earth and premature human ventures into the heavens. Only when the scientist lifts his eyes from the microscope and asks himself about motivations and means of acquisition for the knowledge sought and its wider validity and implications can his studies be justified.

Einstein was instrumental in furthering development of the atomic bomb, its design based on his discovery of the relationship between energy and matter explained by the theory of special relativity. In August 1939 physicist Leo Szilard wrote a letter to President Roosevelt, signed by Einstein, urging President Roosevelt to undertake a development program, expressing concern that Germany might be progressing on the bomb's development. This was followed up in 1940 with another letter, once again written by Szilard and signed by Einstein, to the Briggs Committee that was appointed to study uranium chain reactions, but which Szilard and others feared was proceeding too cautiously. The bomb was ultimately constructed under the Manhattan Project, and two of them were dropped on Japanese cities in 1945, bringing an end to World War II.

After the war Einstein led the World Government Movement, which sought to outlaw production and use of nuclear weapons. "I know not with what weapons World War III will be fought, but World War IV will be fought with sticks and stones."[221] In July 1955, Einstein and Bertrand Russell jointly issued the Russell-Einstein Manifesto: "In view of the fact that in any future world war nuclear weapons will certainly be employed, and that such weapons threaten the continued existence of mankind, we urge the Governments of the world to realize, and to acknowledge publicly, that their purpose cannot be furthered by a world war, and we urge them, consequently, to find peaceful means for the settlement of all matters of dispute between them."

Einstein deeply regretted his role in creating the bomb, as

expressed in November 1954, five months before his death: "I made one great mistake in my life ... when I signed the letter to President Roosevelt recommending that atom bombs be made; but there was some justification—the danger that the Germans would make them."[222]

COMPARTMENTALIZATION AND DIVISION

The transition from natural philosophy to science has resulted in a virtual compartmentalization of acquisition and application of knowledge, the cause of much degradation of Earth and lives of its inhabitants. While the field of vision of science and its offshoot, technology, have narrowed in accordance with their utilitarian objectives, they have revolutionized culture, leading to unprecedented accumulation of wealth by a minority, subordination of the interests of vast numbers of humans by an industrial and commercial behemoth, and hazards to life on Earth in the form of environmental pollution, grinding poverty and ignorance among the masses. These developments have led to hostility among social classes, ethnic groups and nations, fostering the rise of terrorism, proliferation of weapons of mass destruction and the propensity to use them. In the hands of humanity, applications of scientific knowledge and technology, as awesome as they may be in improving some aspects of life, have managed to vastly increase insecurity across the globe.

The general public is not very well equipped to exercise control on the scientific juggernaut. The system has fortified itself by projecting an esoteric aura in the public mind. The concerns of lay people are like the flea on the back of the scientific elephant. Cautions on applications of scientific knowledge lack potency because the nature of arcane scientific achievements are largely incomprehensible to the general public, obscured in the argot of the insiders club, with very little attempt to translate the nature of a development and its consequences to lay language.

Another indication of the absence of holistic thinking within the "scientific community," which is needed to maintain favorable prospects for the future of life on our planet, is the plethora of specializations. The proliferation of academic disciplines seems an inexorable phenomenon, like a tree sprouting limitless branches.[223] Each specialization has a way of dividing, something like mitosis in cell division[224], into an array of subcategories, which in turn are candidates for a repeat of the process, ad infinitum. Just taking into account what are currently considered respectable scientific disciplines, are the following[225]: (1) natural sciences: space science, earth science, life science, chemistry, physics; (2) formal sciences: mathematics, computer science; (3) social sciences: anthropology, archaeology, area studies, economics, ethnic studies, gender and sexuality studies, geography, political science, psychology, sociology; (4) professional and applied sciences: agriculture and forestry, business, education, engineering, family and consumer science, health sciences, journalism, media and communication, law, library and museum studies, military sciences, personal service professions, public affairs, social work.

As an example of the branching related to just one of the above areas of knowledge, life science as a sub-category of natural science: aerobiology, anatomy (comparative, human), animal communications, biochemistry, bioinformatics, biology, biophysics, botany, ethnobotany, cell biology, chronobiology, cryobiology, ecology (human ecology, landscape ecology), endocrinology, entomology, evolutionary biology, genetics, limnology, linnaean taxonomy, marine biology, microbiology, molecular biology, mycology, neuroscience, paleobiology (paleontology), parasitology, pathology, phycology, physiology, systematics (taxonomy), virology (molecular, epidemial), xenobiology, zoology (cryptozoology, entomology, ethology, herpetology, ichthyology, oology, ornithology, primatology, zootomy).

There are further subdivisions at the next level for some of these. An aspirant to a scientific career has a multitude of areas in which to learn more and more about less and less. The consequences for Planet Earth are profound. An old adage is that "a little knowledge is dangerous." While a particular researcher may spend her entire life diligently investigating and discovering, the external significance of what is learned seems to be of little concern, except in regard to maintaining the approbation of those responsible for supporting research.

CONSEQUENCES OF COMPARTMENTALIZATION

There is a spectrum of possible approaches to the pursuit of knowledge—from unstructured to highly focused, and from casual observation to philosophical inquiry to scientific study. There are pursuers of common sense, philosophers, philosopher-scientists of all gradations, and scientists, most of the latter engaging in what might now be called "applied (or utilitarian) science."

When knowledge is pursued in a narrow context, such as at Peenemunde (V2 rockets), at Los Alamos (atomic bomb) and in many contemporary laboratories of universities and industry, the outcome is very often disastrous for humans and for life in general. Scientists responsible for knowledge leading to wondrous miniature electronics, for example—lap top computers, cell phones, games, cameras—do not seem to be concerned that they are unleashing a flood of enormous waste, as these devices wear out or become obsolete and are discarded, much of it toxic (see Chapter 8). The launchers of spacecraft do not seem to be concerned that their creations will eventually come down to earth, contaminating the air, land and waters and even perhaps dropping in on quiet neighborhoods. The ton of solid waste per capita per annum collecting in landfills in the United States and other industrialized countries is mute (and odiferous) testimony to the insensitivity of the scientific community responsible for much of its creation.

The narrower the context in which knowledge is pursued, the more likely it is that it will turn out badly. This is not hypothetical. Just consider what a few hundred years of science have wrought on Earth: means of melting snow caps, endangering and driving to extinction many species, the capacity to destroy all of life by pushing a few buttons, billions without adequate food and water, mountains of waste—radioactive, solid, liquid and gaseous. This is the "Von Braun syndrome" (see below) of scientific inquiry and its aftermath—what a beautiful rocket launch, and who cares where it comes down?—replicated in countless numbers of academic, industrial and government laboratories around the world.

In contemporary life, the scientific method is considered not only the secure path to knowledge, but also the most reliable foundation for deciding what to do about critical issues of the day. For lay people, the scientific method is considered a precise approach to proof, even though scientists acknowledge the tentativeness of any conclusion and that nothing can be really "proven" owing to inherent uncertainties in phenomena and measurements. The lay public is mesmerized by the authority of scientifically justified pronouncements, usually too intimidated by the arrogance (dismissal of other paths to knowledge) and arcane jargon emanating from the scientific community to protest.

The problem is not that the scientific method itself is flawed, but the narrow context in which it is usually applied leaves much to be desired. When issues are examined within the compartmentalized system that prevails in most research institutions, the results are tainted because they normally ignore conditions outside the rigid confines of the micro-discipline. When this is clearly preposterous, scientists collaborate or even cross boundaries, albeit with trepidation—fear of reprisal or at least condemnation from their disciplinary rivals.

The science of chemistry has provided humanity with many thousands of synthesized substances employed in agriculture, industry and medicine. These materials are unknown in nature, many of them resistant or impervious to biological degradation, so that they persist in the environment indefinitely, accumulating in the land, air and waterways. While they ostensibly produce beneficial effects such as increased food production, useful products and health improvements, the buildup of these substances in the environment is a time bomb. According to the World Health Organization[226], 47,000 people die per annum from direct exposure to toxic chemicals, but the actual toll is far greater and will increase as the environment becomes even more heavily laden with these toxic and persistent substances.

There is widespread reverence on the part of the general public and within the scientific community for facts and relationships derived from scientific investigation. The scientific method is regarded as indispensible for secure knowledge about how nature can be harnessed to fulfill human aspirations. Science is even regarded as the instrument for resolving problems created by science: e.g., environmental pollution can only by alleviated by applying more science and technology. Rather than return to a more holistic, philosophical vantage point, conventional scientific/technological solutions are prescribed: the solution to carbon-emitting coal plants, for example, is to apply technology to clean up emissions rather that to return to the basic issue about whether or not strip mined fuel for them is in our long-term interests.

SPACE EXPLORATION—A SPECIAL CASE

During the 20th century, aerospace technology had reached the point of shooting rockets into space, largely as a consequence of missile and rocket developments undertaken by Germany during WWII as a means of pounding Britain into submission with aerial assaults that maimed about nine thousand Londoners (a third fatalities). Interest in outer space was stimulated in the United States by the launch of an unmanned satellite, Sputnik, by the Russians on Oct. 4, 1957. President Dwight Eisenhower in 1958 created the National Aeronautics and Space Administration (NASA), which became the central institution for scientific space exploration. Then on April 12, 1961 the Russians placed their first cosmonaut, Yuri Gagarin, into Earth orbit.

After developing a number of unmanned programs involving communications and weather forecasting systems, NASA, in conjunction with parallel military organizations, became involved in the use of satellites for intelligence gathering and other military purposes such as anti-missile defense systems. Not to be outdone by space accomplishments of the Soviet Union, shortly after John Kennedy was elected president of the US in 1960, he set a goal of landing men on the moon before the end of that decade. NASA began with a series of suborbital and orbital flights of John Glenn, and finally in 1969 with the Apollo program, Alan Sheppard was the first of three astronauts to set foot on the lunar surface.

Did landing people on the moon have any practical significance? According to one study, it was identified as a "societal bubble," a collective excess of enthusiasm based on "public and/or political expectations of positive outcomes...."[227] Support by the public was almost unanimous in the heat of the 'Cold War with the Soviet Union. Those directly associated with the program were exhilarated by the challenge: "political and social factors weaved a network of reinforcing feedbacks that led to widespread over-enthusiasm and extraordinary commitment by those involved in the project as well as by politicians and by the public at large."[228] The Apollo program is one of the most egregious examples of misguided public policy, a project undertaken with no substantial societal purpose except an almost infantile compulsion to flaunt technological prowess.

Once the pointlessness of the moon mission became clear even to man-in-space advocates, NASA then began to concentrate on manned space stations, for what reason is not clear except that like Mt. Everest, it was something to climb. But as we have learned, just because something can be done is not sufficient justification for doing it.

In January 2010, facing massive budget deficits, President Barack Obama announced his intention to change the direction of the space program to rely on privately financed rocket launches.[229] There was also fear that the Constellation Program, initiated by previous president George W. Bush to return to the moon and maybe even Mars, might go by the wayside. One of the major concerns was that 1,500 Huntsville contractor employees and 700 employees at Marshall Space Flight Center working on the program would lose their jobs.[230]

On its own web site, the NASA outlines benefits derived from its space program, described in terms of improvements on the ground rather than in space: e.g., temper foam, enriched baby foods, portable cordless vacuums, freeze drying techniques, and water purification.[231] NASA once identified other spinoffs from their man-in-space program (although apparently no longer touted): home appliances, (more interesting?) museums, accurate thermometers for medical applications, crops and livestock on the farm, sunglasses and facial cosmetics, firefighting and rescue equipment, unspecified benefits for the sports world, virtual reality, airport safety, a safer and more beautiful Earth! (emphasis added) In addition, miniaturized integrated circuits, satellite technology, GPS navigation systems, bone-density measurements, miniaturized heart pumps, water filtration, wireless light switches, remediation solutions for sites contaminated by chemicals, the development of sensors on reconnaissance robots used in Afghanistan and Iraq to deal with improvised explosive devices.

But most, if not all, of these "benefits" that NASA identifies have little to do with space exploration, developments that would have been achieved through the normal process of research and development in universities and industries.

There is little doubt that the national space program has been instrumental in achieving incredible technological breakthroughs. It has provided benefits that could substantially increase hope for the future of life. Global communications systems using space satellites (television, internet, voice messaging) have provided information to people, even in the remotest corners, about a much wider range of life's options than would ordinarily be available. Awesome images of celestial bodies and stellar phenomena have been produced by the Hubble telescope, which should also provide humanity with a little needed humility, and with proper redundancies, would not require human maintenance. Weather systems have allowed farmers and ranchers to improve their decision-making.[232]

Placing humans in space is another matter. The Apollo program was undertaken primarily for geopolitical reasons, as attested by the fact that no further space missions of that kind were undertaken in the next four decades.

Is space exploration worth the cost? The debate about the relative merits of exploring space with humans and robots is as old as the space program itself. One ardent supporter of space exploration, G. Scott Hubbard[233], cites enthusiasm of Werner Von Braun (father of the V2 rocket developed at Peenemunde, Germany during WWII that killed thousands of British citizens), a moving force behind the Apollo Program that sent humans to the moon and the architect of the mighty Saturn V rocket, who "believed passionately in the value of human exploitation [of space]—especially when it meant beating the hated Soviet Empire."

Hubbard points out that James Van Allen, discoverer of the belt of charged particles girdling Earth and held in place by its magnetic field, was an "ardent and vocal [supporter of] robotic exploration." He advances five arguments concerning the utility of space exploration and the roles of humans and robots, in roughly ascending order of advocate support:

> (1) It will eventually allow us to establish a human civilization on another world (e.g., the planet Mars) as a hedge against the type of catastrophe that wiped out the dinosaurs.

The likelihood of this kind of natural catastrophe is so remote as to be almost ludicrous as justification for a man-in-space program. It's much more likely that such a catastrophe would be man-made, e.g., a conflagration involving nuclear warfare.

> (2) We explore space and create important new technologies to advance our economy. It is true that, for every dollar we spend on the space program, the US economy receives about $8 of economic benefit. Space exploration can also serve as a stimulus for children to enter the fields of science and engineering.

While the technology developed in the space program is impressive, these inventions and initiatives did not need the space program as a platform. The economic benefits purportedly derived from the program would most likely have been greater if they were not accompanied by wasteful expenditures on putting people into space.

> (3) Space exploration in an international context offers a peaceful cooperative venue that is a valuable alternative to nation state hostilities. One can look at the International Space Station and marvel that the former Soviet Union and the US are now active partners. International cooperation is also a way to reduce costs.

This implies that the choice is either international hostility between former Cold War opponents or meetings in a space station.

While such catalysts for international cooperation are useful, they are by no means indispensable for political leaders—presidents and prime ministers and other heads of state—and institutions such as the United Nations, to resolve international disputes.

Accordingly, the Russians plan to abandon the space station in favor of a space hotel. Russian Deputy Prime Minister Dmitry Rogozin reported that Russia plans to direct its man-in-space program to other projects after 2020.[234] A Russian firm, *Orbital Technologies*, plans to open the first space hotel in history within five years (by 2019). The "Commercial Space Station" will be located in an orbit 250 miles above Earth, accommodating a maximum of seven people. Special training will be necessary, depending on the type of vehicle used in for travel to the "hotel."

> (4) National prestige requires that the US continue to be a leader in space, and that includes human exploration. History tells us that great civilizations dare not abandon exploration.

Are there better ways to enhance national prestige? How about taking the lead in calling on international leaders to deal with crises on the ground—excessive population growth that is sure to increase the havoc created by already unsupportable human numbers, perhaps three times the level that can be comfortably accommodated; assigning a top priority to figuring out how to reduce and even eliminate global poverty and how to provide more equitable distribution of the world's wealth; pursuing more useful avenues for exploration, e.g., how to live together on Earth in peace, with justice and prosperity?

> (5) Exploration of space will provide humanity with an answer to the most fundamental questions: Are we alone? Are there other forms of life beside those on Earth?[235]

Do we need man in space to answer this question? Are humans going to traverse the vast reaches of space seeking a signal that someone else is out there? Are we to commit an embryonic contingent to this misadventure to the infinities of space without hope of return?

And what's the purpose of this type of information? The likelihood of significant intercourse between humans and other forms of life on celestial bodies is not only remote, but also pointless and foolhardy.

Hubbard offers these additional observations:

> "Personally, I think humans will be better at unstructured environment exploration than any existing robot for a very long time ... There are those who say that exploration with humans is simply too expensive for the return we receive."

Not only is exploration with humans too expensive, but chimerical. Will excess human population be exported to some distant planet? And if you think that a human nucleus will be sent out for some good purpose to occupy celestial bodies, after seeing what humans have wrought on the one planet that we already occupy, is this something that should be replicated elsewhere? Humans are in no condition to populate the rest of the cosmos: one only has to view the condition of the one planet on which we enjoy hegemony to realize that it would be a disaster. Before humans evolve to a state where wisdom is a universal trait, it can only be anticipated that ventures into the reaches of space will result in the same kind of havoc and destruction that our species has wrought on Earth. To answer in the affirmative you have to be the proverbial madman or economist.

> "However, I cannot imagine any US President announcing that we are abandoning space exploration with humans and leaving it to the Chinese, Russians, Indians, Japanese or any other group. I can imagine the US engaging in much more expansive international cooperation. Humans will be exploring space. The challenge is to be sure that they accomplish meaningful exploration."

In confirmation of Hubbard's speculations, President Barack Obama is caught up in the frenzy to expand human presence to the far reaches of the cosmos: "This is the next chapter that we can write here at NASA. We will partner with industry. We will invest in leading edge research and technology. We will set far-reaching milestones and provide the resources to reach those milestones. And step by step we will push the boundaries not only of where we can go, but what we can do."[236]

NASA now looks forward to manned missions in the expanse surrounding the Earth-moon system and beyond: "NASA is embarking on a new era of space exploration in which humans will travel deeper into the solar system than ever before. The International Space Station will be the centerpiece for exploration and will serve as a test bed for research and new technologies and a stepping-stone to future destinations. The commercial industry will transport cargo and eventually crew to the space station while NASA focuses on developing the Orion Multipurpose Vehicle, Space Launch Support and advanced exploration systems. These developments will enable a sustainable human presence in destinations such as the moon, near-Earth asteroids and Mars."[237] That's only for today. Tomorrow the cosmos.

Heaven help us!!!

ENVIRONMENTALISM

Planet Earth auto-assembled from cosmic material about 4 billion years ago. Living things first appeared about a billion years later. During the enormous span of time before humans appeared, nature spawned hundreds of millions of species of flora and fauna, each finding its niche for a time in a dynamic network of interactions and habitats, with most eventually succumbing to inhospitable changes in their domains. Natural and catastrophic extinctions leave Earth at present with an estimated 50 million species.

The first inkling of humanity—the family *homo*—appeared in Africa about 2.5 billion years ago. Then through a veritable avalanche of speciation, at least three or four ancestors (and possibly many more) lived concurrently, and perhaps even as neighbors, each occupying a slightly different niche that enabled them to coexist in relative harmony. The advent of humanity as we know it occurred approximately 200 thousand years ago, which is about 0.005 percent of the total span of Earth's history. To put this in perspective, if all of Earth's history were compressed into a 24-hour day, modern humans would be around for about the last 4 seconds.

According to Judeo-Christian tradition man is above nature, granted stewardship by the god Yahweh over flora and fauna of Earth, free to exploit, consume and even propagate without constraint. As a consequence of our special place in the panoply of life forms we are supposedly exempt from natural exigencies, widely believed to receive our marching orders from inner prodding of soul to behave with morality and altruism. Distinguishing outward traits—self-consciousness, cognitive and analytical powers, speech, manual dexterity, bipedalism—ostensibly confer upon humanity a unique relationship with nature, at once its master and super-benefactor. Our singular role is fortified with self-proclaimed sanctity of divinely inspired manifest destiny.

Only a tuned-in and often activist minority ordinarily contemplates possibilities for the future of humankind; most scarcely consider prospects for the next generation much less posterity or the possibility of extinction[238]. Widespread inaction in the face of momentous degradation in the condition of our planet as it happened attests to this indifference. Wrangling over the costs and benefits of limiting greenhouse gases, the lack of alarm about a burgeoning human population growing by a Germany or Egypt each year, general unconcern for the trash defacing and befouling even the most isolated landscapes and positively inundating urban centers in virtually every country of the world, accepting the stench of effluvia pervading waterways and rendering most fresh water sources unfit for consumption as an acceptable consequence of "progress," indifference to grinding poverty as the lot of a billion wretched human souls and its murderous consequences, to the loss of natural habitat and near-extinction of wondrous creatures and plants in formerly pristine settings, to the accelerating diminution of Earth's forest cover and spreading desertification. Environmental degradation is the consequence of "choices" that either assign greater weight to immediately stimulating general material prosperity by consuming our planet's natural capital or that seek to exploit natural resources without regard for present and future generations of flora and fauna.

No, it's not necessary to insist on scientific evidence to acknowledge the adverse consequences of human hegemony on Earth. Anyone who observes how humans have debased the planet, particularly in the centuries since the industrial revolution (one hardly needs to make an effort to do so) does not need certification to statistical standards that something is desperately wrong. We don't have to count the number of bricks in the ton that is falling on us to know that the building is collapsing.

Yet, that is precisely what is demanded. Those who claim that the house is falling, and do not think it necessary to count the bricks, or cannot because they've been smashed beyond recognition or because they are falling so fast that our counting resources are inadequate, are labeled with the pejorative "environmentalist" by fierce advocates of the status quo—generally the unscrupulous minority that benefits from pollution-inducing exploitation of natural resources and their political collaborators. The same badge is pasted on a few sensitized scientists who attempt to reconnect their severed umbilical by counting the bricks and making their results known, even when current and impending environmental catastrophes are infinitely more evident than the premise that "all men are created equal." Public acquiescence to stigmatizing the messenger is abetted by widespread ignorance and myopia.

There is a way to counter this ploy. The folly of those concerned with adverse consequences of environmental degradation, and for future generations of humans and other living beings upon which our health and well-being depend, is to play into the hands of the short-sighted and ill-willed by loudly and proudly proclaiming affiliation with an environmental movement.

Environmentalists display their colors by behaving much like scientists: they identify as "environmentalists." The problem is that this sets up a barrier between advocates of a more sustainable and wholesome relationship with nature and those whose present state of awareness leaves them unconcerned or even hostile. It would be far more productive to direct attention to specific issues, and to the rational connection between pollution and the magnitude and distribution of its costs. This is not environmentalism, but sanity.

Anti-environmentalists label advocates of a more wholesome approach to life as "environmentalists" (the label is never "partial environmentalist"—an individual is either in or out of the group). If it's sane and rational to be concerned with the quality of one's habitat, upon the physical, social and economic features of the surroundings upon which health and well-being depend, then those unconcerned would have to be insane and irrational. So the proper duality is the sane and the anti-environmentalist. In other words, those in the class of anti-environmentalists are the insane, and should be treated as such.

What is the proper way to deal with the insane? Formerly they were institutionalized, both for their own protection and for what was perceived as the general good of society. Currently the practice is to "mainstream," and this is only fair and just. After all, the insane did not really choose insanity, but were victims of adversity in nature or nurture, or both. A sensible mainstreaming process would include arranging suitable environments in which the insane can function with relative immunity from further emotional and bodily harm, and in which the ability to harm others is precluded.

Anti-environmentalists must be afforded the same consideration. The only way to do this effectively is to protect them from environmental degradation. As they are irrational, arguments based upon the ordinary analytical process would be to no avail. Their participation in this effort must be co-opted with ploys that would appeal to the irrational. Attractive symbols are needed, to which the irrational would respond.

A potentially fruitful area for investigation is professional sports, which thrives on the loyalty of individuals who identify easily with symbols. One is an inveterate Yankee (baseball) fan or devotee of the Chicago Bulls (basketball) not because there is any tangible benefit to be derived, but because identification of this kind responds to fundamental instincts that are beyond what is normally considered rational in the modern world. In fact, loyalty is often strong if the relative proficiency of the team is low, underscoring the irrationality of such an affinity.

The sane (non anti-environmentalists) would sponsor one or more of the national professional sports leagues, with team names such as "Podunk Polluters." Anti-environmentalists, much more numerous than the sane, would thereby be enticed to render support through attendance and purchases of appropriately trademarked paraphernalia. As the sane would be directors and economic beneficiaries, and the anti-environmentalists their loyal supporters, much economic power would accrue to the sane, who would presumably utilize the accumulated resources for the benefit of the environment. Thus, both sane and anti-environmentalists would profit, even though the latter would have little idea, and care less, why. They would continue to berate environmentalists, but their loyalty to the symbol would be much stronger than distaste for their perceived adversaries, so that the quality of the environment would continue to improve, to the everlasting benefit of both sane and anti-environmentalist.

In a more practical vein, the interests of those concerned with the impact of human activity on Earth's natural environment would be better served by rejecting the label "environmentalist" altogether. For one thing, it presents too easy a target for those who would accept despoliation of our planet in exchange for short-term economic and political gain. It allows them to define the environmentally concerned as irrational preservationists rather than perceptive and rational conservers of our natural heritage. Furthermore, the label erects a barrier behind which anti-environmentalists can too easily lure masses of people who are not currently concerned on account of ignorance or economic desperation.

INDIFFERENT SCIENCE

Bisphenol A (BPA) is an additive in production of polycarbonate plastics. This plastic's properties—light weight, transparency, strength, toughness and heat resistance—have been found to be favorable for reusable food and drink containers. In these applications there has been some concern that BPA leaches food initially packaged or refilled within the containers, but its discoverers and producers are apparently unconcerned with its adverse health effects for the large number of people exposed to its toxicity.

BPA mimics estrogen, a hormone that is present in men and women, with higher amounts in women from puberty to menopause. In women the primary function of estrogen is in development of physical and organic sexual characteristics (e.g., ovulation) and in men sperm quality and the sex drive. The hormone also has a role in many other bodily functions, such as bone growth. If an estrogen mimic enters the body there is some concern that the delicate balance of estrogen can cause health problems: a deficit or excess, particularly in utero or early childhood, can affect brain and organ development, leading to health problems in later life.

The use of BPA in plastic food containers had wide public attention in 2008, when many published articles asserted that children were being exposed to dietary toxins. Some retailers pulled these containers from their shelves.

In 2001 the American Chemical Society convened a panel of paid experts to investigate the effects of low doses of BPA on human health. Its final report, in 2004, concluded that the evidence that low dosage exposure to BPA caused health problems was "very weak," relying on results from a few studies commissioned by industry. "By this point, roughly 100 studies on low-dose BPA were in circulation. Not a single industry study found it harmful, but 90 percent of (studies) by government funded scientists found dramatic effects, ranging from increased breast cancer to hyperactivity. Four of the panelists later insisted that the center scrub their names from the report because of questions about its inaccuracy."[239] In 2014 the US Food and Drug Administration (FDA) continues to approve what it claims as are acceptably low amounts in many foods, while some health experts caution avoidance.

The best science that money can buy!

SO, WHAT'S WRONG WITH SCIENCE AS WE KNOW IT??

During the past four centuries, applications of scientific discoveries have radically altered the human landscape. The nature of civilization has been transformed in step with technology, an indispensable component of contemporary social organization. Information technology has been at the forefront, infused into virtually every aspect of private and public life, at home, at work, at play and at war. Transportation technology has extended the domain of humankind into the heavens, vastly increased global trade, and radically changed settlements patterns. Agricultural technology has altered the process of food production, with genetically modified organisms and innovative techniques of cultivation and animal husbandry. Medical science and technology have provided immunities from many viral and parasitic threats, substitutes for defective body parts, and much more effective and less intrusive methods of diagnosis and treatment, leading to longer average life spans for populations in developed economies. These are only samples of the wonders derived from increased scientific knowledge and its technological offshoots.

Despite its potential to achieve the best of worlds—peace, prosperity and justice for all—the pursuit of knowledge via the scientific method has produced quite different outcomes. We see instead, Planet Earth beset with problems that have been enumerated elsewhere. Why point the finger at science? Isn't it the rapaciousness of humankind that is responsible for these excesses? The truth is that science, in its current conformation, has created these problems by foisting on a worshipping and unwitting populace, technology that is inconsistent with the common aspirations of people around the world—solutions that fail to take into account realities on the ground. The mountains of solid waste accumulating all over the world, liquid and gaseous effluents dumped into oceans, lakes and rivers, noxious gases released into the atmosphere, food and water scarcity, economic volatility (with bust becoming more the norm than boom)—all of these attest to the insensitivity of scientists and their technologist collaborators in setting into motion a production and consumption chain that ignores sustainability. The pernicious system of creating scientists, their methods of pursuing knowledge, and their resultant myopia concerning consequences of their discoveries, is responsible.

The practice of science today covers the entire spectrum from pure inquiry to what might be called "applied science," which is virtually indistinguishable from engineering and technology. Very few scientists are engaged in pure research. The reason is that priorities of sponsoring institutions, through the research grant process, determine the priorities of the scientific community. Research topics are most commonly selected to answer questions of the funding institutions. Scientists operate in academia, in industry and in government, most undertaking research projects as directed by those who pay the bills. In 2006, private interests funded 65 percent of research and development (R&D) in the United States.[240]

Anyone who has had direct contact with the academic science mill, either as grist or grinder, can potentially comprehend the destructive nature of the system. Although the pursuit of knowledge is an intrinsic imperative for humans, within this institution the force takes on bizarre dimensions as otherwise competent and discerning people are lured in mainly by the promise of prestige, security and compensation. The most significant flaws, and perils, in the contemporary scientific mode are its divorce from philosophy and compartmentalization, which are really part of the same phenomenon. In the 18th century poet Alexander Pope cogently expresses the hazard: "A little learning is a dangerous thing; drink deep, or taste not the Pierian Spring: there shallow draughts intoxicate the brain, and drinking largely sobers us again."[241]

The academic establishment that has been commissioned to produce scientists by common consent in most parts of the world is structured so that destructive outcomes are virtually assured. Rather than allow a few talented people to pursue their natural intellectual inclinations in freedom and collegiality, what actually happens is that large numbers are recruited by special interests, who are then subject to political and intellectual subordination:[242] Instead of free discourse between mentors and their charges, professors rather serve as judge and jury, administering qualifying examinations and certifying the validity and contributions of research. Students and researchers are favored whose natural inquisitiveness is diverted to issues selected under external pressures and who adopt dutifully the point of view of their superiors (professors), a form of "ideological discipline."

"Any students who instead follow their own interests by only studying things that intrigue them personally are risking their professional future." Rather than permit students to remain immersed in a wide array of issues confronting life on Earth, they are forced into a narrow channel of inquiry, fitted with blinders according to the priorities and exigencies of their sponsors. Through the qualifications and examination wringer, students are forced to "accept alienating work in a hierarchical system."[243] The compromise is not erased from the student's consciousness, and in fact is a source of discomfort. "Although the professional has sidelined his original goals, he usually retains some memory of them. Any such memory inevitably points to the compromises he has made and therefore can be an unrecognized source of unease in the professional's life."[244]

Need more be said about the need to restructure our system of learning and research? One who identifies as scientist under current conditions admits to knowing more and more about less and less, to narrowness in perspective that ignores concern for the consequences of her activity on the welfare of the community. It's one thing to study a narrowly delimited area (the spearhead of inquiry requires this kind of concentration), but to spend one's entire professional life without venturing to the field at right or left is conducive to a kind of myopia—a dangerous condition for one whose conclusions so strongly influence the course of human events.

Rather than producing enlightened repositories of knowledge and wisdom, the "ivory tower" continues to create highly focused functionaries. Critics of academia have generally missed the point that the entire institution needs to be restructured, toward a more philosophically oriented experience and de-compartmentalization. It's not multi-disciplinary inquiry that is required: so long as the plethora of disciplines remains part of the system, the same tensions will prevail. Rather, re-integration of the process of inquiry is required, where students and researchers are free to follow their fields of interest in a collegial relationship with their peers and mentors.

How far can knowledge take humanity? Can we aspire to a seat at the pinnacle of the mountain, where everything is in plain view? Stephen Hawking, an icon of the scientific community in the late 20th and early 21st centuries, states twice in his work *"A Short History of Time,"* that mankind is on the cusp of knowing everything. He alludes to the creation of a model that explains all natural phenomena in the universe.

Is this possible? And how will we know when we get there? Will we be able to completely explain the formation process of stars and planets? If so, how could it ever be confirmed? Is it possible, for example, for humanity to completely know itself? Researchers on the subject agree that there are limits to knowledge, and that the "universe lies beyond the grasp of any intellect, no matter how powerful, that could exist within the universe."[245] There are inevitable impediments to complete knowledge, so that those who seek a "theory of everything" will in the end be frustrated. What are some things we know that seem to inhibit complete knowledge? There is Werner Heisenberg's uncertainty principle—e.g., the more known about an object's position, the less about its momentum; the nature of matter as probability wave, described by Erwin Schrödinger; Kurt Gödel's Incompleteness Theorem, which implies that any logical system of any complexity is incomplete; since each contains more true statements than it can possibly prove according to its own defining set of rules. The concept of Thomas Kuhn that falsifiability is an essential condition for acceptance of any hypothesis—that a theory must be disprovable before it can be accepted—seems to place an impenetrable barrier between humanity and ultimate knowledge. Some things that can be described about nature are not subject to disproof.

Additionally, we humans are caught up in our own petard, insisting that knowledge is only certifiable through the scientific method, this despite the fact that agriculturalists, for example, during many millennia improved their crops and livestock employing "unscientific" processes. Originally the seed pod of teosinte, which even now grows in its native habitat in the mountains of Mexico, was only a few centimeters in length, and was improved over a couple of millennia to the form it has today—maize (or corn) with seed pods up to 10 or 12 inches in length—and a staple for the world. Contemporary agronomists marvel at the seemingly impossible process of the transition.

Some scientists attempt to reconnect with society after having been isolated and fed through the academic sausage grinder, particularly those immersed in issues and phenomena that bear directly on the conditions of human life and those species that have captured the public imagination. For most of them, it would be far better for the future of life if their learning had taken place in unstructured association with mentors and peers lured by the same flickering candle flame.

SCIENCE AND TECHNOLOGY AHEAD OF ITSELF

In the hands of a secure and mature species, knowledge can serve as foundation for social progress and the preservation of life. The divorce of science, along with derivative technology, from its parent philosophy, is unfortunate. While scientific achievements have mesmerized most of humanity, our mythical propensities blot out the fact that the very future of life hangs in the balance. Rather than applying a sufficient portion of the intellectual power that has created microelectronics, global communications, space exploration and smart bombs to resolving the crises confronting all of life on Earth, the absence of a philosophical foundation in the pursuit of knowledge is very likely to have irretrievably fatal consequences.

CHAPTER 8

WASTE NOT, WANT NOT

Even as waste is anathema in the workplace, eating into profits and, consequently, compensation of owners, entrepreneurs and workers in industry and commerce, in the typical American household it is given scant thought. Things from old neckties to balky television sets are discarded offhand if they fail to satisfy an immediate need. The disposition of discarded items is of little concern to average citizens. If they think about them at all, the assumption is that local authorities will see to their disposal. This attitude toward waste is spreading in both developed and economically emerging countries as their consumption patterns emulate the lifestyle in the United States.

Had we humans thought this out and envisioned the long-term consequences of waste, particularly of non-renewables—incessant wars (hot and cold) to establish and preserve control of resources; rapid depletion of earth's natural resource endowment; pollution of land, air and watercourses; climate change that will eventually cause uncountable losses in life and property from inundation of coastal areas and island nations—it's unlikely that we would have opted for the prevalent waste-generating consumerism underlying these catastrophes. However, even in the most deliberative situations (e.g., the business milieu) the planning horizon is notoriously short: as philosopher/economist John Maynard Keynes once reminded us, "in the long run we are all dead."[246]

What *is* waste? As a first approximation, it might be defined as things that are produced and then either discarded because they are believed to be of no further use in contributing to individual or collective aspirations or that are immoderately employed, e.g., fossil fuels and other natural resources exploited in a manner such that the costs (usually externalities) exceed the benefits (e.g., open pit coal mining).

Not all discarded things are forever taken out of circulation. An imperfect apple, unacceptable in a market hypersensitive to anything falling short of an ideal and thus left to the elements, decomposes and contributes to future growing cycles. In fact, organic wastes of many kinds, even paper, are being composted and recycled into agricultural nutrients.

Waste appears to be a uniquely human invention, as no other animal typically converts resources into things that eventually wear out or are discarded for other reasons, even merely obsolescence, and then remain inaccessible for other purposes for extended periods of time. That's not to say that waste is "unnatural." We who generate it are unavoidably integral with nature (whether we like it or not), and comply with its imperatives even though we tend to believe, and act as if, we are free and independent agents.

There is something very unwholesome about human waste. A measure of civilization's failure is the volume of its refuse dumps. In a properly organized economic system, virtually nothing would end up in the trash heap: products would be designed so that they contain biodegradable materials and items that can be disassembled and recycled without material degradation. Other discards would similarly be reused or reprocessed into useful materials. Most plastics would be banned because they both degrade after repeated recycling (and are ultimately discarded) and because their disposition usually creates environmental contamination.

Even human excretions would be returned to the land. The residue of what we ingest after metabolism extracts what is used for energy and growth can generally be reprocessed biologically to be available for the next round of the life cycle[247]. In any event, these materials, and all other organic substances such as animal manures, eventually decompose and so cannot really be classified as waste. Whether the decomposition process is aerobic (with oxygen) or anaerobic (without oxygen), organic materials such as vegetable matter, manures and other excretions eventually are consumed first by microorganisms (e.g., bacteria, fungi, molds, protozoa), and later by larger organisms (e.g., earthworms, beetles, mites). The process of ingestion, metabolism and excretion does involve an increase in entropy (the inexorable trend toward disorder in the universe), and in this sense contributes to the "heat death" assured by the second law of thermodynamics, and might be considered wasteful in the sense that our collective demise is advanced to a small degree.

Medical waste containing potentially infectious microorganisms and other toxins, such as radioactive materials, are generated mainly by health care providers (including veterinarians), medical research and other service facilities. Most medical waste is currently incinerated, posing risks from emissions, particularly if burn conditions are improperly controlled. The volume is increasing with population growth and advancements in medical technology and as health care professionals fail to acknowledge their responsibility to minimize medical waste generation.

WASTE CREATION IN US AND WORLD

Throughout the world, mountains of trash are produced each day. According to one estimate, the Russian Federation and the European Union alone annually produce about 6,500 million metric tons (mMT), including hazardous materials.[248] Estimates of the annual global accumulation of solid waste vary widely. A 2012 World Bank study, "*What a Waste*"[249] reports that the amount generated by the institutions of civilized life—households, industries, recreation—increased from a negligible level at the beginning of the 19th century to the current 4 mMT per day (1,450 mMT per year) and is expected to rise to more than 6 mMT per day in 2025 (2,200 mMT per year)[250]. Depending on demographic, energy and cultural developments, in the year 2100 the amount could grow to anywhere between 8 and 12 mMT per day (to 4,380 mMT per year).[251]

The US EPA reports that 250.4 million tons (mT)[252] were generated in the United States in 2011: 86.9 mT (34.7 percent) were recycled or composted, approximately 29.3 mT incinerated with energy recovery (11.7 percent), and the remaining 134.2 mT (53.6 percent) either burned without energy recovery or deposited in landfills.[253] This amounts to about 4.4 lbs. of trash per day for each woman, man and child in the country, or about the body weight for the average person each month. Japan, with about the same per capita income, generates only 54 percent of the waste as the United States.[254] Rather than mend our wasteful ways, our production of junk has increased 14 percent since 1990 and 35 percent since 1980.

Reducing the amount of waste deposited in landfills or incinerated depends significantly on market forces. "Encouraging ever-higher recycling rates in an imperfect market may impose very high social welfare costs. In such cases it may be far less costly to address the imperfection within the market than to try and bring about increased recycling rates through increasingly ambitious recycling programs."[255] The demand-supply relation for recovered materials weighs heavily in recycling decisions. If competition for collecting and recycling of materials is weak or doesn't exist, a community could incur high costs and little compensation for its efforts. Recycling advocates usually stress economic benefits rather than health, environmental impacts or moral concerns in their public appeals.

One comprehensive study[256] shows that the density of trash as deposited in landfills, a function of its depth from the surface, varies from about 65 lb/ft^3 to 130 lb/ft^3. Assuming the current level of global trash to be 1,450 mMT per year and an average landfill density of 100 lb/ft^3, with a little over half, say 800 mMT, deposited in landfills the volume of trash would be roughly 18 billion ft^3. This would be equivalent to a square piled 150 ft high and 2 miles on each side.[257] Not exactly Mt. Everest, but wait a while.

Space for landfills is becoming problematic. There is usually a great deal of public outcry when one is proposed for a community. Even in emerging countries such as China, Korea, Brazil and Mexico the problem is acute. Typically the larger landfills in these countries that accept more than 10,000 MT per day are either full or close to it.[258]

As development and urbanization proceed, waste tends to reflect the trappings of civilization: not only an increase in the amount of waste produced, but also the wider variety of things that city folk use and discard with shorter product lives than their rural counterparts. As per-capita income increases, people tend to acquire more stuff that eventually is discarded. The amount of waste generated is also affected by the degree of industrialization, culture and climate. "Income level and urbanization are highly correlated and as disposable income and living standards increase, consumption of goods and services correspondingly increases, as does the amount of municipal solid waste generated."[259]

While it's clear that much food and other organic substances in the US and other wealthy countries end up in the trash, the proportion of organic materials in the waste of developing countries is much higher (about 50 percent vs. 28 percent in the US) even though they produce far lower amounts of waste per capita. In the less developed countries populations are neither accustomed nor wealthy enough to accumulate as many things that eventually end up in the trash heap, such as the vast array of goods, typically turned over about four times each year, in any large box store in the US and other industrialized countries. Organic (biodegradable) waste is not particularly problematic, as it will eventually break down. If not composted, but rather mixed with other trash in landfills (as in many developing countries), the result can be a fetid, disease-laden mess.

The growth in trash generation exceeds that of other environmental pollutants. Plastics are a class of particularly problematic offenders, as most are non-biodegradable and persist for years, if not forever. They can be found clogging and fouling waterways and landscapes of some otherwise pristine places, even one of the most exotic in the world, Thimpu, the capital of Himalayan Bhutan.

The world's oceans have served as a dumping ground for centuries, but most notably in modern times. A confluence of currents in the Pacific Ocean—the North Pacific Tropical High from western US to Japan and from California to Hawaii—creates a rotating vortex surrounding a pocket of floating garbage that accumulates from across the Pacific, comprised mainly of non-biodegradable plastics.[260] Much of it has broken up into very small pieces, some invisible without magnification. Another study by an international team took nearly 600 samples from across the Atlantic and Arctic Oceans and in the Mediterranean Sea, from depths ranging from 35 meters to 4.5 kilometers. Litter was found at each test site throughout the Mediterranean, and from the continental shelf of Europe to the mid-Atlantic ridge 2,000 kilometers from land, consisting of plastics (41 percent) and discarded fishing gear (34 percent) plus other miscellaneous glass, metals, wood, paper clothing, etc. [261]

Floating and submersible trash infests the deep oceans, coastal and inland waters around the world. Plastics wash up on beaches, originating as discarded waste that the tides carry into the ocean or that are deposited from barges and transoceanic ships. In Rio de Janeiro, an Austrian sailor preparing for the 2016 Summer Olympics revealed the state of the city's Guanabara Bay. "Garbage bobbed on the surface, everything from car tires to floating mattresses." The bay was so fouled with sewage that he was afraid to step into the water to launch his boat from shore. Others trainees complained of encountering animal and even human remains.[262]

This detritus is detrimental to marine life, which ingests it or becomes entangled in the larger pieces. Birds and other marine animals such as seals, turtles and terns inadvertently scoop up these bits of plastic, mistaking them for foods (e.g., plankton, fish eggs), ingesting some and also feeding their offspring.

Although a conference in Stockholm in 1972 was convened to control dumping of waste into the oceans, it has had limited effect. The *Convention on the Prevention of Marine Pollution by Dumping of Wastes and Other Matter*[263] was implemented in 1975, and a protocol adopted in 1996. Under current Caribbean regulations, as an inducement for the cruise industry to schedule visits to their ports, ships can dump garbage, including metal, glass and paper, three miles (five kilometers) from shore as long as it is ground to less than an inch. Almost anything but plastic can be dumped beyond 25 miles (40 kilometers).

Waste is created when natural resources are converted to the artifacts of civilization without designing in their safe and sustainable ultimate disposition. Except for attempts to reduce production costs by minimizing inputs and disposal expenditures, industries have largely ignored their role in creating waste. As industrialization dominates the tenor of modern life, enterprises are relatively immune to limits or controls on their excesses or demands from concerned citizens to adapt to a sustainable future, continuing to distribute products that are problematic through their entire life cycle. Other public and private institutions—agriculture, mining, industry, government, education—have similarly turned a blind eye to their waste production.[264] Pre-industrial artisans, employing simple technology, were more likely to produce things that were long lasting and safely disposed or biodegradable.

CHEMICAL WASTES

A wide variety of substances have been created only through human intermediation, which did not exist until people learned to create previously inexistent molecules out of the elements of which animal, vegetable and mineral materials are comprised.[265] The science of chemistry, the study of how natural elements are linked into more complex molecular structures, has served as the foundation of an industry that has developed compounds—polymers[266], petrochemicals and inorganic chemicals—unknown before they were synthesized in the laboratory. They are used in households, industrial processes (including food production) and agriculture. Products of the industry, in addition to fuels, are feedstock for downstream processing into familiar appurtenances of modern life: plastics, synthetic fibers, elastomers, lubricants, solvents, detergents, adhesives. Pesticides, herbicides and fertilizers are used in agriculture and animal husbandry. Many of these materials are persistent chemicals with lengthy decomposition periods. They have become household conveniences or have increased production in most cases, but some are toxic and enter the waste stream, often polluting land, water bodies and air. These materials are so pervasive that most would have difficulty in conceiving contemporary life without them.

Petrochemicals are derivatives of "black gold." Deposits of

petroleum form as the remains of ancient plants and animals settle to the sea floor, where there is insufficient oxygen for complete decomposition, creating a reservoir of mainly carbon and hydrogen. Over millions of years, sand, clays, silt and mud cover the carboniferous mass, layer upon layer. The buried and decomposing material is compressed by the weight of the cover and, with transformation stimulated by subterranean heat, forms petroleum. Oil deposits are found in sedimentary rock layers created by geologic action, and also in the intergranular spaces of porous sedimentary and foundation rocks.

The petrochemical industry has revolutionized life on earth. Its produce has permeated every civilized institution—home, office, farm, factory, transportation, entertainment, recreation—to an extent that strains contemplation of a lifestyle without it. In truth, it has been the greatest wasteful endeavor in human history. Within the past two centuries, a mere eye flick in the cosmic timeframe, its resource base has been largely expended. Roughly half of the accessible remains of this ancient plant and animal life—a major part of our natural capital endowment—has been mined and consumed. The "low hanging fruit" has been extracted and the embedded energy expended to virtually "create" a human population far larger than Planet Earth can accommodate, lives that would never have come into being without this concentrated form of energy. It has produced mountains of junk that will persist for the indefinite future and, at the same time, fostered the sixth great extinction of life forms (Kolbert 2014).

In addition to depleting earth's natural capital, the petrochemical industry has been a platform for dispensing wastes into the environment, which occurs in several stages: first, emissions while refining petroleum into fuels and byproducts and then in the various stages of production of industrial and consumer products—ethylene, propylene, benzene, butadiene; acrylics, styrene, formaldehyde; polypropylene, polyurethane, nylon, PVC, polyethylene; and in the end-user stages—automobile components, furniture, polyesters, plastics, paints, lacquers, antifreeze, packaging, adhesives. Some of these emissions contain oxides of nitrogen and sulfur, hydrogen sulfide, methane, ethane, benzene, toluene, xylene, other volatile organic compounds and particulate matter, which are linked to illnesses, particularly in children.[267, 268]

The organic (carbon containing) substances produced by the industry are sources of carbon monoxide and dioxide, the latter a greenhouse gas that has increased from about 315 parts per million (ppm) in 1960 to about 400 ppm in 2013 and, through global warming, threatens displacement of billions of people living in coastal areas and in island nations as ancient glaciers melt and elevate sea levels.

Dioxins (polychlorinated dibenzodioxins, or PCDDs) and furans (dibenzofurans, or PCDFs) are produced in some thermal and industrial processes, for example production of steel and non-ferrous metals. Although the petrochemical industry, *per se*, is not considered a major source of PCDDs/PCDFs, they do discharge into the environment when its products are discarded and then burned in incinerators as municipal, medical and hazardous wastes. Another line of petrochemical products, PCBs (polychlorinated biphenyls), were used widely in industrial and commercial applications (e.g., electrical appliances and electronic devices, lubricants, lighting, insulation, adhesives, paints) until about 1980, when production was banned in most countries.

PCDDs/PCDFs and PCBs are persistent chemicals that do not break down easily into less harmful forms, and so are found widely throughout the environment in relatively low concentrations (many foods have trace amounts). They accumulate to detectable levels in most body tissues of exposed people and other animals through inhalation and ingestion. The highest concentrations are found in liver and fat tissues, although they are present in all tissues throughout the body.[269] They are harmful to health: longer-term exposure adversely affects the immune and nervous systems and disrupts endocrine and reproductive functions. They may also cause cancer.

The half-life of the most toxic dioxin, 2,3,7,8 TCDD, is estimated at 9-15 years on surface soil and 25 to 100 years subsurface. Removal of half of the 2,3,7,8 TCDD from the body is estimated at 7 to 12 years.

Other industrial polymers (e.g., butylated hydroxyanisole or BHA and butylated hydroxytoluene or BHT) are used as preservatives to extend food shelf life (e.g., meat, packaged foods, butter, etc.); although approved by the EPA they are known carcinogens.

Synthesized organophosphates, none of which otherwise occurs naturally, were originally developed as pesticides and insecticides, but have served to kill and otherwise destroy the lives of victims in chemical warfare attacks. Tabun (GA), sarin (GB), soman (GD), and cyclosarin (GF) are among the most toxic chemical warfare agents known. At ordinary temperatures these substances are volatile liquids, and thus can affect victims through both skin contact and via inhalation. They were first synthesized by German scientists in the 1930s and 1940s and then employed in a number of attacks ordered by besieged tyrants such as Bashir Assad in Syria during 2013.

ELECTRONIC WASTE

Around the world people of every stripe and their electronic devices—cell phones, smart phones, personal digital assistants (PDAs), pagers, electronic games and toys, readers—have effectively melded into inseparable entities. These gadgets rival the importance of internal organs: a malfunctioning smart phone brings on about as much anxiety as a balky kidney. Cell phones are so pervasive that the anticipated number of mobile subscriptions in 2014 is expected to surpass the number of people in the world, over 7.3 billion.[270] Other devices—computers, printers, scanners and copiers, televisions and radios—are ubiquitous appurtenances of daily routines.

Vast quantities of electrical and electronic devices are added to the global scrap heap each day. The 300 million computers and billion or more cell phones produced annually (and growing at about 8 percent per year) eventually wear out, or more likely, become obsolete and are discarded. Most of them end up in landfills, and contains toxic materials. By one estimate, in the US alone, about 9.4 million metric tons (mMT) of electronic waste were produced, or 29.8 kg (about 66 lbs.) per capita.[271]

Estimates vary, but reportedly up to 25 percent of discarded electronics are recycled, the rest going directly into landfills and incinerators. However, recycled units are reprocessed, with the residue from disassembly also ending up in landfills and incinerators, so it's likely that no more than 15 percent of the actual tonnage is reused.

Electronic waste processing generates significant hazardous emissions, with severe impacts on the environment and health. Toxic materials in electronics can induce cancer, endocrine and reproductive disorders, and other health problems. Primary emissions derive from embedded hazardous materials (e.g., mercury, lead, cadmium, arsenic, beryllium, bromine-containing flame-retardants, PCBs). Secondary emissions result from treatment of e-waste (e.g., dioxins and furans) formed by incineration of plastics and other substances in the presence of chlorine, bromine, iodine and fluorine (halogen chemical group) that are contained in municipal solid waste (MSW). Tertiary emissions are hazardous substances or reagents used in recovering useful materials during recycling (e.g., cyanide and other leaching agents, mercury in gold reclamation).[272]

Much e-waste is exported to developing countries. However, there is very limited data available on amounts collected and treated through "official" e-waste channels. Undoubtedly significant amounts are unreported in Central and Eastern Europe. In 2012 nearly 50 million MT of e-waste was generated worldwide, about 7 kg for each human. A report by Interpol in 2013 revealed that almost a third of the containers leaving the EU that were checked by its agents contained illegal e-waste.[273] Despite ratification of the Basel Convention by over 150 countries regulating international flows of toxic wastes,[274] although the amount is uncertain, the United Nations StEP study[275] indicates that millions of tons of discarded electronic products are being illegally exported to developing countries. A 2002 study by the Basel Action Network and the Silicon Valley Toxics Coalition, *"Exporting Harm: The Techno-Trashing of Asia,"* revealed that between 50 and 80 percent of e-waste collected for recycling in the United States was exported to these countries. E-waste is piling up in China, Nigeria, Pakistan, Ghana and many more African and Latin American countries, where environmental pollution exposes local men, women and children to toxins.[276] The amount being produced could rise by a factor of five in the next decade (from 2009).[277]

In the Taizhou area of China, e-waste recycling has been a major industry for over twenty years.[278] The air and ground surface in the region is heavily contaminated with heavy metals (e.g., mercury, lead, cadmium, arsenic, beryllium) and persistent organic compounds (e.g., polycyclic aromatic hydrocarbons [PAHs], PCBs, polybrominated dimethyl ethers [PBDEs] and PCDD/Fs). Large quantities of brominated flame retardants have been added to printed circuit boards, plastic covers, keyboards and computer monitors: high levels of PBDEs and PCDD/Fs are emitted when these materials are incinerated, some of the most toxic substances known.[279].

TOWARD ZERO WASTE

Prior to planning an undertaking of any sort, if these questions are asked: is what you are planning sustainable, so that future generations will be able to satisfy their needs and wants to the same extent as the present generation, and, in that sense, compatible with the future of life? Will it maintain, and even protect, the biological diversity that currently exists on earth? If the answers are NO! it's obvious that the project should be rejected.

Underlying all of these concerns is how natural resources are to be regarded. Will they be wasted, ineffectively or inefficiently utilized? Is fairness and good sense served if just a few of the million generations since the advent of modern humans consume the energy contained in fossil fuels millions of years in the making that are our natural capital endowment?[280] Will their use generate material wastes that contaminate land, air and waterways?

John Wesley, founder of the Methodist movement in Britain, touched on the subject of waste in two letters written in December 1772. On December 9 he wrote to the editor of the Lloyd's Evening Post alluding to the austerity besetting Britain at the time: "Only look into the kitchens of the great, the nobility, and gentry, almost without exception ... and when you have observed the amazing waste which is made there, you will no longer wonder at the scarcity"[281] Later, in a letter to a friend, he linked waste with covetousness: "He will waste nothing; but he must want nothing."

In the first letter, needs and wants are the consequence of waste: when resources at hand are not carefully husbanded, they will be unavailable when the need arises. In the second, waste is the precursor of want: if things are not coveted, and hence not acquired, waste will be concomitantly reduced, if not eliminated. If people return to a simple life in which fewer things are wanted, foregoing acquisitions except for those essential to sustaining and enriching the body and spirit, the problem of waste largely disappears (with the likelihood of greater peace and tranquility as icing on the cake).

In the letter to his friend, Wesley is closer to the formulation for a sustainable future. Accumulation of wastes is the inevitable consequence of producing things that are superfluous in a well-functioning community, whose citizens take into account long-term consequences in their consumption patterns. Contemporary civilization could dispense with much of its trappings, while maintaining a healthy and sustainable standard of living.

In the industrialized countries, aspirants to unbounded economic expansion—myopic in the sense that endless material growth under constraints is impossible and fraught with dire consequences—disseminate the growth mantra through powerful and omnipresent media. It's no wonder that people can be mesmerized by the promise of limitless and risk-free consumption. Even in (nominally) democratic societies, the ordinary citizen is typically unprepared for, and therefore vulnerable to, the incessant promotional onslaught of producers and marketers insisting that life can only be beautiful when one is immersed in an ambit of possessions. Practitioners of the psychological arts cleverly disseminate these messages promoting acquisition of a product or service by basically linking its possession to personal status and security, rather than merely describing its characteristics and uses.

On a collective level, the political structure of nominal[282] democracies as they currently function is geared to waste generation. The volume and value of goods and services produced within the economy, generally the Gross Domestic Product (GDP) or GDP per capita, defines the level of prosperity. The GDP roughly tracks consumption[283], so a political administration that fails to keep the pot boiling is quickly deemed to have failed in the public mind. Without a bit of reorientation, people are generally unprepared to properly assess a program that focuses on merely uplifting mind, body and soul.

Considering the havoc heaped upon our planet stemming from inordinate consumption, leaders at all levels of government and industry who intend to act responsibly would assign the highest priority to addressing and spreading awareness of this global threat.

A guide to a more wholesome way of life, one that is committed to the concept of sustainability but which concedes the inevitability of an avalanche of discarded things, is proposed in the principles of waste management of the US EPA: Reduce, Reuse, Recycle as means of improving the environment and saving money, energy, and natural resources.

Waste is to be reduced. How this is to come about? First, remove items that can be recycled or otherwise reused from the waste stream. In a society with economic growth as the *sine qua non* of an acceptable lifestyle, even dedicated adherence to this principle is bound to failure in the end. This type of growth inevitably involves the production of more stuff, so that even when larger percentages of it are somehow removed from the waste stream, the quantity is bound to steadily increase. Furthermore, recycled and reused things in many cases reach the end of the line and have to be discarded. Paper and paperboard comprises a large part of MSW in the United States and other industrialized countries, about 28 percent in 2012.[284] Although much is recycled, "new virgin fiber will always be needed in paper production as each time fiber is recycled it loses quality and thus cannot be recycled indefinitely."[285] The same is true for many plastic items, even those that are thermoplastic and repeatedly used in container production: "Removing labels, print, (is) all but impossible at 100 percent success rate."[286] Plastic waste that is contaminated with residues, labels and other impurities compromises re-use in high tech applications, such as carbonated water bottles. The consequence of contamination of recycled plastic materials is that most of it (apart from producer-recycled material) is reused in lower-grade applications that eventually end up in the waste heap.

Add to this the other major forms of non-biodegradable material waste. e.g., rubber, synthetic textiles, glass and some types of metal, and it's clear that recycling without a major change in consumption patterns, particularly in the industrialized countries, will not solve the problem of waste buildup. Something more revolutionary is required.

ALTERNATIVES TO WASTE GENERATION

The fate of future generations of humans and other inhabitants depends on the present generation's response to alarming levels in Planet Earth's life signs—atmospheric carbon dioxide concentration not seen in at least 800 thousand years, a rate of species extinction highest since the Cretaceous Era, diminishing fresh water availability, increasing pollution from activities such as exploitation of shale and other fossil fuel deposits. Looming threats of further environmental degradation, loss of biodiversity, climate change and population pressures will not be passed off to future generations without enormous risk. Furthermore, if moral standards are to prevail as the basis for humanity's thoughts and actions, whether rationally or divinely inspired, one of them surely is that we current inhabitants of earth must not degrade the quality of life for future generations, some who may be our own descendents.

The pulse of life can be observed by measuring the volume of wastes that our planet is expected to accommodate. Is it necessary that waste is discarded, that trash dumps exist and that waterways and the atmosphere be contaminated with detritus? It is within the realm of human ingenuity to design products that are useful and that make life more interesting and comfortable for all earthly inhabitants, while their ultimate disposition is planned to preclude final consignment to the waste heap and to minimize or even eliminate the need for additional exploitation of natural resources.

So long as a large proportion of people are ignorant or negligent of the need for, or opposed to, sustainable patterns of consumption, only regulation of what can be produced can resolve the problem of waste generation. This is stopgap, as only universal acceptance of the need to live harmoniously within natural constraints will do in the long run.

ZERO-WASTE DESIGN

To transition to a state in which generation of waste is essentially eliminated from the human lifestyle, one of the major alterations has to involve design of products and substances. One approach is design controls that would assure safe and sustainable disposition of anything that is produced. This could be accomplished through a national review board that would set and maintain design standards and that would assure sustainable production under a zero-waste policy[287]. The standards could be applied by mandatory product design review for enterprises over a certain size. Ideally, conversion of any substance to a form that could not be readily reduced to true recyclables[288] and/or biodegradables would be prohibited, so that their disposition would not involve any practice that would degrade the environment. The review board would examine a proposal for production of any item, or any conversion of materials to certify that the criterion of zero waste is inherent in the plan. The system could be implemented initially at the local level, but more effectively at the national and ultimately on the international scale.

Small specialty fabricating shops would be provided with guidelines to follow in the production of individual products or batches. Their production would be investigated if and when it appears problematic in relation to the sustainability criterion.

As matters stand now, a producer of goods generally makes design decisions based on acceptability in the market and on the economics of production. In some countries manufacturers and importers are legally bound to bear responsibility for some types of products throughout their life cycle under Extended Producer Responsibility (EPR) mandates (e.g., autos, tires, batteries, waste oil, electrical and electronic products, refrigerants, construction materials). EPR mechanisms in force[289] include mandatory producer recycling, deposits or up front disposal fees.[290]

Although the societal burden associated with product disposal is considered to an extent in some countries, as a general rule there remains a prevailing mindlessness concerning disposal of unwanted things, as attested by the mounting accumulation of wastes throughout the world. The user of a product that cannot readily be disassembled into constituent parts for reuse or recycling is, in effect, tossing the burden of his decision to consume on the rest of the public, which, if better informed, would likely not be so magnanimous as to accept the responsibility for its ultimate disposal without protest.

It may appear farfetched to think that all products can be designed so that virtually no part ends up in the trash heap. A computer circuit board is comprised of microchips of silicon impregnated with small amounts of minerals and also includes components of electronic circuits that are complex amalgams of various mineral substances. As miniaturization in this industry has progressed, these components have become more integrated and less amenable to disassembly to basic materials. However, with a zero discard policy as a constraint, it's probable that designers and producers would quickly learn to accommodate. Microelectronics might be precluded unless its circuits could be either easily disassembled into reusable or infinitely recyclable materials or biodegradable within a reasonable time frame.

Product designs may radically change compositions and configurations, and some may be precluded, but in the end it's likely that there would be little change in the scope of utilitarian functions available to the public.

It can be argued that it would be impossible to implement such a system without a drastic reduction in the standard of living. It may well be that the cost to the producer of manufacturing products according to a "zero waste" policy would be greater as a result of being restricted to the use of materials and components that could readily be disaggregated for sustainable reuse or recycling. Production is likely to consume more resources in the forward path to the user, but the end result may well be a net saving of resources as adverse impacts of disposal, loss of valuable materials, health threats and aesthetic deterioration would be avoided.

A SIMPLER WAY OF LIFE.

As we continue to foul the earth with the effluvia of contemporary civilization, the consequences are largely ignored: it's convenient to heavily discount the impacts on future generations when there is such intense desire for current consumption. Only when we can regard our own lives in the context of the continuum stretching from the dawn of existence to the indefinite and virtually infinite future may posterity be given its due. These are our children, whose lives we jeopardize with wanton disposal of our cast-offs.

Self-anointed futurists see continual growth in national and global economies as measured by conventional macro-economic indicators, e.g., Gross Domestic Product, undeterred by finiteness of the resource base on which it is predicated. A general assumption is that technology will solve any resource constraints by discovering substitutes, alternative ways of doing things, or completely new approaches to satisfying human needs and wants. The disposition of all the consequent paraphernalia produced and ultimately worn or degraded to the point of uselessness appears to be off the radar screen.

If human life is to continue into the indefinite future, the concept of waste has to be removed from the lexicon, but more important, from the psyche. Of all mortal sins, indiscriminately discarding anything has to rank among the highest. It is tantamount to manslaughter: surely if current practices of disposal persist for very much longer, people will die as a result. In fact, many have already succumbed to the effects of discarding and incinerating trash. Landfills pollute aquifers and surrounding landscapes, and emit greenhouse gases. Incineration produces toxic gases and other emissions that are already responsible for many illnesses and deaths as they are breathed and ingested. Indigent processors of toxic wastes routinely suffer illness and death.

The Bill of Rights, added to the US Constitution after it was ratified and found wanting in respect to a clear enunciation of what citizen entitlements had been ordained from on high, is derelict in at least one respect: the general presumption that what material items one possesses can be discarded at will. Yes, there may be a cost associated with throwing things away, but the authority to discard is inalienable.

Among activists who advocate recovery, reuse and recycling as a means of dealing with waste, the main impetus seems to be esthetic and economic. There is a realization that the steady accumulation of waste piles is becoming problematic as space for its disposition competes with other land use needs such as residential, industrial and commercial development as well as agriculture. There are also costs associated with waste disposal—dumping fees for communities or for individuals in pay-as-you-throw schemes. Another concern is health, not only from pests attracted by mounds of potential breeding grounds and nutrients, but also emissions from incinerators used to diminish the volume of refuse while emitting toxic gases and particulate matter that are inhaled and ingested.

Humanity will eventually have to adapt to a simpler way of life without many of its accustomed material possessions. It will happen one way or another, either through a peaceful and relatively painless transition, or otherwise.

CHAPTER 9

CONFLICT, CONFRONTATION AND VIOLENCE

The proclivity of humans to wage war to the death, rather than settling differences with less draconian methods, is unique in the animal kingdom; a few other primates do share a modicum of this bloodletting predilection. Confrontations between most animal adversaries are settled with displays of one sort or another and rarely lead to death or dismemberment. Humans tend to take confrontation over the brink, undoubtedly the outcome of frailties already identified—at root, outsized propensity for mystification. Whether in one-on-one or in collective confrontation, biased to highly imaginative interpretations of circumstances and events of possible scenarios take over, and perceived threats easily assume proportions of unacceptability. In collective settings a scenario that serves the interests of a charismatic leader is often disseminated, mutually reinforced in the collective frenzy so that it permeates the marrow of each and every member. This is how genes overcome prudence—the emotional response trumps rationality.[291]

The Holy Scriptures are replete with episodes of violence. For example in Deuteronomy, Chapter 7 KJV: "When the LORD your God brings you into the land which you are entering to take possession of it, and clears away many nations before you, the Hittites, Girgashites, Amorites, Canaanites, Perizzites, Hivites, and Jebusites, seven nations greater and mightier than yourselves ... and when the LORD your God gives them over to you, and you defeat them; then you must utterly destroy them; you shall make no covenant with them, and show no mercy to them ... And you shall destroy all the peoples that the LORD your God will give over to you, your eye shall not pity them; neither shall you serve their gods, for that would be a snare to you."

The covenant is further elaborated in Deuteronomy, Chapter 20: "But in the cities of these peoples that the LORD your God gives you for an inheritance, *you shall save alive nothing that breathes* (italics added) ... but you shall utterly destroy them ... as the LORD your God has commanded."

During the Roman Empire the favored method of dealing with enemies of the state and other miscreants was crucifixion, preceded by scourging of the naked prisoner—whipping with a short lash embedded with stones on back legs and buttocks—after which the victim would be nailed to a cross through hands and feet and left hanging without vertical support so that the diaphragm would be distended making breathing difficult if not impossible.

Thomas Hobbes, English philosopher (1588 – 1679) regarded life in material terms—merely matter and motion. The natural state of humankind, in the absence of civilized, political organization, was seen as a brutal struggle for existence. Only the social contract, whereby individuals tacitly or explicitly consent to subordinate their freedom of action to the authority of the state in exchange for a degree of protection, ameliorates the tendency toward violent resolution of competing aspirations. "Whatsoever therefore is consequent to a time of Warre, where every man is Enemy to every man; the same is consequent to the time, wherein men live without other security, than what their own strength, and their own invention shall furnish them withall."[292]

Absent the pacifying effects of civilization, humans would be pitted against one another in an elemental and endless round of wanton advantage seeking: the will of the strongest and fittest would prevail. Cultural development would be arrested, if not precluded. "In such condition, there is no place for Industry; because the fruit thereof is uncertain; and consequently no Culture of the Earth; no Navigation, nor use of the commodities that may be imported by Sea; no commodious Building; no Instruments of moving, and removing such things as require much force; no Knowledge of the face of the Earth; no account of Time; no Arts; no Letters; no Society; and which is worst of all, continuall feare, and danger of violent death; And the life of man, solitary, poore, nasty, brutish, and short."[293]

That humans are inherently disinclined to violence was a philosophical theme of the 18th and 19th centuries, embodied particularly in the concept of the noble savage of Jean-Jacque Rousseau. For example, in *A Dissertation on the Origin and Foundation of the Inequality of Mankind* of 1754: "it may be justly said that savages are not bad merely because they do not know what it is to be good: for it is neither the development of the understanding nor the restraint of law that hinders them from doing ill; but the peacefulness of their passions, and their ignorance of vice."

But not all primitive people practiced such pacifism. Of native dwellers of the North American plains of that period, members of neighboring tribes feared the Western Sioux for their brutality and sadism (Drury 2013). For a Sioux brave "A good death did honor to an entire life, and thus on the battlefield he was an exhibitionist with no sense of modesty. When he took a scalp, gouged out an eye, or severed a penis, he screamed at the top of his lungs to proclaim his greatness." With acquisition of the horse, introduced into North America by the Spanish conquistadors, the Sioux extended the scope and range of their brutal excesses. "Now dazzling Sioux war parties riding painted mounts rapidly and overwhelmingly extended their savage and relentless subjugation of neighboring tribes." To exercise their burning hatred of the enemy Crow, Sioux fathers instructed their sons in the most excruciating tortures. "A favorite was not only to gouge out a Crow's eyes and hack off his ears, arms, feet and penis, but also to punch a hole in his bladder and urinate or defecate into it."

Steven Pinker (2011) asserts that violence has diminished with the advent and progress of civilization. One indication is the fact that prehistoric remains, such as the Kennewick Man (a nine-thousand-year-old body found in Washington State) and Lindow Man (a well-preserved two-thousand-year-old body discovered in England in 1984) suggest that they invariably met their ends through violence. "What is it about the ancients that they could not leave us an interesting corpse without resorting to foul play?" However, Pinker reviews the prevalence of violent confrontation in early civilizations such as Homeric Greece, the Roman Empire, the Middle Ages, early modern Europe and even the early years of the United States, and proposes that contemporary life is much less prone to violence, despite the global gore disseminated by the media. However, this secular trend may be in the process of alteration, as conflict and political violence have dramatically increased in the year 2014 in as many as 48 countries, with popular revolutions and regime change as the main themes.[294]

The most primitive animals live only in space, contemplating neither past nor future. Through the evolutionary process, space/time has become the existential framework found most decidedly in humans and to a lesser extent in some of our closest kin—it's one thing to sense the prowling lion, quite another to be fearful even though it is not now menacing because it could attack in an hour, or to consider what one might have done had it arrived an hour ago. In this context, whether in one-on-one or in collective confrontation, biases and/or highly imaginative assessments take control of responses, as perceived threats easily assume unacceptable proportions requiring some form of defense or retaliation.

A charismatic demagogue often succeeds in conjuring up a scenario that serves to arouse the masses to do his bidding, one that typically amplifies the magnitude of a potential external threat, identifies internal subversive elements to be expunged, or that promises salvation and more (vindication, enrichment) if prescribed actions are scrupulously followed. Enthusiastic allegiance to the cause is mutually reinforced in the collective frenzy.

At the root of most hostility is conflicting material, social or territorial aspirations. During his successful campaign to unseat president George H. W. Bush in 1992, with issues such as the environment and government regulation in the forefront of debate, then governor of Arkansas Bill Clinton astutely remarked (essentially repeating a phrase coined by Democratic strategist James Carville), "It's the economy, stupid!" In essence, people function under "ontogenetic economics," broadly defined as the means employed by individual organisms (including humans) to satisfy their real and perceived needs and wants.

When two people or two groups share aspirations, generally they will get along peaceably. But even if there are common goals, possibilities for hostility lie in the method. For example, prior to the US entry to World War II, most citizens shared the goal of keeping the country out of the conflict, interventionists by assisting Britain and France to fend off the Nazi onslaught and non-interventionists (America Firsters) by avoiding assistance to any of the warring powers. The dispute was vitriolic and, in some cases, violent. (Olson 2014)

Even if conflicted parties don't agree, hostilities can be avoided if the other's apparent intentions are considered not sufficiently threatening to one's fundamental objectives and goals. A strictly rational assessment would require that each participant take into account the costs and benefits of actions through the range from unqualified acceptance to outright rejection of the other's point of view. However, as discussed in Chapter 1, emotional reactions often tilt the assessment of the other's intentions into the realm of irrationality.

PROPENSITY TO VIOLENCE, HISTORIC ROOTS AND SELF-DECEPTION

Beneath the veneer of accommodation and flexibility in "civilized" human relations lies a propensity to maim and kill when one's aspirations are threatened. Violent confrontation is *the* salient feature of the entire span of human history. There is evidence of mortal encounters occurring routinely in prehistoric times. History is replete with uprisings, inter-tribal massacres, wars and genocide. The advent of civilization has had little effect on the prevalence of mayhem and murder, although "advanced" societies justify their violence by the need to eliminate real and imagined threats to their allegedly indispensable socio-political paradigms.

Often a state justifies engaging in war on ideological grounds. A socialistic threat to capitalism was ostensibly the rationale for interventions by Western powers in Korea and Vietnam during the 20th century. The truth had more to do with egotism and political expediency than with principle. One of the major proponents of war in Vietnam as part of the struggle against imperialistic "communism," Robert S. McNamara (President John F. Kennedy's Secretary of Defense), later in life admitted that fighting the Vietnamese was a horrible error. A senior official in the administration of president G. W. Bush in regard to the rationale for the war in Iraq: "The only reason we went into Iraq, I tell people now, is we were looking for somebody's ass to kick. Afghanistan was too easy." (Baker 2014)

The pervasiveness of taking conflict over the edge is indicated by the incidence of violent deaths around the world. At least 526,000 people meet a violent end each year (data for 2011), 55,000 in direct conflict, 396,000 through intentional homicides, 54,000 unintentional homicides, and 21,000 during legal interventions. Ten percent of violent deaths are attributable to terrorism or other conflict settings. Globally, in 2004-9 the average annual violent death rate was 7.9 per 100,000, so for a person living 75 years the likelihood of violent death is about 1 in 200.[295] In the US the overall odds of being murdered during a lifetime decreased from 1 out of 157 in 1978, 240 in 2000, and about 280 in 2012;[296] in 2012 the rate of all violent crimes in the US was 387 per 100,000 residents (down from a peak of 758 in 1992)[297].

During the 20th and 21st centuries approximately 130 wars claimed in the order of 170 million lives.[298] Wars erupt over real or imagined threats to economic aspirations, transmuted to political or religious credos that are bound to a society's cultural superstructure with "hoops of steel." At root of almost all wars is access to resources: land and property for living space and agriculture, mineral deposits, water. Germanys aggression in the early stages of WWII was predicated on the quest for *lebensraum* (living space) to accommodate a growing population of "superior" Germanic peoples by displacing allegedly inferior people in territories taken from them by the victorious powers according to the Treaty of Versailles after WWI.[299]

Invariably there are ontogenetic forces at play: the needs and wants of *individuals* are often pursued collectively as a result of inherent social inclinations, accommodated and subordinated to more comprehensive strategies proposed (or, more commonly, demanded) by demagogues and other aggressive power-seekers. However, the fundamental, evolutionarily derived imperative for any organism, including a human, is to survive and propagate. Collectives such as clans, tribes, cities and nations are no less driven by natural forces, but how they play out is a function of social organization. From the most autocratic structure to pure democracy, threats to the status quo are viewed with alarm and often evoke violent reactions to perceived threats—defensive assaults, retaliations and preemptive strikes.

Modern civilization is not far removed from its tribal antecedents. It's comforting to be surrounded by people who are familiar, who share culture and aspirations, and who participate routinely in group activities, including confrontations with rivals. Primitive hunter-gatherers lived precariously, so commonly disputes among bands over territory or trade resulted in violent confrontation. Even while cultural complexity and diversity, and advanced technologies of civilized society offer a more efficient and less risky path to conflict resolution, tribal identity patterns seem to prevail after thousands of years of civilized experience.

In war at any level there is the possibility of losing everything, though the potential rewards may seem appealing. The irrationality behind the risk-reward calculation often results in a fight to the finish, a tendency that has carried over through the various stages of human social "progress."[300]

One aspect of the irrationality behind most violent conflict is the self-deception that is so thoroughly ingrained in the human character. For example, in the Oxford Dictionary the word "humane" is defined as "having or showing compassion or benevolence; inflicting the minimum of pain; or intended to have a civilizing or refining effect on people." It's inescapable that to exhibit humane behavior is quintessentially human. But nothing could be further from the truth than the proposition that humans typically exhibit humane behavior in accordance with this definition. In fact, to cast aspersions on another's morality, pat him on the back with the words "you're a real human being."

LARGER STAKE, GREATER RESPONSE

When pushed to the limit, almost anyone will lash out to protect or preserve a cherished thing, idea or person. The propensity for violent confrontation varies with personal traits derived from nature and nurture—courage, sociability, emotional stability—and the risk/reward assessment.

One's immediate emotional state is an important factor: expected behavior can be dramatically altered by proximate circumstances such as a traumatic experience seemingly unrelated to the relationship at hand. When an otherwise even-tempered individual exhibits unexpected violent behavior, the explanation is often hidden, as one's demeanor may reflect the state, but not the source, of animosity. Random neural phenomena resulting in behavioral indeterminacy can also factor in.[301]

In sub-Saharan countries of Africa during the transition from colonialism to independence, aggressive and ambitious individuals gained control of governments, most of them having emerged from poverty and obscurity, often by demonstrating courage and fortitude in battle. Many were illiterate, or nearly so, and ruled by force of their personalities. Having arisen from the ashes, these Phoenixes were bent on maintaining status, and subdued opponents with terror, torture and murder to solidify political and economic control. The stakes were high, with severe penalties for failure but extraordinary benefits if successful in attaining political power. Typically these "strongmen" confiscated earnings from exports of natural resources (timber, oil) to support lavish lifestyles and to maintain the loyalty of subordinates. Political opponents would be liquidated, often publicly, not only to eliminate threats but also to impress upon the population the perils of supporting the opposition.

Of all the post-independence African leaders who combined politics, intimidation and murder, Idi Amin of Uganda has to rank among the most brutal and sadistic. He was "virtually illiterate, with no schooling and limited intelligence," but was accepted into military service in 1946 as a trainee cook in the King's African Rifles. He was physically imposing, impressing his British superiors with prowess in sports and marksmanship. He was national heavyweight boxing champion for nine years. Although his proclivity for violence was cause for concern, he was accepted as an officer candidate as the British were hard pressed to find alternatives.

Amin was commissioned from the ranks as a lieutenant in 1962, and rose to the level of lieutenant colonel in 1964 as a battalion commander. Having seized power in a coup against then Ugandan president Milton Obote, he organized death squads to eliminate army officers and civilians that he suspected of opposing him. In short order he directed mass killings of Langi and Acholi (tribal groups that supported the deposed Obote). On the day of the coup he proclaimed himself "His Excellency President for Life, Field Marshal Al Hadji Doctor Idi Amin, VC, DSO, MC, Lord of All the Beasts of the Earth and Fishes of the Sea, and Conqueror of the British Empire, in Africa in General and Uganda in Particular."

He was described as the "Butcher of Uganda" as testament to the atrocities committed under his orders. His "killer squads" were employed to eliminate hundreds of his opponents and the members of their families. His cabinet secretary, Henry Kyembu, later wrote that 'It was impossible to dispose of the bodies in graves." Ugandan nationalists finally deposed Amin with help from the Tanzania People's Defense Force mobilized by Tanzania president Julius Nyerere in 1979. He fled first to Libya, and then settled in Saudi Arabia, where he was provided sanctuary and support.

Almost all post-independence African leaders employed similarly bloody approaches to maintaining political control and to facilitate extraction of national wealth—Mobutu Sese Seko of Democratic Republic of Congo (Zaire), Ahmed Sekou Toure of Guinea, Charles Taylor of Liberia, Robert Mugabe of Zimbabwe, Kamuzu Banda of Malawi, and Jean-Bedel Bokassa of Central African Republic.[302] It's not particularly noteworthy that they were all Africans, as their methods have spread in various permutations across the globe, except as tacit confirmation that colonialism set the stage for despotism throughout the continent.

Brutality and venality of these leaders and their failure to address inequality and poverty in their countries after independence set the stage for the chaos that followed: rapacious militias controlled by warlords, and concessions granted to transnational enterprises to exploit natural and mineral resources in exchange for personal gain and to strengthen favorable political and military alliances.[303] These developments have provoked violent confrontations with neighboring countries and foreign powers seeking to protect their economic and geopolitical interests, and ethno-political confrontations in some countries concerning exploitation of mineral resources.[304]

During the Cold War from the end of WWII to the breakup of the Soviet Union in 1989, the superpowers contended in the geo-political arena, unwilling to go so far as open warfare for fear of mutual annihilation, but rather using proxies to fray the edges of their adversary's domain in the hope that cumulative damage would eventually weaken them to the point of exhaustion. In the United States during the administration of President Ronald Reagan, a military buildup was intended to force the Soviet Union to commit matching resources from a much weaker economic base. Whether or not this accounts for the collapse of the Soviet bloc is debatable, as autocracy and economic inefficiency was already undermining its viability. However, opposing arrays of superpower nuclear weapons came close to activation during the Cuban missile crisis, with a threat of mutual (and global) annihilation.

CONFRONTATION IN THE NON-HUMAN WORLD

Primates

Our nearest relatives provide a window on our own behavior patterns. Taxonomists classify us, *H. sapiens*, along with apes, monkeys and a few other lesser-known species as primates—placental mammals (the placenta channels nutrients and other substances between parent and embryo). It should not be surprising that behaviors of the great apes—chimpanzees, gorillas and orangutans—are very much like ours. In fact, in the Malaysian language *orang utan* means man of the forest. Recent studies based upon genetic mutation rates during the evolutionary path to humanhood indicate the last common ancestral species of humans and chimpanzees lived 7 to 8 million years ago and possibly as much as 13 million years ago, and that the human-gorilla split occurred from 8 million to 19 million years ago. These large ranges are attributable to uncertainty about mutation rates over time.

The genetic structure of an organism (genome) is a blueprint for its construction. Genetic mutations are permanent alterations of genetic sequences. Favorable mutations (in regard to survival and propagation) tend to spread among a population, and are responsible for changes in an organism that lead to speciation when an offshoot of the population is isolated. Mutations can occur when copying errors occur during replication of cells; if in sperm or egg cells they would be passed on and are present in every cell of the offspring for its entire life. If the mutation occurs in a cell of an embryo, only some cells will contain the mutation. Mutations can also occur during a person's life from radiations or other environmental effects or from replication errors, but these are not passed on to offspring.

The genome of the chimpanzee, mapped in 2005, turns out to be remarkably similar to that of humans, sharing 96 percent of DNA base pair sequences (containing four types of nucleic acid bases, designated A, G, C, and T plus U substituted for T in RNA); much of the rest is non-gene segments of the genome.[305] Comparing only gene segments, the similarity is 98 percent.

Consequently, humans and great apes are very similar in physical conformation, with virtually identical bone structure and organs, susceptibility to some common diseases, and sharing some blood traits. The small difference between human and chimpanzee genomes gives rise to distinguishing features: intelligence, brain size and organization, speech, digestion, sensory characteristics, and disease susceptibility.

One feature of chimpanzee life seems to be replicated among their nearest relatives. Jane Goodall spent years starting in 1960 in the Gombe forest of Tanzania studying behavior of chimpanzees. As reported In a paper published with colleagues in 2008 on the Kasekela community, from records of 220 chimpanzees and 130 observed deaths, they found that 20 percent of deaths were from intraspecific aggression—murderous confrontations among the members within the troupe and also with neighboring bands.[306]

The Bonobo (*Pan. paniscus*) diverged from the chimpanzee (*P. troglodytes*) line about three million years ago. This species, in some respects, is more human-like than the chimpanzee, although it is generally smaller in stature. Bonobos have highly distinctive facial characteristics much like humans. Once considered more pacific than its sister species, hunting and consuming the meat of various medium-sized terrestrial mammals caught only opportunistically by single individuals[307], now it is considered likely that bonobos are also omnivorous (as are chimpanzees and humans), and include group hunting of other primates[308] to round out their diets.

With the intellectual capacity of three or four year old humans, it's unlikely that Chimps live very much in the time domain. They may have a sense of the immediate past and future, but do not engage in long term planning. Their actions and attitudes might more appropriately be described as impetuous, responding to relatively short term threats, although alliances and feuds may be more long lasting.

Social relations among chimpanzees are remarkably similar to humans. They create friendships, teach their children, and engage in leisurely frolics and pastimes. They form cliques that vie with one another for dominance and food, seemingly predicated on personality types, with extroverts in one and introverts in the other.[309] Some chimps in a group seem to have an affinity for one another, and create friendships very much as humans do.

Chimps are inventive, using stone hammers to break shells of nuts and use twigs to extract the last morsel of nutmeat, honey from a beehive or as a lure to collect a succulent mouthful of ants. They have been observed using wooden spears in hunting or ferreting prey out of their dens, and separating rice grains from sand by floating them on sea water. Mothers cleaning their babies have used leaves for scooping drinking water from streams and crevices. These behaviors are learned and spread through local populations.

Chimps also share another trait with humans, the proclivity to wage war to the death, particularly when the odds are in their favor. During the 1970s several researchers noted similar behavior patterns:

The Kasekela community In the Gombe National Park of Tanzania consisted of about 40 to 60 members. Typically, as resources dwindle in the home area or incompatibilities occur between aspiring dominator males, some members of a chimpanzee community organize under a new male leader (or dominant group) and go their separate ways. By 1973, after a period of dwindling contact, a group designated as the Kahama community separated completely from the Kasekela and moved to an adjacent territory. Afterward, as is the rule, a Kasekela band, usually of males but occasionally accompanied by one or more females, every few days checked their own borders seeking intruders. On several occasions, a lone male or female spotted close to the border would be attacked, with beating and clawing almost always leading to fatality.[310] When an isolated female carrying an infant was attacked, usually both were killed, with the attackers eating the baby.

Even more ominously, on occasion a band of Kasekela would undertake a foray into the Kahama territory and engage in combat when the "enemy" was encountered. Even though the Kahama were all former group members, allies and "friends" of the Kasekela, after the split they were treated as enemies, to the extent that eventually all the adult males (six) of the Kahama were dispatched. The only remaining adolescent male was subsequently attacked and murdered. Within a period of about four years, the Kahama band ceased to exist. The remaining Kahama females rejoined the Kasekela, who expanded their domain to include the former Kahama territory.

Toshisada Nishida has been observing chimpanzees in Tanzania's Mahale Mountains National Park since 1965. Just as at Gombe, Nishida's team has seen border patrols, violent charges toward strangers, and furious clashes between male parties from neighboring communities. From 1969 to 1982, seven males of one community disappeared one by one, until the community was extinguished. Nishida and his team think that some and perhaps neighboring bands killed most of those who disappeared.

In Senegal's Niokola-Koba National Park, Stella Brewer in 1977 attempted to "repatriate" a group of ex-captive chimps. After a series of attacks on the intruders by native chimps the project had to be abandoned.

Christophe and Hedwige Boesch have been studying wild chimpanzees in the Tai Forest of Ivory Coast since 1979. They have observed territorial aggression among chimpanzees similar to the Gombe, extra-territorial raids as a means of preempting competition for resources and creating additional *lebensraum* as populations expand or accessible resources dwindle.

Gilbert Isabirye-Basuta has studied relations between northern Kanyawara and southern Wantabu bands in the Kibale Forest of Western Uganda. The same pattern of border monitoring and incursions into neighboring territories were observed between these bands, resulting in fatal attacks. In one instance in 1988 four Wantabu males stalked and charged a small Kanyawara party. In 1994, tourists found the dead body of a (previously) robust male chimpanzee, obviously the victim of a cross-border attack.[311]

So, it would appear that something in the blueprint gives rise to inordinate intra-species aggressiveness both among primates and their human cousins. It's one thing to treat fauna of one's external environment as fair game, but quite another to attack, maim and destroy close relatives.

Most other animals

The number of species living on Earth has recently been estimated to be about 8.7 million, roughly 7.7 million animals (others are fungi, plants, protozoa, chromists).[312] Compared with humans, primates, some of the canines and a few insects, intra-species conflict among other species tends, in a sense, to be more rational. For most animals, egotism doesn't enter into the picture, but rather potential gains and losses from conflict are assessed from the perspective of the very basic criteria of survival and procreation. In most animal conflicts, the degree of confrontation—from mere probing up to mortal attack—proceeds gradually so that contestants have a chance to assess the potential gains and losses and withdraw if the likelihood of success and the risk of serious injury or death are not favorable. "One of the striking things in highly gregarious and also highly aggressive animals is that a considerable amount of overt aggression is redirected ... When an aggressively interacting pair of (intraspecific) animals comes to an impasse, instead of continuing the contest, one of them will frequently fight or threaten some third and disinterested party. As a result, the third animal usually flees, the impasse is ended, the two original contestants return to non-aggressive activities."[313]

In some species aggressive acts are an important part of Darwinian strategy, often limited to snorting and posturing. Computation of the most appropriate means of resolution—e.g., to take confrontation to the point of physical combat or not—depends upon signals related to possible outcomes. While this may not be equated to contemplation, it might be said that intuitive mechanisms, derived in the evolutionary process for the species, operate to decide on the appropriate course of action. If the mechanism is working properly the animal makes the right decision. But not all machines are equally proficient. Occasionally one goes awry with fateful (maybe fatal) consequences (see Chapter 9).

In intraspecific lethal violence among animals, typically the confrontation is one-on-one (dyadic) rather than between groups or group-on-one (coalitionary or polyadic). Aside from mammals, only social insects—some species of ants—routinely kill their species-mates through coalitionary aggression.[314] Why a dyadic encounter, when ganging up on a solitary enemy would considerably reduce risk? Each of us has natural allies, primarily family and bosom buddies, and can often recruit others who share similar goals.

It boggles the mind to contemplate the evolutionary steps that gave rise to the social complexity and specialized behaviors of members of an ant colony. There is obviously a lot of "intelligence" there, though not of the conventional variety with discretionary behavior as its hallmark. Intelligence is apparently not a criterion for coalitionary raids. So sociability has a down side—the propensity to gang up on opponents to subdue and kill them as a means of attaining aggressors' objectives.

For almost all species intraspecific killing is rare. In a small number such killing occurs more frequently, but encounters are always dyadic. Intraspecific deaths tend to occur among Red deer (*Cervus elaphus*), estimated at 29 percent of adult male mortality[315], apparently over access to females (what else is new?) When "a major part of a contestant's reproductive success is at stake," no holds are barred. However, these confrontations are always dyadic, presumably because the social structure doesn't allow for special interest groups to form. Ants are among the relatively few species that frequently undertake coalitionary raids into enemy territory. There are known to be only about ten mammalian species engaging in forays of this type that are commonly responsible for adult deaths—a few primates, the wolf *Canis lupus* and the spotted hyena *Crocuta crocuta* of Sub-Saharan Africa, and most notably, us.

CONFLICT AND CONSEQUENCES IN SOCIETIES

There is little doubt that the proximate cause of most human conflict is frustration of aspirations that derive essentially from our long history of physical and cultural development. To clarify what lies beneath our confrontational episodes, Maslow (2011) provides a reasonable framework for examining what we seek and how we go about attaining our objectives. The essential operational mode is ontogenetic, but social inclinations can easily shift individual conflict toward group identity and competitiveness.

A fair assumption is that the intensity of conflict is a function of the level of need: frustration in attempting to obtain a life-dependent necessity elicits a more energetic and persistent response than the need for improving one's image. As we shall see, this is not necessarily the rule, as two important factors upset this logical applecart: human self-consciousness and imaginative speculation. How significantly these characteristics affect the intensity of conflict depends on how deeply they reflect the personality and the real or perceived needs of competitors.

Life-threatening deprivation is the most serious challenges

that an individual can face. Inaccessibility of fundamental needs—nourishment, shelter, sex, sleep—is a clear and present danger to the most fundamental of human aspirations, survival and propagation. In poor countries riots break out when the price of a staple is increased, generally a confluence of individual responses cascaded into mass demonstrations through sympathetic resonance. In the melee people vie with one another for basic needs in very short supply, sometimes to the point of mortal combat.

People are deeply concerned with security, as the fear of loss of life and limb intensifies with greater uncertainty in the external environment. So law and order and political stability are usually coveted. Demagogic and charismatic politicians are adept at exploiting the quest for security, typically inventing fearful scenarios with lurking bogeymen or that divide ethnicities or social classes, intended to stir up their constituencies as a means of securing their own positions of privilege. Allegations of imminent danger spread like wildfire, so that individual judgment coalesces around their pronouncements and dictates, often with disastrous consequences.

Intergroup confrontations arise when impediments to social access create conflict, e.g., Hatfields vs. McCoys, Catholics vs. Protestants in Northern Ireland, Muslims vs. Eastern Orthodox in Bosnia. When charismatic leaders hype up exclusionary attitudes and practices, group identification becomes paramount and all hell breaks loose. Murder and mayhem are the result, as we have seen throughout the course of human history, on scales ranging from family to community to state to nation to the world.

The result of such fears and frustrations is often a type of coalitionary violence, intensified by imaginative extrapolations of which the human mind is uniquely capable. Those identified as outsiders are attacked and killed by frenzied rioters; in some cases the demagogue is able to foment an assault by marauding groups or armies on territory of the enemy with the intent to either destroy them or render them impotent.

At very young ages, children tend to form groups to satisfy their need for security and identification. Alliances serve the ontogenetic imperative of a secure external environment—better to be surrounded by friends rather than unpredictable strangers. Children seek to be accepted, admired and loved by their peers, often wearing clothing distinctive for the group, and creating in-words, phrases and codes to solidify their sense of belonging. In some cases children, mostly disadvantaged but also privileged, form gangs that stake out territory and engage in violent confrontations to defend them. In adult life networks are created among family, close associates and work-mates, predicated on the same social imperatives. The motivation inevitably is satisfaction of individual needs and wants, but *per unitatem fortitude* (roughly, there is strength in numbers).

Beyond the mundane and parochial pursuits associated with mere physical survival and growth, philosophers are inclined to wax poetic regarding the nobler dimensions of human existence, suggesting that we seek self-actualization, knowledge and beauty only for their esoteric qualities. Mt. Everest is to be ascended only because it is a challenge to our loftiest physical and spiritual aspirations. To George Sand, "Art for art's sake is an empty phrase. Art for the sake of truth, art for the sake of the good and the beautiful, that is the faith I am searching for."

People are generally most content when feeling good about themselves, and when they have standing and are admired by others. We revel in our achievements, particularly if they are widely acknowledged, and are elevated emotionally by a sense of having attained prestigious status. These needs are so compelling that when unrealized they are "created" with one-upsmanship and other mechanisms such as rewriting history.

Attacking another's standing is a recipe for confrontation, often violent, depending on the depth of the insult. At one point in time it was common for the offended party to challenge the offender to a duel, usually ending in the death of one of the combatants. Instinctive physical retaliation is not uncommon in such situations, and with the prevalence of firearms in the United States, neither is murder.

Under most any circumstance people have a craving for knowledge, particularly about the nature of the external environment. Greater understanding inevitably confers greater security. There is also concern for the internal environment: when one is afflicted with illness or a bodily malfunction, a need for understanding the human organism arises. However, the pursuit of knowledge at both individual and collective levels is a source of conflict. First, there is the question of what needs to be known. Scientists often contend about which areas of knowledge are to be pursued. In the current climate of funded research, competition for grants can be fierce. In the United States The Bayh-Dole Act of 1980 facilitated technological and financial relations between industry and academia, with selection of areas of investigation presumably the prerogative of researchers. With heavier reliance on industrial funding, studies of the biomedical field at universities discovered problematic conflicts of interest between traditional academic activities involving research, teaching and public service, and demands of grant-providing industry sponsors, whose interests are disproportionately served by academic research (see Chapter 7).

Tragic outcomes associated with poor research tend to correlate with financial relationships between academics and industrial sponsors. Some medications developed under industry sponsorship have resulted in great risk for patients and others. One case that drew a great deal of public attention was thalidomide, originally developed in Germany as a sedative, but then proposed as a remedy for morning sickness in pregnant women, and used widely in the United States and other developed countries. The drug was eventually tied to severe birth defects—absent or deformed limbs (*phocomelia*) and internal organs, blindness and deafness. In 1962 Frances Kelsey, an inspector of the US Food and Drug Administration (FDA), was widely praised for having prevented approval of the drug despite pressure from the pharmaceutical industry and supervisors of the agency (FDA) in which she was employed. Despite her efforts, the drug was used off-label In the US, Europe and some other countries. Thousands of children were born with deformities, with a mortality rate of about 50 percent.[316]

Knowledge beyond what is immediately useful is pursued when conditions are ripe—when more pressing demands that affect one's security or well being do not intrude. Although people are internally wired to seek comprehension of the threads and patterns in the tapestry of one's external environment, these details may seem superfluous when there is little or no external pressure. A sense of freedom to divert one's attention to loftier matters arises when threats are not imminent, or when the external environment is sufficiently controlled to the extent that some relaxation is warranted.

People are comforted when surrounded with things that are familiar, or that conform closely to idealized conceptions of form and function, suffering pangs of fear and doubt when confronted with objects that appear discordant in the accustomed environment. Abnormal fears abound in the human psyche —xenophobia (the unknown), agoraphobia (unfamiliar surroundings), social phobia (human interaction) and the like. All are manifestations of heightened sensitivity to external threats, conditioned by experience and genetic disposition. What is unfamiliar is unpredictable, and thereby potentially dangerous. The subjectively beautiful and balanced (and unthreatening) is preferred: for some, natural surroundings—mountains, forests, glens, lakes—reflect the comforting sense that nature's bounty is at one's disposal; others are more uplifted by a city skyline.

Conflicts arise from differing conceptions of beauty. A public project decision is imposed on all members of a community, and becomes a factor of contention. The presence of wolves in the wild is a source of pleasure to lovers of natural surroundings, but anathema to others. Naturalists have tried to protect a fledgling wolf population in Norway, while opponents have tried to destroy them. Wolf advocates search for and remove poison bait traps set out by opponents, presumably sheep ranchers who have suffered losses to their flocks from attacks by marauders. Ranchers, on the other hand attempt to protect their herds by shooting and poisoning. While clashes between proponents and opponents of the wolves have thus far been limited to verbal assaults and appeals to authorities, as the gnawing gets closer to the bone violent confrontation is in the offing.[317]

Beyond status, most people have a craving for fulfillment; its pursuit is possible only when more pressing needs have been satisfied, but often people even at basic levels of subsistence engage in creative endeavors. Cro-Magnon people living over forty thousand years ago created some of the most impressive artwork in human history in dark caves of various parts of what is now Europe (e.g., France, Italy, Romania). These achievements support other aspirations, e.g., self-esteem and recognition. Creative attainments bring on a sense of peace and security, by expanding comprehension of one's surroundings—something like erecting a wider secondary perimeter defense—or from a sense of having the wherewithal and latitude to deal with issues far removed from immediate threats.

The extremities of human performance, as seen in the fine arts—painting and sculpture, musical composition and rendition, dance, drama and poetic expression—and in intellectual achievements, in athletics and other creative endeavors of every stripe, overwhelm the senses and strain belief in their natural underpinnings, suggesting, instead, divine inspiration.

A sober analysis suggests something quite different: notable characteristics of our species, yes, but with no more claim to uniqueness than maneuverings of sea urchins. As products of evolution, along with every other species living and extinct, we are compelled to follow the rules that nature has imposed on our creation, development and behavior. The "higher" pursuits are inspired by the need to understand one's capacities and to comprehend and manage interactions with the external environment. They are hedges against adversity, counterparts to the search for alternative sources of needed resources during times of plenty to offset future shortages. Martial arts hold the clue that the "finer" pursuits are utilitarian, in the sense that exploring the limits of human performance has survival value.

But does mastery of a Chopin etude have survival value? Yes, in the sense that extending one's musical universe can be useful in other domains. Musical virtuosity confirms one's uniqueness and social standing; but it has also been associated with mathematical and other cognitive skills. Research has shown a connection between musical participation and brain activity, and that listening to music affects spatial-temporal reasoning.[318] So pursuit of the arts is a way of exploring and honing one's capacities to deal with a variety of challenging situations.

That aesthetic values are deeply engrained in the human psyche is attested by the degree of conflict they can arouse. Culture is apparently one of the factors affecting the *propensity* for violence as part of the fundamental human repertoire for dealing with threats and settling disputes. In the eighth and ninth centuries, violent conflict arose in the city of Constantinople (now Istanbul) after Emperor Leo III instituted a policy of Byzantine Iconoclasm, which prohibited the use of religious images. Murderous confrontations between Christian factions erupted after images in the Hagia Sophia[319] that were considered blasphemous were destroyed. When Islamic Ottoman Turks seized the city in the fifteenth century they removed or plastered over artistic works. Some of the murals are now being restored.

INTERPERSONAL VIOLENCE

That nature and nurture influence behavior is widely acknowledged, along with the questionable assumption (see Chapter 1) of latitude in choosing how to react to an external circumstance. In societies where economic status, ideology or ethnic identity is polarized, when privilege is threatened the reaction is usually extreme.

Human history is replete with episodes of massive torture, rape and murder, and genocide. To cite just a few who were victimized late in the past century: people of the former Yugoslav republics of Bosnia and Herzegovina, Croatia and Serbia, African countries of Congo and Rwanda and Chile and Guatemala in the Americas. It's difficult for one who has not experienced or witnessed these atrocities to imagine the degree of pain and suffering of victims as recounted by survivors.

However, interpersonal violence has been responsible for a greater number of fatalities globally than collective violence (war). In 2000, for example, about 310,000 died as a direct result of war injuries, but 520,000 died from dyadic (one-on-one) encounters.[320]

VIOLENCE IN THE UNITED STATES

Violence has always been a part of the American way of life. The slaughter of Native Americans in the 18th and 19th centuries was perpetrated (Brown 2007)[321] with little regard for the pain and suffering inflicted on the original occupants of the area, by settlers of the west and by the military contingents that cleared the way for their invasion. Now in the 21st century the prevalence of violence cannot be avoided without completely closing off access to any and all media, particularly television and electronic gadgetry, whose producers make a living on it. Young people appear to be mesmerized by flashy presentations in computer games and other forms of "entertainment" that reek of gratuitous violence, in many instances with sexist overtones.

Violence was a way of life in the old South. A code of honor prevailed during the antebellum period, when the south was primarily agricultural while the north became industrialized. Southerners engaged in herding were found to be more prone to violence than those engaged in farming: this hazardous undertaking apparently required its practitioners to be overly aggressive as a means of protecting their investments from rustlers and the hungry. Even children in the south were encouraged to engage in aggressive acts and roughhouse antics as a means of securing their identity, as reflected in their rigorous adherence to a code of honor: better to suffer pain of a thrashing rather than meekly accept the taunts of an oppressor.[322] Alexis de Toqueville (1835) commented on the military prowess of southerners as compared with northerners—greater expertise in committing violent acts of aggression.

Weapons prevalence

The people of the United States are, by and large, culturally oriented to the use of firearms. The US is the leader by far, in private gun ownership, with over 270 million at last count.[323] Among developed countries gun ownership per one hundred inhabitants is as follows: US ~ 90 (so, on average, almost every US resident has a firearm); Finland and Switzerland ~ 45; Germany, Iceland, Austria, Canada, France Norway and Sweden ~ 30. In all other developed countries the number is about 20 or less. Countries with the highest levels of gun ownership, aside from the US and other developed countries are Yemen, Serbia, Cyprus, Iraq, Saudi Arabia and Uruguay, the first four having experienced wars during the past few decades.

Why the United States leads the world in gun ownership is undoubtedly related to the "wild west" syndrome that developed during the period of expansion from the original eastern colonies. In the extended territories, with land, minerals and other natural resources there for the taking, law enforcement was minimal, so that impromptu and lawless settlement of disputes was common.

The Second Amendment of the US Constitution, somewhat ambiguously, prohibits infringement on the right to bear arms. Although the original intent of the founding fathers was to promote the formation of militias among the states for national defense, it was widely interpreted as license to use firearms for private purposes. In fact, the US Supreme Court decided in June, 2010 that the right to bear arms could not be denied by local or state legislatures. Justice Samuel A. Alito Jr. wrote the majority opinion in a 5-4 vote: "The right to keep and bear arms must be regarded as a substantive guarantee, not a prohibition that could be ignored so long as the States legislated in an evenhanded manner.... It is clear that the Framers ... counted the right to keep and bear arms among those fundamental rights necessary to our system of ordered liberty."

Members of the National Rifle Association (NRA) of the United States are drawn from the firearms industry and proponents of private gun ownership (hunters, target shooters and a few with more alarming intentions) with a compelling need to own and use guns, as witnessed by the intensity and political potency of their lobbying efforts when attempts have been made to curb gun usage.

Even after a deranged student used a rifle to kill 26 children and teachers at an elementary school in Newtown, Connecticut in December of 2012, President Barack Obama's appeal to the Congress to take modest actions against gun violence fell on deaf (or more correctly, quivering[324]) ears. The solution proposed by the NRA was to arm schoolteachers.

Were it not for the affinity for firearms in the US it would be ironic that NRA membership surged to five million in the wake of the Newtown massacre. Inordinate militancy of large swaths of the American population is undoubtedly part of the explanation, but also part of a vicious circle: people who would otherwise be peaceful and non-violent feel compelled to keep firearms in their households as protection against intruders, who, in consonance with the culture, almost invariably carry them as "persuaders."

Firearms prevalence is not a very good indicator of interpersonal violence. Although US citizens own more firearms than those of any other country, they are not nearly leaders in intentional homicides by firearms. That "distinction" falls to countries in Latin America. Honduras, El Salvador, Colombia, Mexico, Brazil and Nicaragua have far higher rates (68.4 to 5.9 per 100.000 inhabitants compared with 3.0 in the US).[325]

Native American holocaust

The legacy of atrocities committed against Native Americans by European invaders beginning in the fifteenth century remains to this day. Violence in Mesoamerica was particularly brutal, as the Spanish conquistadors—Pizzaro, Cortes, de Soto, their subordinates and successors—recognized no moral bounds in their quest for gold and silver. "The inhabitants of America (in pre-Columbian times) ... had occupied all habitable zones from the Arctic tundra to the Caribbean isles, from the high plateaus of the Andes to the blustery tip of Cape Horn. They had developed every kind of society: nomadic hunting groups, settled farming communities, and dazzling civilizations with cities as large as any on earth. By 1492 there were approximately 100 million Native Americans—a fifth, more or less, of the human race ... Within decades of Columbus's landfall, most of these people were dead and their world barbarously sacked by Europeans." (Wright 1992)

In the United States and Canada lands and resources of Native Americans were occupied and expropriated by Europeans beginning in the sixteenth century. Indigenous people were compelled to resort to violence as their way of life was continually threatened and undermined by encroachments on their traditional hunting and fishing grounds by settlers, miners and business interests (e.g., railroads). Often European incursions were marked by atrocities against native occupiers of the land, resulting in repeated and escalating deadly conflicts between them.

The US attitude toward the indigenous peoples of North America is revealed by the pronouncement of future president Theodore Roosevelt in 1888: "The most righteous of all wars is a war with savages, though it is apt to be the most terrible and inhuman ... The rude, fierce settler who drives the savage from the land lays all civilized mankind under a debt to him." (Zimmerman 2002)[326] Demonizing is a convenient device for rationalizing oppression of those who stand in the way of manifest destiny.

But it was really no contest. Eventually the force of numbers weighed heavily in favor of the invaders. Perhaps 75 percent or more of native populations were wiped out by pestilences, e.g., smallpox introduced by infected but immune Europeans; the survivors' ranks were decimated in numerous clashes as peace treaties, intended mainly to provide the Europeans a temporary respite from the bloodshed, were violated. Invariably Native Americans were compelled, in the face of superior force, to accept further encroachments on their territories. The cycle of conflict, treaty and violation by Europeans continued until eventually virtually the entire continent was under control of the invaders. However ethnic and cultural pockets of Native American culture remain to this day.[327]

KNOCKOUT

Although some psychologists have warned that malleable youths become more attuned to violent means of settling disputes through ubiquitous video games and visual media offerings[328], oddly enough the prevalence of violent crime has decreased since 1992, peaking at 494 murders and non-negligent manslaughters, forcible rapes and aggravated assaults per 100.000 population down to 274 in 2012, a reduction of about 45 percent. This decrease has occurred during the period when violence in video games and media content has increased dramatically. Perhaps youth vicariously experience the violence through these mechanisms that they would otherwise inflict on others. This begs the question: what will occur when the lights go out?[329]

A behavioral fad that has swept through the ranks of youth is a game known as "knockout," in which "players" select helpless targets at random and try to knock them unconscious with a single blow. Typically the victims, for some of whom the attack is fatal, are homeless vagrants and even women. The status of targets perhaps reflects the lowly self-appraisal of perpetrators, who are reduced to seeking status among their peers by evincing dominance over hapless victims. In a more bucolic setting status-seekers would challenge only higher-level males; demonstrating supremacy over lower castes would be perfunctory and bloodless.

Law enforcement and social analysts have attempted to determine the cause of this phenomenon. One expert on youth violence attributes this "extreme aggression" to the public media and poor parenting. "America loves violence and so do our kids ... We market violence to our children and we wonder why they're violent. It's because we are." Not only are youth oriented to violence, but also "They want to get arrested. They want to get caught, because they want that notoriety."[330]

By this assessment, children are cast in the same mold as their seniors, lacking only the full complement of physical development and experience. In late adolescence physical immaturity doesn't seem to be a hindrance to inflicting great damage when deciding to attack innocent bystanders: their strength and agility are up to it, even to the extent of causing death.

What prompts adolescents and young adults to attack others in such a violent manner? Limited experience clouds their assessment of the pros and cons of any action: they are more likely to resort to aggressive behavior in conflict situations when they feel insecure in the absence of a reliable support structure. In a number of instances, child soldiers have engaged in ruthless attacks against people as directed by diabolical leaders: the holocausts in Cambodia and Rwanda in late 20th century are two examples, but there are many others. The child perpetrators appear to lack empathy—concern for adversity, injury or death—for their victims. Some studies indicate progress in development of empathy from childhood to adulthood is highly variable, and that there appears to be a stage in late childhood to early adolescence when the capacity for empathy is stagnant;[331]

its development in children is a function of environmental factors, such as genetic makeup, ability for facial mimicry and imitation, neurodevelopment, the quality of parent-child relations (or, more broadly, relations with caregivers and mentors). "If one or more of these factors function atypically, they may contribute to empathy deficits, such as those present in autism spectrum disorders or psychopathy. The empathy deficits present in autism spectrum disorders may be more indicative of impairments in the ability to take the perspective of others, while the empathy deficits in psychopathy may be more indicative of impairments in responsiveness to others' emotions."[332] It's no wonder that children growing up in an environment where violence is condoned and promoted are devoid of empathy. This suggests that nurturing of children cannot sensibly be left to chance (see Chapter 3).

ANATOMY OF US WARS OF THE 20TH AND 21ST CENTURIES

During the last and current centuries the United States was involved in at least seven major military conflicts plus a number of lesser bloody altercations. Strictly rational criteria for waging war would presumably be security and welfare of citizens—territorial incursions, threatened or actual assaults from abroad, and economic aggression, e.g., damage to infrastructure or production facilities. The calculation on engaging in or foregoing war would also take into account the extent to which the external threat would be alleviated, and casualty estimates (fatalities and injuries). The consequences of an adversary gaining control of the state would be a prime consideration, particularly if cherished democratic liberty or expropriation of the country's economic resources are threatened.

One of the first casualties of adversarial politics is the welfare of constituencies. After successfully vying in the political arena, each new occupant of the seat of power is strongly motivated to confirm superior status. It's not unusual for political victors to justify a place in history by conveniently finding or creating a war. While politicians proclaim the imperative of vanquishing an "enemy"—usually from a safe seat in the arena for themselves, their backers, kinfolk and associates—the rank and file are designated to slog it out on the "playing" field.

In the US, Franklin Roosevelt (1932-1945)[333] presided over and was widely accused of fomenting World War II. Harry Truman (1945-1952) dropped atomic bombs on Japan, engaged in the Cold War with the Soviet Union and launched his own hot war in Korea. Dwight Eisenhower (1953-1960), on many occasions voiced his abhorrence of war, having already established his warrior credentials as Supreme Commander in Europe during World War II, but hostile relations with the Soviet Union continued. John Kennedy (1961-1963) presided over the Bay of Pigs fiasco against Fidel Castro's Cuba, and also commissioned advisors to the South Vietnamese army in its conflict with North Vietnam, setting the stage for what became a major conflagration. Lyndon Johnson (1963-1968) escalated the smoldering conflict in Indochina to full-scale war. Richard Nixon (1969-1974) approved bombing of Cambodia. Gerald Ford (1974-1979), who ascended to the presidency when the Watergate scandal forced his predecessor to resign, was not around long enough to launch his own war. Jimmy Carter (1977-1980) was caught up in the hostage crisis with Iran. He ordered a military rescue mission that failed, after which the hostages were peaceably released shortly after Carter's successor, Ronald Reagan, was sworn into office. (Carter also sponsored the Camp David accords in 1979 that established a shaky but enduring truce between Egypt and Israel). Ronald Reagan (1981-1988) vastly expanded military expenditures as a means of challenging the Soviet Union, and launched his own mini wars in Grenada, Central America, Lebanon and Libya. George H.W. Bush (1989-1992) was handed a war-making opportunity when Iraq invaded Kuwait. He also committed US troops as part of a U.N. mission to quell tribal warfare in Somalia, with disastrous consequences. After the U.N. Security Council was unsuccessful in arranging weapons inspections, Bill Clinton (1993-2000) ordered four days of air strikes on Iraq. US troops were also committed to ethnic conflicts (under NATO auspices) between Serbia and Bosnia in 1995 and in Kosovo in 1999. After the attacks on the World Trade Center and the Pentagon on September 11, 2001, George W. Bush found ample opportunity to exercise his belligerent tendencies in Afghanistan and Iraq. Barack Obama gradually wound down US involvement in Iraq, but escalated the conflict in Afghanistan.

Of all of these engagements, only United States intervention in World War II could be justified on reasonably rational grounds. The Axis Powers, principally Germany and Japan, had created military behemoths with the potential to crush Allied defenses. At the time of US entry into the war Britain was reeling from German bombing and missile campaigns. France had already succumbed. The Japanese had annexed Korea and Taiwan and occupied Manchuria. In their European and Asian invasions the Axis Powers had occupied, brutally oppressed and in some cases enslaved the populations and destroyed much of their infrastructure. Perhaps of greatest concern was that each had adopted dictatorial, anti-democratic political structures that had already been imposed on the countries that they occupied.

In no other war was the security of the people of the United States directly threatened, nor was there an attempt to confiscate national resources. There were certainly links to security and economic issues, but in all cases they could more effectively have better been addressed with surgical precision rather than massive military campaigns.

World War I

The spark that ignited WWI in 1914 was the assassination of Archduke Franz Ferdinand, heir to the throne of Austria Hungary, and his wife Sophie in Sarajevo, Bosnia on June 28, 1914. A Serbian nationalist, Gavrilo Princip, associated with the organization Unification or Death, popularly known as the Black Hand, was the perpetrator. The goal of this organization was liberation of Slavic populations from control of Austria-Hungary, which had annexed the predominantly Serbian states of Bosnia and Herzegovina, Slovenia and Croatia in the early 1900s, and more broadly, establishing a pan-Serbian state comprised of all areas in which their ethnic members resided.

Although Europe at the time superficially enjoyed a perpetual state of peace and prosperity, escalating tensions roiled in the Balkans and among the multitude of independent states vying for predominance, generally constrained only by their size and available resources. It's a wonder that World War I didn't erupt sooner. Germany and France had traditionally been at odds, most recently in a war of 1870 when Germany defeated France and claimed territory along their common border. The French still harbored notions of grandeur and glory that prevailed under Napoleon.

The most powerful European states, Germany, France, Britain, Austria-Hungary, Russia and Italy, struggled over diplomatic and colonial issues as they attempted to maintain and elevate their military and economic status. When Austria-Hungary declared war on Serbia on July 28, 1914, alliances and treaties drew the other powers into the conflict. Russia was ethnically tied to Serbia, and France was allied with Russia, so the French prepared to join the conflict. French-German animosities, in turn, decided on which side they would come down, so very soon Russia, France and the United Kingdom (the Triple Entente, or Allied Powers) were arrayed against the Central Powers, principally Austria-Hungary and Germany. Italy initially sided with the Central Powers, but subsequently joined the Entente. It was just a matter of time before most all other states fell into one line or the other.

Under President Woodrow Wilson, the United States took sides by providing munitions and financial assistance to the Allied Powers. Germany retaliated by conducting extensive espionage and with submarine attacks on US merchant ships that were feeding the Allied war machines. Wilson became further incensed when the "Zimmerman telegram" was intercepted by British Intelligence on January 19, 1917 (although not revealed to the Americans until February 24), in which Germany tried to induce Mexico to join the conflict by promising to help restore territories taken by the United States after the Mexican-American War. Wilson had already decided to arm merchant ships for protection against German submarines, which was considered by Germany a violation of international law and an act of war that justified renewed attacks against American shipping. President Wilson finally asked Congress for a declaration of war against Germany, which was passed in April 1917.

Globally, in the "war to end all wars," approximately 17 million people lost their lives, including military personnel and civilians (7-8 million). There were a total of 37 million military casualties (8.5m deaths, 21m wounded, 7.7m MIA).[334] This doesn't account for incalculable losses of infrastructure, and medical costs and psychological damage to military and civilian survivors. United States casualties totaled 350,000 (126,000 deaths, 234,000 wounded and 4,500 MIA).

World War II

Just fifteen years after the end of hostilities in 1918, former army corporal and house painter Adolph Hitler, became German chancellor by linking the severe economic depression that beset the country with onerous reparations payments to the victorious Allied countries as prescribed by the Versailles Treaty. When President von Hindenburg died in August 1934, Hitler and his National Socialist (Nazi) party took control of the country. His appeal featured racial superiority of Germanic people over "lesser breeds" such as Jews and Slavs. *Lebensraum* for pan-Germanic people (including Austrians) would be gained through control of Eastern and Western European countries. After annexing Austria, Hitler seized the Sudetenland, parts of Bohemia and Moravia occupied largely by Germanic people, which had been incorporated into the new nation of Czechoslovakia after WW I.

Poland was next on the list, invaded in 1939, which prompted England and France to declare war on Germany. The Nazi blitzkrieg then swept over most of Western Europe, imposing its dictatorial regime on the conquered peoples. Jews were rounded up in all these countries and sent to concentration camps, where six million were systematically slaughtered as part of the Nazi ethnic purification program.

After breaking a non-aggression pact with Russia, German troops crossed the Russian frontier in the summer of 1941. The battle at Stalingrad (August 1942 to February 1943) was a turning point in the war, as the Russians held out despite enormous cost in lives and property. The Germans, with their supply line stretched to the breaking point, also suffered heavy losses, forcing them to withdraw troops from the western front and perhaps changing the outcome of the war. The Nazi invasion and its aftermath were responsible for an estimated 14 million civilian deaths from intentional violence, forced labor in Germany and famine and disease in occupied areas. Russia suffered perhaps 20 million military and civilian casualties (this doesn't include the millions of his own citizens executed or victimized by Stalin before and even during the war on the grounds of political unreliability).

The US population was split between those favoring assistance to the Allies (mainly Britain and France) to fend off the Nazi threat, and an anti-British faction, The America Firsters, who were inspired by Charles Lindbergh (the Lone Eagle widely revered for his groundbreaking solo flight across the Atlantic in 1927). Lindbergh advocated friendly relations with Germany and opposed support for Britain. After repeated appeals from Prime Minister Winston Churchill, President Franklin Roosevelt devised a lend lease program to provide Great Britain with armaments to fend off the Nazi onslaught that threatened annihilation of the British people. War was inevitable, but the issue came to a head when Germany's ally, Japan, launched a surprise attack on Pearl Harbor in the Hawaiian Islands on December 7, 1941.

Both Germany and Japan evinced alarming dictatorial aspirations and brutality toward their enemies. Japan had launched a vicious attack on China, sacking and committing atrocities in cities such as Nanjing and Shanghai. The Nanjing massacre took place during a six-week period from December 13, 1937: in addition to the murder of up to 300 thousand Chinese civilians, Japanese military forces carried out widespread rape and looting. During the war the Japanese murdered as many as 30 million people in the countries that they occupied: Philippines, Malaysia, Burma, Indonesia, Vietnam and Cambodia.

After the fall of Bataan in the Philippines, the Japanese rounded up surviving American and Filipino defenders and forced them to march sixty-five miles over a period of five days to a detention center. In the oppressive heat and humidity, stragglers were shot and bayoneted. The Japanese guards killed up to 10,000 American and Filipino soldiers during the march, in addition to Filipino civilians who attempted to help the emaciated prisoners. During internment at the concentration camps, 26,000 of the 50,000 Filipinos died. As liberating American forces approached in 1944, American prisoners were moved to Japan and Manchuria as slave laborers in factories and mines. By the time the

Japanese surrendered in 1945, two thirds of the American prisoners had died.

News of German and Japanese atrocities was disseminated widely and repeatedly. Fear and loathing of these adversaries was almost universal among the populations of the Allied countries. Although there had been some opposition prior to the outbreak of war, the Japanese attack on Pearl Harbor of December 7, 1941 was considered by the vast majority of the US population as a stab in the back, justifying the most intense and severe retaliation. It evoked an acute sense of imminent political and economic threat and solidified commitment to defeating the Axis Powers.

The toll of deaths and injuries, and destruction of infrastructure during WW II is almost incalculable. By some accounts, over 72 million military personnel and civilians died, and very likely a similar number of people were injured. Much of Europe and Japan were in ruins.

Korea

The Korean peninsula, annexed by Japan prior to World War II, had been arbitrarily divided at the 38th parallel after the war, the north under control of the Russians (who had declared war on the Japanese near the close of the war), and the south controlled by the United States, which had borne much of the burden of defeating the Japanese in the Pacific theater. As the Cold War developed, North and South Korea became effectively protectorates of Russia and the United States, respectively.

Under President Eisenhower, and then Pres. Truman, the US was obsessed with the "Domino Theory"—that if one Asian state were swallowed up into the communist orbit, the stage would be set for others to follow. The fall of Korea would threaten Japan, which had become a major trading partner for the US. Another concern was the imperial aspirations of the Soviet Union and its major ally, China, where Mao Tse Tung's communist forces had ousted the governing Kuomintang under Chiang Kai-shek in 1949.

The US surrogate presiding over South Korea, Syngman Rhee, proclaimed the need to unify the divided country and threatened to invade the north. Many of the South Korean military leaders had been part of the Japanese army that occupied Manchuria during World War II, and were apparently imbued with the aggressive posture that the invasion entailed. So the North Koreans preemptively invaded the South.

The prevailing Cold War mindset offered Truman a framework for committing US troops to defend South Korea as the major component of a United Nations force, which was authorized by the UN Security Council when the Soviet Union boycotted the meeting and was not able to exercise its veto power. After about three years of brutal conflict, in which the Chinese became the major adversary, the parties fitfully arrived at a truce, which was signed at Panmunjom on July 27, 1953.

The toll of dead and injured for the countries involved: United States: 54K (thousand) military deaths (36K in-theater), another 103K injured; South Korea: 217K military and 1 million civilian deaths plus 700K wounded; North Korea: 406K deaths and 300K wounded plus 600K civilian casualties; China: 600K deaths and 350K wounded.[335] All told, about 5 million people were killed, injured or missing, including military personnel of other U.N. countries that had committed troops to the conflict.

Vietnam

The Japanese army occupied French Indochina (Vietnam, Laos, and Cambodia) during WWII. After the war, with United States complicity, France reoccupied their former Vietnamese colony (they had occupied at least part of the country since the mid 19th century), in the face of opposition of the Vietnamese independence movement, led by Ho Chi Minh, who was instrumental in creating the Democratic Republic of Vietnam in 1945. Discussions on independence between the nationalists and the French broke down, whereupon the French forcibly took over the country. This precipitated the First Indochina War, which ended when the French were defeated at Dien Bien Phu in 1954. In the Geneva Accords the country was partitioned at the 17th parallel, the north under control of the victorious Viet Minh and the south under the leadership of Ngo Dinh Diem, a Roman Catholic and staunch anti-Communist who, with US support created the Republic of (South) Vietnam in 1955.

As an outgrowth of the Cold War, the United States gradually became involved by supporting the South Vietnam military in their skirmishes with the North, which increasingly came under the influence of "communist" Russia; traditional animosity stemming from their historical intrusions limited collaboration of the Chinese.

With support from Cold War enemies of the US, the imaginations of Congressional leaders and the population in general were easily stirred to accept the proposition that the Vietnamese represented a clear and present threat, even though many experienced analysts identified the movement of the North Vietnamese to unify their divided country as purely nationalistic. Instead, the Vietnamese leaders, and particularly Ho Chi Minh, were successfully painted as communists, although it was clear that they were driven to the Russian bosom because they were so thoroughly rejected by those whom they sought as friends. The entire episode of North vs. South was, in reality, a proxy global confrontation between Cold War adversaries (a testament to the widespread prevalence of irrational behavior).

As the US became more involved militarily in the conflict under Presidents John Kennedy and then Lyndon Johnson, the US population gradually supported intervention, convinced of imperial aspirations of the communist states, even though the Viet Minh were essentially nationalists seeking independence from French control. Ironically, Ho Chi Minh used the US Constitution as a model for the Vietnamese governing framework. Prior to intensification of hostilities between the US and North Vietnam, a number of analysts such as Tad Szulc of the New York Times, attempted to counter the jingoistic posture of US leaders by explaining the nationalistic foundation for North Vietnamese militancy.

On August 2, 1964, the U.S destroyer USS Maddox was attacked by North Vietnamese torpedo boats in the Gulf of Tonkin while performing intelligence gathering, close to or within North Vietnamese territorial waters. An alleged second attack two days later, apparently fabricated by the Johnson administration to justify intervention, was followed by a Congressional resolution permitting military operations that became the legal basis for escalating the war against the North. With increasing national debt absorbing the brunt of the cost of war,

President Johnson convinced the people that they could have both guns and butter. For the average individual the calculation was a no-brainer. War had its merits in terms of an ostensibly growing economy, plus the feeling, apparently of the majority of the US population, that a threat was being expunged.

The Viet Minh were able to set up collaborations with South Vietnamese opposed to American intrusion. Eventually the Viet Cong became a potent opponent of US intervention and were instrumental in finally forcing the US to abandon South Vietnam in one of the most astounding military defeats of US history. Unchallenged control of the air, and incessant bombing of the north ("by the end of the war, 7 million tons of bombs had been dropped on Vietnam, Laos, and Cambodia—more than twice the amount of bombs dropped on Europe and Asia in World War II"[336]) were unable to pound the North Vietnamese into submission.

The US agreed to a settlement to withdraw its forces from South Vietnam until a coalition government would be put in place, which was rejected by the South Vietnamese authorities. Subsequently the US undertook a massive bombing campaign against Hanoi and Haiphong harbor, which did little to stop the Viet Minh. Secretary of State Henry Kissinger then signed an original agreement in Paris, and US forces were withdrawn. But after the North Vietnamese launched a series of attacks on cities of South Vietnam, the Saigon government collapsed and North Vietnamese troops took over the city in April 1975. In a chaotic withdrawal the US embassy staff and Vietnamese collaborators abandoned South Vietnam, which was then unified into the Democratic Republic of Vietnam under control of the Viet Minh. Saigon was renamed Ho Chi Minh City.

Casualties attributable to the war in Vietnam, Laos and Cambodia (approximately): US: 47K in combat plus another 10K from various non-combat causes, 315K wounded and MIA; South Vietnam: 186K deaths and 500K wounded; North Vietnam and the Viet Cong: 925K deaths; civilians in north and south: 415K killed and at least 935K wounded. Over 3 million people either lost their lives or were wounded during the war (Bowman 1989).

In 1995, just two decades after the US debacle, diplomatic and trade relations were normalized under President Bill Clinton with the Socialist Republic of Vietnam.

Afghanistan and Iraq

By 1973, as the war in Vietnam concluded, US military services had been transformed into an all-volunteer force. With the exception of the military intervention in Kuwait after the Iraqi army had invaded the country in 1993, the wars in Afghanistan and Iraq were the first major actions conducted by predominantly non-drafted service members. For the general American population, these wars might have been taking place on another planet. Sons and daughters were no longer pressed into service, nor did those who did participate represent a significant proportion of the population. News of the wars occasionally made the front pages, but for the most part descriptions of the fighting and dying were hidden in the recesses of the media. Congressional representatives could show their mettle by continuing to fund these adventures with borrowed money, by pronouncement of support for attending to the security of the American people, and an occasional jingoistic phrase confirming their commitment to US global supremacy.

On September 11, 2001, shortly after George W. Bush took office as president early that year in a contested election finally decided by the US Supreme Court, the New York World Trade Center was struck by two commercial jetliners that had been commandeered by Islamic extremists. United Airlines Flight 175 and American Airlines Flight 11, Boeing 767s, slammed into the South Tower and North Tower, respectively. Another plane, American Airlines Flight 77, a Boeing 757, crashed on the west side of the Pentagon, the US military headquarters in Washington, D.C. A fourth plane was also hijacked, United Airlines Flight 93, its intended target uncertain but possibly the White House, the Capitol Building or a nuclear plant along the eastern seaboard, but passengers interceded, causing the plane to crash in Stonycreek Township, Pennsylvania, about 130 northwest of Washington, D.C. About three thousand American citizens and a few other nationals died in the attacks.

The hijackers were sponsored by the Islamic fundamentalist

extremist organization al-Qaeda headed by a wealthy Saudi, Osama bin Laden. Of the 19 hijackers, 15 were Saudi Arabians, and the others citizens of Egypt, Lebanon, and the UAE.

The Taliban, an Islamic fundamentalist group had succeeded in gaining control over much of Afghanistan; Osama bin Laden was allegedly conducting training programs there for al-Qaeda terrorists, who were linked to the September 11 attacks. When negotiations with the Taliban for extradition of bin Laden failed, the US and its NATO allies launched Operation Enduring Freedom in conjunction with friendly Afghan forces. The Taliban were ousted, but most of them and al Qaeda members fled to neighboring Pakistan and the remote mountainous areas of the country, where they were essentially immune from attack (the US troop commitment eventually reached 100,000 in mid-2010, when President Obama sent in additional troops to deal with escalating violence).

In December 2001, the United Nations Security Council got into the act by establishing an International Security Assistance Force (ISAF) to set up and train the Afghan national army. Hamid Karzai was appointed to head the interim government, and was elected to the presidency of the Islamic Republic of Afghanistan in 2004.

The conflict eventually spilled over into Pakistan, with clashes between the army and isolated tribes that were accommodating Taliban and al-Qaeda. US and NATO forces continued to fight against incursions and increasing support from dissident Afghans opposed to the NATO presence. The US sent drones into Pakistan targeting Taliban and other insurgents, which had the unintended consequence of widening the war into Waziristan, a mountainous region in northwestern Pakistan on the Afghanistan border under control of Islamic fundamentalists. Suicide attacks and roadside bombs became almost a daily occurrence.

The Taliban and al-Qaeda have not disappeared (2014). They, and Afghan dissidents fed up with attacks by NATO forces that have killed many innocent civilians, have continued to wage a guerrilla war in the country with suicide bombings and ambushes. The Taliban have been able to exploit the weak and corrupt government to maintain a presence in rural areas.

Through 2013 over 4,000 ISAF military and contractor personnel have been killed, and over 10.000 Afghan soldiers, in addition to many thousands of civilians.

Afghani political activist Malalai Joya provides a cogent assessment of the outcome of US intervention in Afghanistan. [337] Joya is a former member of the Afghan parliament, ousted as a subversive under pressure from the Karzai government: "Eight years is enough to know better about the corrupt, mafia system of [President] Hamid Karzai ... My people are crushed between two powerful enemies. From the sky, occupation forces bomb and kill civilians ... and on the ground, the Taliban and warlords continue their crimes ... It is better that they leave my country; my people are that fed up ... Occupation will never bring liberation, and it is impossible to bring democracy by war."

In March 2003, under allegations that Iraq was building up its store of "weapons of mass destruction," President G. W. Bush launched "Operation Shock and Awe," intended to force Saddam Hussein, the mercurial Iraqi leader, from power. Ironically, as a member of the Ba'ath Party, which emphasized pan-Arab nationalism, the Iraqi ethos under Saddam was anathema to al-Qaeda, with its Islamic fundamentalist orientation. The bombing campaign was followed by invasion in April 2003. The Iraqi army quickly succumbed. Saddam Hussein was arrested and executed by the new Iraqi regime.

The conflict dragged on. After eight years of fruitless attempts to pacify the country by the US military and their trained Iraqi security force, it was business as usual as far as internal conflicts were concerned. The Shia-led government of Prime Minister Nouri al-Maliki professed inclusiveness for the Sunni minority that had dominated Iraq under the leadership of Saddam Hussein, but it became clear after departure of foreign troops that the Sunnis would not share political power or social status under al-Maliki's Shia-dominated government.

US forces withdrew completely from Iraq by December 2011. Internecine conflict has continued. According to U.N. assessment, over 8,000 people were killed during 2013, most of them innocent civilians caught up in the tempest of violence that grips their country. Repression of the Sunnis sparked the formation of the al Qaeda-linked Islamic State of Iraq and Syria (ISIS)[338], which was able to establish a presence in Anbar Province, in the heart of the country. Iraq post-Saddam Hussein did not return to tranquility. Sunni-Shia animosities continued. Under the US backed government of al-Maliki, who identifies as Shia, warfare continued to claim the lives of many civilians from car bombs in Baghdad and other major cities, allegedly carried out (according to Shia leadership) under Sunni direction. ISIS has taken control of large areas of the country, including the city of Mosul, inspiring President Obama to once again commit up to 900 military advisors to assist the Iraqi government, and once again to authorize air strikes to thwart the ISIS territorial expansion.

About 4,500 US service personnel lost their lives during war in Iraq, and 32,000 were wounded. Iraqi losses are estimated at about a half million, including military and civilian deaths and injuries

War—the ultimate folly

During the 20th century, wars were directly or indirectly responsible for up to 175 million deaths worldwide (Brzezinski 1995). The number of injured was even greater. To sense this level of carnage imagine that every woman, man and child currently living in the United States was either killed or injured in these wars.

Direct military costs of major US wars of the past and present centuries have been estimated (in 2011 US dollars through FY 2010): World War I $334 billion; World War II $4,104 billion; Korea $341 billion; Vietnam $738 billion; Persian Gulf $102 billion; Iraq and Afghanistan (including other costs such as enhanced security at domestic US military bases to FY 2009) $1,147 billion, a total of about $6.8 trillion.[339] The Gross Domestic Product in 2010 was about $15 trillion; so direct cost of these wars was almost half the value of everything produced in the country during that year. However, cost of military operations by no means tells the whole story. US federal expenditures for the Iraq war alone, including benefits for veterans' over their lifetimes—medical and disability, education, housing, etc.—has been estimated at about $2.2 trillion. The Veterans' Administration budget runs close to $150 billion per year, and these costs will continue for decades to support disabled and retired war veterans. Other costs are interest on war related debt and assistance to allies.

The Harvard University Kennedy School of Government estimates that the wars in Afghanistan and Iraq alone would cost the US as much as $6 trillion, or $75,000 for every American household. If the same ratio of actual to direct costs is applied to all US wars since the beginning of the 20th century, the amount is staggering—in the order of $35 trillion, or about twice the current level of annual GDP.

The US engages in senseless wars at the cost of blood, tears and wasted resources, but many others also pay a very stiff price:

- Death and injury to US and foreign contractors, security forces, journalists, humanitarian workers and civilians;
- Damage to infrastructure of countries within war zones—transportation facilities, buildings, health maintenance systems, education systems, environment;
- Displacement of populations as refugees, many relegated to life in resettlement camps for extended periods;
- *Economic opportunity costs* have to be considered, the value of goods and services not produced when resources are instead employed for war materiel, which has no lasting value. Instead of producing bombs, which are exploded into useless fragments, while at the same time wreaking destruction on their targets, suppose the resources had, instead, been invested in infrastructure, such as a mass transit system, or in human capital, e.g., providing first class nurturing for every child in the country.

The human constitution almost guarantees that most violent conflicts, including war, are irrational in the sense that potential gains do not exceed costs. US leaders, from Presidents Wilson through Obama, led the country into new or expanded wars using their imaginative and creative faculties to justify military engagements to the vulnerable minds of their constituents, wars that were, for the most part, responses to their own egotistical criteria and almost guaranteed to result in more regret than satisfaction. Franklin Roosevelt was no less guided by personal criteria, but was immersed in a situation for which there was little alternative for the country but to fight for its life. For those who suffered as a result of wars that were rationally unjustified, that they sacrificed so much with so little to show for it is a tragedy beyond measure.

In a lecture at Stanford University in 1906, William James[340] despaired of the human propensity for war: [341] "Modern man inherits all the innate pugnacity and all the love and glory of his ancestors ... Showing war's irrationality and horror is of no effect on him. The horrors make the fascination. War is the strong life; it is life in extremis ... Our ancestors have bred pugnacity into our bones and marrow, and thousands of years of peace won't breed it out of us."

MASS KILLING AND GENOCIDE

Organized killing, whether considered genocide or crimes against humanity, is not a new phenomenon, but was "refined" during the 20th century through "advancements" in the means of killing and dissemination of information. The most intensive mass murdering episodes have usually involved attempts to wipe out entire populations. *The impetus is invariably economic*, even though the campaign is ostensibly justified on ethnicity, religion, political leanings and the like. Wholesale destruction of Native Americans in the 19th century by the US military and civilians caught up in the frenzy for land, the Nazi attempt to exterminate German Jews, ethnic cleansing in Bosnia and Kosovo, can be characterized as genocide.

What are the ingredients in the witch's brew that precipitates mass murder? First, discrimination, directed at large numbers of people based on their ethnic identity or another distinguishing feature; weak to non-existent leadership of the targeted population, whose distinctive characteristics may be real or imagined; a demagogic and charismatic individual capable of creating fear and loathing of the target group; an incident, commonly staged or fabricated, that snaps the barrier between hatred and overt aggression.

In Rwanda-Burundi, Belgian colonialists had fomented ethnic tensions by first encouraging dominance of the Tutsi minority over the majority Hutu population, and then switching their preferential treatment when the Tutsi favored early independence, which was attained in 1962 as Rwanda and Burundi were separated.

In 1994, Rwanda's population of seven million was composed of three ethnic groups (approximate percentages): Hutu (85), Tutsi (14) and Twa (1).[342] In the early 1990s, Hutu extremists within Rwanda's political elite blamed the Tutsi for the country's increasing social and economic malaise. Tutsi were also accused of supporting a Tutsi-dominated rebel group, the Rwandan Patriotic Front (RPF), operating from a base in neighboring Uganda.

A Hutu, Juvénal Habyarimana, assumed the presidency after a 1973 military coup. Through propaganda and political maneuvering, Habyarimana continued to increase tensions between the two ethnic groups, building Hutu animosity by stimulating fear and resentment of Tutsi dominance.

On April 6, 1994, a plane carrying Habyarimana was shot down near the Kigali airport. Violence erupted almost immediately, as Hutu extremists planned to destroy the entire Tutsi population. Everyone even suspected of being Tutsi was killed at home or as they attempted to cross roadblocks set up across the country. Entire families were killed; women were systematically raped. An estimated 200,000 Hutus were involved in committing these atrocities. People were hacked to death with machetes or horribly killed with a burning tire "necklace" around the arms and torso filled with combustibles. Moderate Hutus were not spared: an army comprised mainly of young and illiterate peasants also murdered thousands of Hutu politicians and others who opposed the genocide. In just a few weeks about 800,000 men, women, and children were cut down, perhaps as many as three quarters of the Tutsi population. The genocide ended when the RPF managed to overcome Hutu opposition, with its leader, Paul Kagame, taking over the presidency.

Prior to the slaughter Hutu dominated radio was used to incite violence, overtly calling for elimination of the Tutsi minority. World leaders in the US, France, Belgium, and even in the United Nations, were loath to acknowledge impending genocide because it would require intervention according to UN regulations. This hands-off attitude continued during the perpetration of genocide.

Even with a population of only seven million, Rwanda was one of the most densely populated regions in the world. As families continued to divide their arable land among offspring, most Rwandans found themselves hard pressed to eke out a living. With most at the margin of sustenance, it's little wonder that the country was a powder keg ready to ignite with a little prodding from demagogic opportunists. Rwanda is one of the poorest countries in the world: in 2011 about 82 percent of the population lived on the equivalent of less than $US 2 per day.

The Rwanda calamity is not unlike that of Cambodia under the Pol Pot regime. After the election of Richard Nixon to the US presidency in 1968, with the US military heavily committed to war against North Vietnam, Operation Menu was launched as a covert bombing campaign in neighboring eastern Cambodia and Laos from March 1969 until May 1970, with the aim of destroying sanctuary bases used for supply and training of the People's Army of Vietnam (PAVN) and the Viet Cong, who operated mainly in South Vietnam (the US had begun bombing in Cambodia as early as 1965 during the Johnson administration; Operation Menu was an intensification of this campaign). The US also conducted air raids close to the capital of Phnom Penh, with thousands of urban civilians killed.

In July 1968 the mercurial Cambodian sovereign, Prince Norodom Sihanouk, had formed the Government of National Salvation under pro-US General Lon Nol, who became the effective head of state after a vote in the National Assembly on 18 March 1970.

Lon Nol was not a popular leader, and requested bombing of sites that actually targeted his political opposition. Many Cambodian hamlets and villages were destroyed and about 150,000 civilians killed by B-52 bombers, which created great resentment and paved the way for the radical Khmer Rouge to seize power.

The civil war that ensued after the rise of the Khmer Rouge was ended in 1975, when Lon Nol abdicated and left the country. The US embassy was evacuated. The Khmer Rouge marched into the capitol, Phnom Penh, cheered on by the people, who had little inkling of what horrors lay before them.

The Khmer Rouge regime, or Angkar, led by Pol Pot, ordered the complete evacuation of the capitol. The entire population of intellectuals, business people, students and tradesmen were forced into the countryside to fend for themselves. The majority of dispossessed urbanites, particularly children and elderly, ill equipped to eke out a living in the countryside, perished from starvation and exposure to the elements.

A "re-education" program was the fate of those considered to have committed crimes—any hint of dissatisfaction with the aims of the regime. A "transgressor " receiving more than two warnings was consigned to the killing fields. For pre-revolutionary activity involving free-market or any type of foreign contact, the usual penalty was consignment to one of the detention areas for torture and execution.

Methods of execution included poisoning or inflicting wounds with spades or sharpened sticks. Children were often killed by bashing their heads against tree trunks or walls. Victims were sometimes required to dig their own graves. The perpetrators were recruited largely from among young, illiterate male and female peasants.

The Khmer Rouge tyranny came to an end only when the Vietnamese army, spurred on by ancient animosities with the Cambodians, invaded the country in December 1978, occupied Phnom Penh and formed a new government, the People's Republic of Kampuchea (PRK).[343]

Researchers studying global violence claim a decidedly diminishing secular trend, which they predict that will continue over time, despite modern incidences of incessant war, terrorism, mass murders and urban crime.[344] The reasons? Cultural improvements—better educated people who are less prone to resolve disputes through confrontation—and peacekeeping efforts at all levels of governance. Another factor cited is the increasing prevalence of democracy and decreasing number of autocracies (see Chapter 3 and Magaloni 2007). While the extension of modern communications through satellite television, radio and the Internet may indeed have expanded the visions of millions of people around the world to recognize the futility of violence, the decreasing trend may already have begun to reverse: as an example, the steady decline in the US violent crime rate since the early 1990s has shown an increase in the most recent years.[345] As Earth's already excessive packing density is projected to continue to increase throughout the current century, the likelihood of violent confrontation is bound to follow. Many other global issues will have to be addressed before violence is contained: neglect of the nurturing needs of children, growing disparity in wealth and income, mindless resort to military force to alleviate real and imagined threats to national security, among many others.

CHAPTER 10

THE EDIFICE COMPLEX

Something there is that doesn't love the small.[346] While modest stature has advantages in some instances, for example, a compact, agile person is better able to scamper up a palm tree to gather coconuts, in most cases people aspire to large physique. Few parents wish to beget small offspring, usually taking pride as the height of their scions increases. There is no mystery here: in the essential struggle for survival and growth an imposing frame is often a decided advantage in the pursuit of preeminence, and with it a greater capacity to attune the external environment to real and perceived needs.

The inexorable quest for physical prominence has its psychological counterpart. Megalomania has been widely considered a psychopathological condition, characterized by delusions of power, omnipotence and self-esteem.[347] In truth, it's anything but abnormal, residing in virtually everyone in varying degree, even in outwardly self-denigrating individuals who are merely attempting to lower the barrier to social acceptability. As any other characteristic, this delusional trait is distributed among individuals over a range from minimal to average to extreme.

Louis XIV, who ruled France for 72 years (1643-1715) proclaimed "l'etat, c'est moi" (I am the state). In other words, Louis *was* France, its sole decision-maker, at least in matters of state. Absolute despots may be omnipotent, but not necessarily omniscient: Louis is credited with advancing the country's culture, but also committing grievous errors. His *Edict of Fontainebleau* denied religious rights to French Protestants (Huguenots), of whom about one million lived in France at the time, resulting in mass emigrations that denied the country a significant economic force.

This penchant for impressive stature has behavioral counterparts. Ostentation is one means of projecting dominance, particularly when one's economic underpinnings are shaky. A large home, lawn, automobile, even home appliance (television or refrigerator) conveys a sense that the owner has "arrived."

As population on a finite globe continues to increase, consequences of winning and losing become more acute, inspiring greater impetus to avoid relegation to the ranks of the also-rans.

Under neo-globalization, commerce and industry are the arenas for attaining real status and power. "Consolidation of forces" has become a strategic mantra for those seeking a competitive edge, usually by those already well positioned through heritage or cunning. There is truth in the old saw "the bigger they are, the harder they fall," as we have seen when giants of the financial services industry came crashing down in the global economic debacle starting in 2007. However, even as the world stood in awe of the spectacle, most of these mammoth enterprises were resurrected for fear that they were "too big to fail"—that their demise would have too devastating an effect on economic life to allow them to wither and die.

So "bigness" has become the formula for attaining dominance where it now counts: in the economic arena. Intense competition of the 21st century opens the path to genuine acquisition of power and wealth for a relatively small number of aggressive, insensitive and risk-oriented individuals—the one percent. As the global system has continued to serve their interests by channeling most incremental wealth to their coffers, indications of resistance have occasionally surfaced, but in most cases have not been sustained.

The Occupy Wall Street protest in New York City's Zuccotti Park erupted on 17 September 2011, spread to other venues, but eventually faded as an overt expression of discontent. The movement reflected a deep desire on the part of the dispossessed to correct economic imbalances, but the sobering reality of an unresponsive "system" apparently tempered enthusiasm for direct participation. Municipal, state and national legislative bodies are too dependent on political contributions of the highest income-earning "one-percenters" (often via their political action committees or PACs) to redress inequities by redistributing the wealth and income that sustain their privileges.

Popular uprisings were common in the in the early 21st century: "Arab Spring" revolutions and protests in Algeria, Bahrain, Egypt, Libya, Morocco, Syria, Tunisia, and protests in some European countries—France, Greece, Spain, Italy, Ireland, Portugal and the United Kingdom. Although some of these appear to have been fomented by fundamentalist religious movements or opponents of repressive regimes, all essentially reflect dissatisfaction of marginalized citizens in the global shift toward capital concentration and greater inequality in distribution of wealth and income that has been ongoing for many decades.

Some deadly incidents *appear* to be outside the protest framework, actions of fanatics bent on irrational destruction of life and property. In March 1995 members of a religious movement AUM Shinrikyo carried out an attack on a Tokyo subway using the highly toxic nerve gas sarin, resulting in thirteen deaths and over 5,000 injured. In July,2005 Islamic fundamentalists carried out suicidal attacks in the London public transport system during the morning rush hour. Four bombs were detonated, three in cars of the London underground and one in a bus in Tavistock Square, killing 52 civilians and wounding over 700. The perpetrators of the September 11 attacks on the World Trade Center in New York City in which three thousand lives were lost were mainly fairly well to do and "educated" Saudi Arabians.

THE AFFAIRS OF MICE AND MEN

What has all this to do with "bigness"? Economic "gigantism" leads to intellectual "dwarfism." Civilized, democratic society can't function in a climate of ignorance and repression, where ordinary citizens are merely grist for the mill rather than full participants in the social machinery. Global capitalists have little stake in the character of their host venues, except to skew the system to their needs and to avoid security risks; genuine edification of the masses is not in their interests, so instead they do all in their power to suppress it.

An approach to achieving an unobstructed field of operations for absentee investors is to co-opt the energies and abilities of members of the host community; one method is to identify what they are seeking, and to lure them into compliance by asserting monopolistic competence to satisfy those aspirations. To broaden the range of possibilities, clever opportunists recognize that needs are not necessarily intrinsic, but often can be "created."

Politicians whose allegiances have been locked in by global investors in exchange for support at the ballot box have taken the lead from the advertising industry to employ similar techniques to achieve their ends: know your audience and its psychological vulnerabilities; tailor the message accordingly; subtly threaten cherished ideas and/or possessions if the thrust of the message is not followed.

So, as in any modern marketing campaign, the successful global capitalist, aided and abetted by well-oiled and compliant politicians, both creates needs and wants and also conveys his unique ability to satisfy them. People are merely cogs at each end of the process—consumers and workers: the more thoroughly repressed (dissuaded from exercising their true inclinations), the better attuned to serving their appointed functions.

Whether repression is exercised locally, nationally, regionally or globally, the result is usually similar—subservient behavior of subjects, with personal and societal interests either expunged or suppressed. Although people can be repressed by overt intimidation, a form of indoctrination in the guise of "education"—the antithesis of enlightenment or edification—is easier and more effective. Social media constitute a very effective mechanism both for disseminating propaganda, mainly via the Internet, and also for defusing dissent as users expend their psychic energies in "tittytainment."[348]

Some escape the net, at least temporarily, and still have the wherewithal to protest. Others are lured into subservient roles and do the bidding of their capital-wielding[349] masters, aided and abetted by compliant public administrators and legislators. Still others are easy prey for charismatic fanatical leaders, who typically adopt a religious framework for exercising repression through intimidation and indoctrination. This is discussed at length in Chapter 6. [350]

EMPIRES

Throughout history individuals have combined political or business acumen, intrepidness and inflated egos to create political, commercial and industrial empires, so firmly entrenched in some cases to transcend the life of the originator.

Most of the expansion of ancient Rome took place under the Republic, but after Octavian (Julius Caesar's nephew and heir) was declared Augustus Caesar in 31 BCE, he cut the mold for a line of successors to conquer and annex territory. By 116 CE, when Trajan annexed the Fertile Crescent region, the empire stretched from Mesopotamia in the east to the Iberian Peninsula in the west, and from North African coastal areas to Britain. By one definition the Roman Empire endured for at least 500 years, until 476 when it fell of its own weight as Germanic invaders swarmed over the western areas of the empire, although the Ottomans conquered the Eastern Byzantine offshoot a millennium later in 1453.

There was a time when relatively modest gigantism could be attained in the arena of commerce and industry by methods that appear tame compared to the high-flying schemes of contemporary entrepreneurs: astute traders could buy low and sell high; those fortuitously sitting on stores of commodities with demand much greater than supply could form monopoly cartels that fixed prices to assure a steady transfer of wealth from consumers; financiers could apply leverage, covering much of their portfolios with borrowings from depositors and loans from central banks so that their control of assets was much greater than their capital would ordinarily allow; innovators could amass wealth by introducing technologies with novel features that were indispensable to households or industries.

John Pierpont Morgan was perhaps the poster boy of traditional empire building. As his father was already one of the most successful financiers in the world, he had a head start on his contemporaries from birth in 1837. Along the way to fame and fortune, he launched his banking enterprise in 1871, which continues operating to this day. Morgan was sufficiently perceptive to recognize the potential of electric light, collaborating with inventor Thomas Edison in forming the Edison Electric Company. Through acumen, guile and power of the purse, he created General Electric, which grew into one of the largest conglomerate enterprises in the world, later incorporating the alternating current invention of Nikola Tesla, a much more efficient system for energy transmission. He also recognized the potential of freight handling, so that by the turn of the century he controlled half of the railroad tracks in the United States. Morgan also created US Steel in 1901, after buying out another titan of industry, Andrew Carnegie. J. P. Morgan & Co. was so powerful that it could even bail out the United States government, providing financial backing in the depression of 1895 and also in the financial crisis of 1907.

The current incarnation of the company, J.P. Morgan, Chase & Co., by its own admission, swallowed up more than 1,200 institutions in arriving at its present configuration. Among those were firms in commercial and consumer banking, and also brokerage and investment banking (after repeal of the Glass-Steagall Act of 1933 that separated commercial and investment banking), cash clearing and global energy trading.

At about the start of the current century, leaders of the company along with those of sister financial services institutions in banking, brokerage and insurance, such as Lehman Brothers, Citigroup, Morgan Stanley, AIG and the like, discovered that when conventional sources are insufficient to meet commercial targets there is always the possibility of creating innovative products as newfound sources of revenue and profit growth, further justified to government and market participants on the basis of their purported capacity to reduce or spread risk. There are derivatives, by means of which an investor can access potential gains from large amounts of capital with a relatively small investment, and also other financial instruments such as the credit default swap (CDS), which a creditor buys (pays a premium) for credit protection and the seller guarantees the credit worthiness of the debt instrument. Default risk is transferred from the holder (buyer) of the fixed income security to the seller. For many banks and insurance companies these instruments seemed like an infinite source of found money, until wholesale defaults sent the global economy into a tailspin, rendering the CDSs and other financial inventions either worthless or impossible of determining their value.

Home mortgages packed into marketable securities seemed a reasonable way to diversify risk: when one borrower defaults, it's only a small piece of the pie, so relatively insignificant. But suppose most, if not all borrowers default simultaneously because their balloon loans (interest only until maturity, when the principal is due) were stretching their budgets just to pay interest, in the expectation that real estate prices could only increase. In this case the bubble burst, the end of the "greater fool" line, which ultimately had to be reached when mortgagees found property values declining and their properties worth less than the balance of their loans ("under water").

Some mega-enterprises lost their figurative shirts as traders in these and other instruments. The US Congress passed the Toxic Asset Relief Program (TARP) to save the economy. Then Secretary of the Treasury Henry Paulson was handed a blank check for $700 billion (in borrowed money since the US budget was chronically in deficit). Rather than use the money to assist families in danger of losing their homes, Paulson and the Chair of the Federal Reserve Bank decided to bail out the largest banks that they considered "too big to fail." At the same time, the Fed opened its discount borrowing window to the banks, adding much more liquidity to the economy with the equivalent of monopoly money.

Although the TARP program was considered a success by the US Treasury Department, which reported that a large percentage of these funds had been recovered,[351] some funds were used by recipients to subsidize profits and to pay out bonuses to those whose reckless financial dealings had created the crisis. As one example, American International Group (AIG) received over $170 billion in TARP funds and subsequently paid out about $165 million in bonuses to the very executives who were responsible for bringing the company close to bankruptcy.[352]

The people of the United States have been in a state of denial regarding the quest for global dominance, a recurrent theme throughout the country's 200-plus year history. In 2014 American military forces are spread throughout the world in about 150 countries, 75 percent of the nations in the world. Some of the more striking examples (in thousands of troops): Afghanistan (68.0), Japan (50.9), Germany (47.7), South Korea (29.5), Kuwait (15.0), Italy (10.9), United Kingdom (9.3). But there are also US forces deployed in places such as Spain, Turkey, Kyrgyzstan, Cuba (Guantanamo) and Qatar. Current US allies Japan and Germany were enemies in World War II that ended almost 70 years ago. War in South Korea ended in 1953, over 60 years ago. But the American military tiger has been enervated by ill-advised engagements with mythical enemies in Korea, Vietnam, Iraq and Afghanistan, to the point that in 2014 Russia was able to wrest Crimea from Ukraine without so much as a strong whimper.

Former US President Theodore Roosevelt tended to conflate his persona with the nation he led, a kind of extended megalomania, and sought any pretext to expand the country's geo-political reach, e.g., Cuba, Mexico, Philippines and Venezuela, actually preferring hostilities to more benign paths to empire. "In his more bellicose moods it sometimes seemed that just about *any* war would do." In 1889 he wrote to a British friend (Thomas 2010), "Frankly, I don't know that I should be sorry to see a bit of a spar with Germany; the burning of New York and a few other seacoast cities would be a good object lesson on the need of an adequate system of coastal defenses."[353]

MONUMENTS

Erecting mammoth structures has historically been the means for tyrants, despots and the merely wealthy to make a statement about the significance of their existence. Some seeking enshrinement have been content to have a library or other public building named in their honor, but for those of means a major criterion is visibility.

The Pharaohs of Egypt and some Amerindian rulers discovered the pyramid as an imposing and durable structure to commemorate and celebrate their prominence. Political luminaries and others of their ilk, who followed in their footsteps, construct magnificent edifices as testament to their preeminence in human affairs.

Nicolai Ceausescu, former despotic Romanian leader, constructed the Palace of Parliament in Bucharest, reputedly the world's largest building devoted to public administration (a multi-purpose building containing both chambers of the Romanian Parliament).[354] According to the World Records Academy, the Palace is the world's largest civilian building with an administrative function. Ceausescu also ordered construction of the Transfagarasan Highway (1970-74)—Ceausescu's Folly, as it came to be known—after the Soviet Union invaded Czechoslovakia in 1968. The road runs across the highest sections of the southern Carpathian Mountains for 90 km, between Transylvania and Wallachia. The epithet was inspired by the high cost and loss of life (mainly military personnel) in its construction, as well as its limited utility. His rationale was to provide military access across the mountains in the event of Soviet aggression against Romania, but there is little doubt that delusions of omnipotence played a part. At the time, Romania's economy was reeling under the strain of Ceausescu's economic policies, which featured his determination to create a completely self-sufficient economic base, including heavy industry and elimination of foreign debt.[355] He was inspired to move the under-utilized rural population to urban areas to serve as industrial workers. However, the country lacked the resource base to maintain this program, and soon the labor force was faced with a lack of employment opportunity and reduced food supplies and consumer goods. Ceausescu's megalomania allowed for no flexibility in his policies, which induced economic collapse. He paid the ultimate price, ignominiously dispatched to his eternal "reward" by his own people.

The idea of the presidential library arose when then US president Franklin Delano Roosevelt turned over to the government a museum created to preserve his papers and memorabilia at his family estate in Hyde Park, New York in 1941. Since then it has become *de rigueur* to create a library for each national leader, ostensibly to preserve historical records of their administrations, but more pointedly to build monuments as lasting testament to their greatness. There is on the books a Presidential Libraries Act, dating from August 12, 1955, apparently inspired by a sense that presidential papers and memorabilia should be preserved for posterity. The act allows for the building of a library for each president at no public expense, which would then be turned over to the federal government to administer (at public expense), justified by the desirability of preserving national history for research, and presumably to avoid repeats of past errors. But would it be to the country's advantage to suppress historical records of failed presidencies, e.g., Richard Millhouse Nixon, Jimmy Carter, William Jefferson Clinton, the Bushes, Barack Obama, and the like? Will there ever be a president who says "no library for me, please. It's best that posterity forget the blunders committed on my watch!"

GLOBALIZATION

A phenomenon that glaringly exposes the human megalomaniac affliction is the trend toward global reach of enterprises and markets since about the end of World War II. Extending operations, markets and distribution of commercial and industrial enterprise to include virtually the entire world has vastly increased the wealth and power of those in a position to avail themselves of the opportunities created by geo-political realignments coupled with technological revolutions. Business magnates found it now possible to extend commercial links through advanced information, transportation and communications networks, and to integrate labor markets through outsourcing and migrations. The breakup of the former Soviet Union created opportunities for well-positioned bureaucrats to seize control of state enterprises at a fraction of their true worth, or even less, At the same time, the rest of humanity has essentially stood still or even declined economically.

Since the end of the war economic policy-makers have tended to change their view of the world from an assemblage of relatively isolated economic nation-units to a more unified and integrated whole. Free markets and deregulation have predominated in economic policies of industrialized countries, spilling over into the developing world as it found entries to prosperity via the "maquiladora"[356] role in the global production network.

Global markets

Global markets for goods and labor have paved the way for some countries and transnational enterprises to vastly increase the scope of their industrial and commercial operations. Workers are either imported to fill gaps at all skill levels, or else enterprises have outsourced jobs when justified by cost considerations. Along with newfound prosperity, these countries and enterprises have exercised their political clout to their great advantage.

For example, US corporations have been able to rig rules that allow them to avoid taxes on income from foreign subsidiaries if the earnings remain in the country of origin. Analysis of 60 large US corporations found that they shielded more than 40 percent of their earnings from US taxes.[357]

As part of the neo-globalization process, cultural norms of Western countries, and particularly the United States, have been widely adopted, even in parts of the world that ostensibly reject them. The spread of this cultural *pandemic* has been greatly facilitated by breakthroughs in communications technology, particularly satellite television and the Internet, which have opened windows to the world from the remotest corners, and which compresses virtually all spatial and temporal dimensions of contemporary life. Adaptation has been uneven: if there *is* a rising tide, it has not lifted all boats. There have been winners and losers, the latter comprising a growing cohort of people whose capacities and opportunities have diminished in both a relative and absolute sense.

Global markets are nothing new, having been around since well before the beginning of the industrial revolution. Commodities were exchanged among disparate population during many previous centuries. Trade links existed between ancient Sumer and the Indus Valley in the third millennium BCE. The Great Silk Road, which linked

East Asia with Europe and North Africa, provided lucrative trading opportunities for the Chinese of the Han Dynasty dating from the same century, and also access to sea routes to East Africa, India and Southeast Asia. By the thirteenth century the Mongolian Empire under the Khans (Kublai, Genghis and others) dominated trade from Northern China, across the Eurasian land mass and into Eastern Europe, trading luxury items, fabrics and furs. During the fifteenth century the Chinese mariner Zheng He led expeditions to India, Indo China, the Persian Gulf and East Africa (in some accounts his exploits also ranged to the Americas and Australia). As an outgrowth of explorations of European maritime powers such as England, Spain, Netherlands and Portugal during the fifteenth century, material and cultural exchanges developed with the Americas, Africa and Eurasia in the following century.

Whether or not these early exchanges represented globalization is debatable. Basically three elements distinguish global commerce of the late 20th and 21st centuries: virtual disappearance of national boundaries, mobility of production factors, and speed of transactions. Economic planners and their industrial counterparts, driven by the power of obsessively acquisitive investors, are more than ever focused on efficiency—the most "bang for the buck"—to be facilitated by centralized, specialized production units with economies of scale in the lowest cost venues to serve extensive markets. Production units are located and relocated to areas or countries with marginally more favorable investment conditions—lower material and/or human resource costs—so long as production efficiencies outweigh increased transportation costs. As national demand is usually too small to absorb the output of these production units, markets have to be expanded beyond the borders of the host country.

This neo-globalization, a departure from a few millennia of traditional international commerce comprised of balanced, mutually beneficial exchanges predicated on reciprocal competitive advantage, has now taken on onerous tones. It has created a polarity of winners and losers; rather than improving the quality of life for both sides of international exchanges of goods, capital and people, it has been transformed into a mechanism for increasing disparities in income and wealth, somewhat obscured by apparent economic gains of some countries that have been absorbed into the system. Growth in indicators such as GDP or GDP per capita for these countries masks the fact that increased international traffic has disproportionately benefited political and economic elites.

Controllers of wealth and power make the rules. Despite benefits attributed to globalization for some developing countries—a sense of reduced isolation, better standard of living, longer life span, access to knowledge well beyond the reach of even the wealthiest of a century ago, factory work that is "better than staying on the farm and growing rice—the West has driven the globalization agenda, ensuring that it garners a disproportionate share of the benefits, at the expense of the developing world." (Stiglitz 2002) The benefits, at least in a relative sense, are illusory, as the disparity in wealth and income around the world continues to increase. Fifty years ago the ratio of CEO/factory worker income was something like 40:1. It is now closer to 400:1, and perhaps even greater.

SMALL IS BEAUTIFUL

E. F. Schumacher, noted British economist, expounded on the virtues of avoiding "gigantism" in his landmark work (Schumacher 2010). He warned of that mammoth enterprises would take any sense of creativity out of the workplace, and deal with people as anonymous cogs in the economic machinery. He decried economic policies predicated on profitability and the shibboleth of growth, rather than human need. He warned that human happiness would not derive from material wealth, but that only societies functioning on a human scale with close relationships can foster ethical behavior and protection of the natural environment.

In regard to urbanization, Schumacher saw megalopolises as a threat to human need, warning that cities shouldn't have more than a half million people, and that such huge concentrations and sterile workplaces would lead to human misery in terms of mental stress, depression, anxiety and panic attacks.[358]

Absentee ownership, an inevitable consequence of capital concentration, is a formula for disaster. When movers and shakers of industry and commerce have little to no stake in the social consequences of their investments, they focus on attempts to rig the political system to avoid unfavorable policies or political upheaval that might upset the applecart rather than to uplift the status of the community.

For centuries perceptive investors have employed the concept of diversification to mitigate risk. As we have seen in the global economic turbulence starting in 2007, "gigantism" and its underpinning of capital concentration is the very antithesis of risk avoidance. To meet the challenge of intensified global competition, capitalists have assumed the character of gamblers, opting for high risk, high reward projects rather than relatively secure investments. In this way they seek to clear the field by obliterating the competition. When they fail, they fall very hard, with the rest of society pummeled by the debris.

PART III

THE ROAD AHEAD

CHAPTER 11

TO BE OR NOT TO BE

Life on Earth is up for grabs. Whether or not humanity and the other creatures inhabiting our planet survive into the foreseeable future is a tossup. We have reached a state that the future is essentially in our own hands, barring some as yet unrecognized pending cosmic calamity, as our activities impact climate and all other qualities of the biosphere. We are unwitting players in this drama: the incomprehensible dealer not only doled out the cards we hold in our hands, but also manipulates the way we play them, while deluding us into believing that we can win or lose based on our own decisions.

Some aspects of the human behavioral repertoire favor continuation of life:

- An innate propensity for cooperation, part and parcel of nature's strategic legacy predicated on mutual collaboration for survival and growth;
- The capacity to reason profoundly about consequences of actions and attitudes;
- Ability to innovate, to find revolutionary solutions to problems, far superior to any other creature known;
- Acute sensitivity to form and function, conducive to immersion in the finer things of life.

Others carry the threat of extinction:

- A tribal instinct to follow the leader;
- Polarization, too easily intensified by demagogues;
- Resort to violence to redress real or imagined offenses by "others";
- Prevalence of mysticism, linked to the conflict between our brain hemispheres;
- Excessive presence—the tendency to overpopulate;
- Child neglect—by far the most serious threat to continuation of life on Earth

OPPORTUNITIES

Cooperation

Nature bestowed on humanity a legacy of collaboration. Our evolved body type, as part of our strategic bequest, was inadequate to challenge the largest competitors or prey, but this deficiency was compensated in some degree by a predilection for cooperation in the care and protection of offspring and in securing food supplies. The long period of dependency of human children required support by the male parent for the female bearer, so the family structure became a mainstay of human social organization. In securing food, the larger and stronger males participated in the hunt, but were compelled to join forces to corral and to bring down large prey. Gathering also required cooperation in protection of stores while the search for food was in progress. Transference of this cooperative trait to all spheres of interaction and at all levels of organization would go a long way toward assuring extended continuity for life.

Rationality

The human central processing unit—the brain—is divided into left and right hemispheres, as are those of other primates and some animals. Although somewhat controversial, there are indications that the left hemisphere provides a more orderly approach to information processing, and the right brain the more imaginative and speculative ideations. To whatever extent this is true, there's little doubt that humans have uniquely powerful analytical capacities—the ability to reason out the consequences of an action or event taking into account both internal and external aspects of the process or phenomenon. There are rivals to rationality, mainly the more imaginative dimensions of human thought processes—intuition and mysticism—which can be applied in both information gathering and in assessing the consequences of actions: in a strongly connected social environment they would either be strengthened to the point of dominating collective decision-making or else set aside as significant factors, depending on the sophistication of citizens and the orientation and capacities of community leaders. Although shaky baselines, or sets of assumptions, can undermine the validity of any sober analysis, rational assessment of phenomena almost usually (at least more consistently) lead to more satisfactory solutions to problems than those dominated by other modes of thought.

Innovation

Change is natural: we are faced with a roiling, swirling and unpredictable environment that often presents challenges to our well-being and even to our survival. Other animals have been observed to find new ways of dealing with issues, but humans stand alone in the complexity and range of innovative systems and processes to stave off impending threats and to provide for greater future security. Achievements in medicine, communications, transportation, food production, have been truly staggering by human standards, revolutionizing the lifestyles of most people on Earth, while in the process already forcing into extinction, and further threatening the existence of, many other species. Now as the world is imminently faced with enormous challenges to the future of life—vastly excessive numbers, massive poverty and deprivation, widespread terrorism and violence, severely degraded and polluted land, water courses and air—our capacity to discover new processes and modes of organization can be called upon to get us out of the mess and into a more sustainable mode of existence. The skills and talents of those at the cutting edge of change—the innovators—could be reoriented to solving problems here on Earth rather than narrowly focusing their attention on issues of limited impact or ventures into other parts of the cosmos.

Sensitivity

We humans are perceptive in the extreme. Other animals have sensory organs that more acutely acquire information—sounds, smells, images—but humans have evinced a capacity to sense qualities in our external environment above the mundane, which inspire loftier pursuits in music, art, theater, literature, philosophy. While our inherently competitive tendencies sometimes get in the way, in general the humanities have been a unifying social force, bringing people together while focusing on something outside themselves rather than immediate necessities for sustenance. Prospects for the future of life would be more secure with widespread involvement of people in the arts, requiring a process of not only of spreading the virtues of sensitivity to beauty, but also providing access for participation. An international organization such as the United Nations (e.g., UNESCO) could serve as the instrument for creating access to the finer things in life for people throughout the world.[359]

THREATS

Tribalism

A legacy of evolutionary development, more strongly predominant in some respects among humans than even our primate cousins, is the tendency toward obsequious subservience to dominant individuals. As we are never very far from our roots, even in the most advanced civilizations, charismatic figures can hold sway over masses of people. The promise of acquiescence to prescriptions of such dominant individuals is, of course, a greater sense of security attributable to their proclaimed powers to ward off threats. Some evangelical religionists are particularly adept at feathering their own nests by exploiting this tendency in particularly vulnerable people (see Chapter 6), fomenting the march against demons and other evil spirits rather than enemies lurking in the bush. There's not very much wrong with seeking security, but a tribal leader may be oriented toward peace or war, even though peace is invariably better. In any case, diversity in thought is just as powerful at mitigating risk as diversification of other assets.

Polarization

People are incessantly confronted with natural dualities—night and day, left and right, up and down—and thus are susceptible to manipulation by opportunists who recognize the potential residing in this characteristic. The ruse employed to serve the interests of power-seekers is to create false dichotomies, imaginatively strict divisions between concepts or entities that are alleged, in the aggregate, to represent all possibilities that are out there—ins and outs, Hutu and Tutsi, believer (in Islam) and infidel. Demagogic politicians make a lot of this vulnerability by insisting that you are either "with me or agin' me." If the former, all good things will ensue; if the latter, hell is on the horizon. Religionists use similar ploys. "I am the way, the truth, and the life: no man cometh unto the Father, but by me," (John 14:6, KJV).

Presenting the external world as limited to two distinct and all-inclusive camps plays on susceptibility to security threats. One does not wish to be left out in the cold, and so is easily lured by assertions of a warm and comforting environment inside the sphere delimited by the beckoning seducer.

Charismatic, power-seeking politicians have had a field day in African countries newly emerging from colonialism (see Chapter 9), but even in what are considered well functioning democracies, extreme political polarization has become the norm. The increasingly competitive globalized economy may be responsible, with the stakes very high for winning or losing, so "selecting" the right camp may be a monumental choice. In the US Congress the infighting has reached a crescendo, each party granting no quarter to the other. Rather than tackling issues demanding deliberation and cooperation, the principle objective of each party is to destroy the image of the opposition. Numerous attempts to deal with fiscal crises have brought the country to the brink of default on its massive debt, which precipitated reduction of the credit rating of the global economic powerhouse. Lack of cooperation has been costly, both in terms of impeding sensible legislative initiatives and also in erecting wasteful showcases.

Polarization is not limited to the political domain. Throughout the world wealth and income distribution are widely unequal, and growing (Picketty 2014, Stigliz 2013). The economic duality of the 1 and 99 percenters is creating a growing barrier that will only be demolished painfully.

It would be better to allow a thousand flowers to bloom.

Violence

It's apparent that violence is natural. Fatal intra-species confrontations are not uncommon, so it should be no surprise that humans follow the pattern. Only the threat of mutual annihilation has inhibited the world's superpowers from using their awesome firepower to blow each other to smithereens, but these constraints don't appear to function very well on a smaller scale. Injuries take a toll of 5.8 million lives per year, about 3 million violently. Of the total number of fatalities: about 1.3 million in road accidents (which indubitably often have violent undertones), 174,000 in wars, 638,000 homicides and 870,000 suicides.[360] Excluding road fatalities, the human toll of global violence is over 1.6 million lives lost each year through interpersonal, collective and self-directed violence.[361] Of the variety of means employed to do away with ourselves and one another, one-on-one (dyadic) violence is exceeded by self-inflicted death, which far exceeds the numbers killed in collective (polyadic) violence such as wars, terrorism and other violent political conflicts, genocide, abduction and torture, and organized crimes (gang conflict and banditry). Although armed conflict has declined in recent years, the number of people killed by firearms has not. More than 740,000 men, women, and children die each year as a result of armed violence, the majority (490,000) in countries without armed conflicts. [362]

Steven Pinker and Joshua Goldstein believe that global violence is on the wane. Pinker explains: "Beginning in the 11th or 12th [century] and maturing in the 17th and 18th, Europeans increasingly inhibited their impulses, anticipated the long-term consequences of their actions, and took other people's thoughts and feelings into consideration. A culture of honor, the readiness to take revenge, gave way to a culture of dignity, the readiness to control one's emotions. These ideals originated in explicit instructions that cultural arbiters gave to aristocrats and noblemen, allowing them to differentiate themselves from the villains and boors. But they were then absorbed into the socialization of younger and younger children until they became second nature."[363]

Goldstein claims three reasons for the decline of war in the international system. One is the evolution of social norms described by Pinker. "Things like dueling or human sacrifice just aren't cool anymore." Another is widespread recognition that trade is a surer method of acquiring riches than war. Thirdly, global cooperation, such as United Nations peacekeeping activities, has been effective in reducing the incidence and longevity of inter-state and civil conflict.[364]

While the secular trend of violence may be in decline, over recent decades this is not so certain. It may well be that some of the factors that Pinker and Goldstein identify are overpowered by growing inequality in wealth and income[365] and the pressures of population. "Although six years of data, covering 2004-09, is not enough for detailed trend analysis, it is possible to tease out some possible patterns. In 2009 Sri Lanka experienced the highest violent death rate and the greatest increase since 2004, mainly due to the intense armed conflict that year. But other countries also exhibited significant upward shifts between 2004 and 2009, including Afghanistan, Honduras, Iran, Mexico, Pakistan, Palestine, Panama, Peru, and Uganda. The violent death rates in these countries in 2009 were at least twice the rates of 2004, although some countries (Burundi, Georgia, Iraq, Lebanon, Nepal, and Somalia) experienced significant decreases in lethal violence between 2004 and 2009."[366]

Violence begets violence. The longer the twin sins of poverty and child neglect are allowed to perpetuate the cycle, the more assured is an early demise for humankind. As Einstein predicts (see Chapter 7), without major initiatives to arrest our propensity for violence we will end up (if any remain) fighting with sticks and stones.

Reduction or even elimination of weapons of all types (biological, chemical, nuclear) in public and private hands (mainly firearms) would tend to reduce violence, but it isn't the cure-all by any means. The primary factors of child nurturing, poverty reduction and disparities in wealth and income have to be addressed worldwide: relative poverty may be an even greater impetus to violence that absolute poverty.

Reducing or containing global violence won't happen in a vacuum. National and global plans have to start at square one—serious attempts at addressing the primary factors. It would also be useful to promote national and international collection and dissemination of information on the extent, causes, consequences and means of prevention. Victims of violence have to be provided the opportunity for exposure and to seek restitution from perpetrators. How to get there from where we are is a formidable political challenge.

Mysticism

Nature dealt humankind a flaw in its makeup that counteracts its extraordinary intellectual prowess. It's a kind of split personality, one supremely rational, the other imaginative and prone to fantasizing—a flaw that doesn't bode well for the future.

For most of us, the left and right cerebral hemispheres each has primary control over different functions. The two hemispheres are connected by the equivalent of a coaxial cable, the corpus callosum, a band of nerves that provides channels of communication between them. That the two are not independent, and attempt to coordinate their functions, is responsible for much of the upheaval that humanity has created on Earth.[367] As a consequence the human animal is endowed with heightened self-awareness or self-consciousness,[368] employing both words and body language to project an image, such as facial expression, posture and gestures, to a degree far beyond the capacities of our primate cousins.

The tug of war that exists between the left and right brain hemispheres seems to be related to their division of responsibilities: the left brain as the rational, logical, factual, comprehending, realistic, orderly and strategic partner, and with most of the verbal responsibility as well, while the right brain controls emotions, imagination, impetuousness and fantasizing. An individual interacts with the external world essentially through speech and actions. Ideas inspired by the right brain are communicated largely through verbal capacities of the left brain. Conversely, left brain-inspired activities are rarely "pure"—coordination with the other hemisphere is usually unavoidable.[369]

Because language is linked to Broca's area of the left, rational hemisphere, perceptions originating in the right hemisphere are mediated by the rational and effusive left hemisphere, which tinkers with the message according to its own criteria. This tug of war gives rise to mystical visions and spiritual fantasies within the human psyche, the social cement that was part of our strategic evolutionary heritage and crucial to our survival: "under the spell of our carefully programmed spirituality, we cannot help falling in love, yearning for sexual gratification, nurturing our children, forging tribal bonds, suspecting strangers, uniting against common enemies and on occasion laying down our lives for family, friends or tribe."[370]

Since it's apparent that some of our ancestors survived, our logical faculties apparently took a back seat during crisis episodes, when unmediated genetic responses were required. The surviving human genome, filtered through nature's sieve over the ages, provides the basis for the predominance of mystically inspired, irrational behavior. "There is little doubt that during the past two million years of human evolution the cold-blooded processes of Darwinian selection would have unerringly weeded out many a deep-thinker in favor of the wild-eyed fanatic—among tribal leaders especially. The clinical eye and the cool head would have its uses, but only as optional extras that could be called upon to solve tactical or technical problems and then be relegated to their usual subordinate role—just as they are today." [371]

One only has to regard humanity's resolution of critical contemporary issues of global import to confirm that rationality has been relegated to subordinate status. While selectively preserving the mystics among our ancient ancestors was crucial to survival during the developmental stage, at the same time it was a formula for eventual existential crisis. "Only our obsessive yearning for significance, spirituality and the supernatural, and consequent auto-adoration, could blind us to the dangers of overpopulation and environmental degradation and prevent us from taking corrective action ... Let us recognize human mysticism for what it really is—the rusting Excalibur of our species, an old and vital streak of genetic madness that once rescued our kind from the brink of extinction, took us to the moon, and will run us through with due dispatch when our play is done."[372]

So the individual presents to the world the behavioral consequences of history, genes and memes (the cultural equivalent of genes; see Dawkins 2006), filtered by internal wiring that is itself derived from a combination of genetic inheritance and experience. In turn the individual receives feedback from the external environment, being altered in the process and responding in accordance with genetic and cultural imperatives.

Despite having at its disposal reliable information, and with the capacity to accurately analyze the consequences of one or another response to an external stimulus, the human organism will often "select" a path that's irrational in relation to its best interests. The flaw gets in the way, either allowing the myth-creating right brain to choose according to its own criteria while its counterpart is diverted, or permitting ideas originating in the rational left brain to predominate, but often undermined by interference from its emotional and fantasizing partner. Not often does the individual or the collective arrive at the most sensible course of action.

Evidence that humans have rarely responded to their rational prodding is overwhelming. As discussed in Chapter 9, almost all of the wars of the current and past centuries were fomented by mythical assertions of national leaders that were readily accepted by the general public, e.g., the "Domino Theory" of a menacing juggernaut, about to convert the global economic system to "communism." The entire episode in Indochina during the mid-late 1900s (including both French and US involvement) was, in reality, a proxy global confrontation between Cold War adversaries, which itself is testament to the widespread predominance of myth as justification for actions large and small. On a less grand scale, UFO sightings have routinely been reported and accepted, starting from the time in 1947 when debris from an airplane accident in Roswell, NM, was interpreted by military, the press and the public as evidence of an incursion by extra-terrestrials. The "blood libel," originating in twelfth century medieval Europe, and promulgated by adversaries of Jews to this day, asserts that Christian children are killed so that their blood can be used in making unleavened bread used in the Passover celebration.

Myths are instruments employed by scoundrels to coerce uninformed and gullible people to do their bidding. Vulnerability to this kind of manipulation can only be reduced or eliminated by widely increasing the powers of observation and analysis among the human population. It will not happen by accident, but rather is something that we have to work on diligently.

Population overkill

An ominous development is the increasing clamor for growth in population on the basis of country demographics. In the US the ratio of workers covered under the social security program compared with the number of beneficiaries decreased from 159.4 in 1040 to 2.9 in 2010. In 2011 there were only 1.75 full time private sector workers for each recipient of benefits.[373] Alarmists have called for changes that would arrest the trend of insupportable growth in the number of retirees as compared with the number of workers paying into public and private pension systems. Some proposed changes include reducing pay-as-you-go pension financing that relies on current income to cover retiree pension benefits. Retirees would be encouraged, or even required, to set up private pension accounts, taking responsibility for their own retirement savings. The retirement age could be gradually increased in consonance with increasing longevity. But the most ominous proposals, in the face of a world awash with people (see Chapter 2) would encourage countries to arrest the trend of declining birth rates and to *increase* their populations to redress the alleged imbalance between workers and pensioners.[374]

Despite a human population far in excess of a level that can be comfortably accommodated, the Chinese government relaxed the ban on families having more than one child.[375] The changes are intended to deal with the rapidly decreasing working age population. A fourth of the population will be over 65, and presumably pensioned, by 2030, up from one in seven now. Based on current demographic trends, the working age population is expected to decrease by eight million per year starting in 2023. It is expected that the changes in the law will increase the number of births by up to two million per year, a substantial addition to human population growth.

Since we assumed the status of "plague mammal" at the onset of agriculture some 10-12 thousand years ago, the increase in human population has been characteristic of a species under conditions of stress. The typical pattern is boom and bust, and we are moving inexorably toward that eventuality. From the current level of about 7.3 billion of us, the United Nations Population Fund (UNFPA) projections on global population in 2100 are up to 29 billion (constant fertility), with 17, 11 and 7 billion respectively for more realistic the high, medium and low projections.[376]

Our encroachment and despoilment of habitats of other species not in a position to defend themselves, owing to our exponentially growing numbers and life style of consumption, has precipitated the sixth great extinction of species. The litany of environmental abuses places all other life forms and us in peril. Global warming, with alarming possibilities for positive feedback as methane-laden polar ice caps melt, threatens inundation of the most fertile lands alongside watercourses.

A warning signal of ultimate climax and crash typical of plague (inordinately expanding) species is the current diminishing per capita grain supply. While China and India have managed to maintain production on pace with population growth, in the most recent years global grain production per capita has begun to slide, a trend that technology will not be able to fix. In fact, technology has provided a false sense of security. The Green Revolution that averted a crisis in the 1960s provides the dangerous presumption, all too readily accepted, that it can be replicated whenever the need arises. But high yields have high costs. Applications of high rates of nitrogenous fertilizers and synthetic pesticides have resulted in other environmental problems—excessive nutrients, pesticides, erosion, acidification of soils, salinization (from excessive irrigation) and soil imbalances in micronutrients and trace elements. Biotechnology poses another set of dangers: emasculated viruses used to immunize crops have somehow recovered missing genes from transgenic host plants; food crops have been inadvertently pollinated by sterilized varieties. Eventually the agricultural "chicken" will come home to roost, leaving the world with a food crisis of epic proportions.

Child neglect

As discussed more thoroughly in Chapter 3, to avoid global calamity as pressures build during the rest of this century, a complete nurturing program for children has to become the first priority of all societies. The fact that no country has adopted such a course is an indication that this pressing need is being sacrificed to short-term demands of the current generation for improved standards of living and security.

An entirely different system for nurturing children is required, one that doesn't involve stultifying institutionalization, but rather maintains a connection to the everyday life of the community. What the factories of our "education" system need is the wrecking ball.

Children are a society's treasure. Failure to foster the physical and mental health of every young person, to provide the means for intellectual development and refinement of character, and to inculcate societal values, virtually dooms a society to decline and ultimately even to extinction. If democracy is cherished as a precious form of social organization, it has to be recognized that it cannot function for a population that is uninformed, intellectually deprived, and in a poor state of mental and physical health. Development of the greatest potential for every child has to become *the first priority*—taking precedence over any other commitment of resources, certainly in the United States as a model for responsible leaders throughout the world. Achieving a well-functioning democracy has its price, but the advantages to be gained by this expenditure in human capital are incalculable.

Where do we go from here?

Awareness of our "condition" is the first and essential step to allowing a reasonable tenure on Earth for humanity and for the other species that share it with us. The essence of our condition is that we are not in control, but rather follow the dictates that nature ordained. There are too many of us, and our adverse impact on the biosphere too great, to allow a sustainable future for all of Earth's life forms.

The outgrowth of our condition is an array of behaviors, predicated on our genetic endowment and history. How we respond to the opportunities and threats described above will write the epilogue.

We can tinker with possible alterations in our destructive behavior—environmental awareness, acknowledging sustainable capacities of Earth, fostering appreciation of the value of other forms of life, but so long as we remain the same kind of animal the outcome will likely not change very much. Our fundamental characteristics are too well ingrained, reinforced by the notion that we can fix whatever we break so long as we have the will. What is needed instead is something transcendental, ascendancy to a completely new plane of understanding about what makes us tick.

The likelihood of a sharp reduction in human numbers during the current century seems inevitable. Although our spiritual faculties tell us that this would be a tragic and unthinkable outcome, particularly when we contemplate the fate of our own progeny, there seems to be no way out. Rather than view our existence on this insignificant orb in the cosmos as a miracle that should be preserved through cooperation and magnanimity, events seem to be moving in another direction, with competitiveness gaining in intensity. The ironic side is that continued domination of the current strain of *H. sapiens* is detrimental to biodiversity, and would have the most devastating impact upon evolution itself.

The human plague may have been triggered by the advent of agriculture, and accelerated by the industrial revolution, but oil was undoubtedly the bullet in the barrel—probably two thirds of us are made of it. Exploitation of fossil fuels, just as any other natural phenomenon, was not written in the stars. Had this not occurred, the fury of the plague, if it is indeed to exact its toll in relatively short order, may well have been expressed in a more benign manner, so that a vestige of the humanity we know would end its tenure in some other way, maybe even in the inevitable fiery holocaust of the solar supernova.

Is it too late in the game to alter the outcome? If catastrophe strikes, but humanity does not completely disappear from the face of Earth, will the population emerging from the collapse have characteristics less dismissive of nature's imperatives, able to use its rational faculties to greater benefit of life? Or can the collapse be averted by a twist of fate that raises our species to the necessary level of perceptiveness? In any case, randomness in nature precludes any definitive prognosis.

We are handicapped by monumental misconceptions arising from the mysticism that is pervasive in our thoughts, and which therefore affects our deeds. In attempting to peer into the future it's useful to consider a few things that aren't obvious: a human organism is an integral mind-body entity whose behavior is genetically driven, as any other animal, but mediated by culture, experience and environment; although our self-consciousness engenders the illusion of choice, we do the only thing we can do under the circumstances; most environmental damage is the inevitable consequence of excessive numbers of humans, a phase in our species' population cycle; environmental issues do not have technological solutions; in our present state of development virtually all human activity, "good" or "bad," adds to environmental degradation—excessive exploitation of natural resources and pollution.[377]

So what is in store, for us, and the rest of life on Earth? It's not easy to be sanguine about our future, even in the relatively near term. Our numbers continue to grow, with no commensurate increase in the means of providing sustenance for the human population with already a billion at the point of desperation. The suggestion of finding an alternative planet to host our starving minions is chimerical. Extinction of species continues at an alarming rate, while some who sense the significance of this loss seek to preserve them through study and confinement to artificial habitats; but greater awareness of their habits and habitats could be a mortal embrace, a kiss of death, as human "lebensraum" takes precedence over their needs. Climate change induced by greenhouse gas emissions is bound to wreak havoc as rising sea levels inundate coastal areas, extreme weather destroys property and disrupts existing agricultural patterns. Modern media may yet provide the means for greater dissemination of knowledge, with sufficient feedback to alter the course of events in favor of life. But whether the future is a joyful chorale, a dirge, or something in between isn't matter of choice: nature will call the tune.

BIBLIOGRAPHY

INTRODUCTION

Carroll, Lewis. *Through the Looking Glass*. Bel Air, CA: Hesperides Press, 2008.

Dawkins, Richard. *The Selfish Gene: 30th Anniversary Edition—with a New Introduction by the Author.* Cambridge: Oxford University Press, 2006.

Gregg, Allan. "A Medical Aspect of the Population Problem." *Science* 121 (1955): 681-82.

Knoll, Andrew. "How Did Life Begin?" *NOVA*, July 1, 2004. Accessed July 12, 2014. http://www.pbs.org/wgbh/nova/beta/evolution/how-did-life-begin.html.

Lovelock, James. *Gaia: A New Look at Life on Earth*. New York: Oxford U. Press, 2000.

McKibben, Bill. *Eaarth*. New York: Times Books, 2010.

Morris, Desmond. *The Naked Ape: A Zoologist's Study of the Human Animal.* Los Alamitos (CA): Delta, 1999.

Nelson, James Carl. *The Remains of Company D: A Story of the Great War.* New York: St. Martin's Press, 2009.

Olson, Steve. *Mapping Human History: Discovering the Past Through our Genes*. New York: Houghton Mifflin Co., 2002.

CHAPTER 1 A MATTER OF CHOICE

Bargh, John A. and Ezequiel Morsella. "The Unconscious Mind." *Perspectives on Psychological Science* 3(1) (2008) :73-79.

Bernstein, Peter L. *Against the Gods: The Remarkable Story of Risk.* Hoboken: John Wiley & Sons, 1996.

Brooks, Michael. *13 Things that Don't Make Sense*. New York: Doubleday, 2008.

Einstein, Albert. *Albert Einstein, the Human Side: New Glimpses from his Archives*. Edited by Banesh Hoffman and Helen Dukas. Princeton: Princeton University Press, 1981.

Greer, Philip T., ed. *Identity and Difference: Studies in Hegel's Logic, Philosophy of Spirit, and Politics*. Albany: SUNY Press, 2007.

Hume, David. "Liberty and Freedom." In *Enquiry Concerning Human Understanding: With A Letter from a Gentleman to His Friend in Edinburgh and Hume's Abstract of A Treatise of Human Nature*, edited by Erick Steinberg. Cambridge (MA): Hackett Publishing, 1993.

Johnson, George. *Fire in the Mind; Science, Faith and the Search for Order*. New York: Vintage, 1995.

Kowalski, Maria. "Hegel: Abstract Right and Duties to Self." Paper presented at the annual meeting of The Midwest Political Science Association, Palmer House Hilton, Chicago, Illinois, Apr 15, 2004. Accessed August 6, 2014. http://www.allacademic.com/meta/p82865_index.html

Popper, Karl R. *Conjectures and Refutations*. Abingdon (UK):Taylor and Francis, 2002.

Rummel, R.J. "Determinism and Free Will." In *Understanding Conflict and War, Vol I: The Dynamic Psychological Field*. Beverly Hills: Sage Publications, 1975.

Viorst, Judith. *Imperfect Control: Our Lifelong Struggles with Power and Surrender*. New York: Simon and Schuster, 1998.

Watzlawick,Paul.*HowRealisReal?Confusion,Disinformation,Communication*. New York: Vintage Books, 1976

CHAPTER 2 FECUNDITY TO A FAULT

Carson, Rachel. *Silent Spring* . New York: Mariner Books, 2002. (Original release 1962)

Sachs, Jeffrey D. *The End of Poverty: Economic Possibilities for Our Time*. New York: Penguin Press, 2005

Wilson, Edward O. *The Future of Life*. New York: Vintage, 2003

CHAPTER 3 SOCIETY'S JEWELS

Hughes, Kent. *Building the Next American Century: The Past and Future of Economic Competitiveness.* Baltimore: The Johns Hopkins University Press, 2005.

Koen Vleminckx and Timothy M. Smeeding, eds. *Child Well-Being, Child Poverty and Child Policy in Modern Nations.* Bristol (UK): The Policy Press, 2001.

Kotulak, Ronald. *Inside the Human Brain: Revolutionary Discoveries of How the Mind Works.* Kansas City: Andrew McMeel Publishing, 1997.

Leidloff, Jean. *The Continuum Concept.* Cambridge (MA): Da Capo Press, 1986.

Magaloni, Beatriz. "Comparative Autocracy." Paper presented at conference *Research Frontiers in Comparative Politics.* Duke University, April 27-28, 2007.

Schwartz-Nobel, Loretta. *Growing Up Empty: The Hunger Epidemic in America.* New York: Harper Collins Publisher, 2002.

Kossinets, Gueorgi, and Duncan J. Watts. "Origins of Homophily in an Evolving Social Network." *American Journal of Sociology* 115 (2009): 405–50.

Sedlak, Andrea and Diane D. Broadhurst. "Fourth National Incidence Study of Child Abuse and Neglect (NIS-4)." *US Dep't. of Health and Human Services* (2010). Accessed August 6, 2014. https://www.childwelfare.gov/systemwide/statistics/nis.cfm

CHAPTER 4 RIGHTS ARE WRONG IN DEMOCRACY

Morrison, Samuel Elliot. *Oxford History of the American People.* New York: Oxford University Press, 1965.

Stevens, John Paul. *Six Amendments: How and Why We Should Change the Constitution.* New York: Little, Brown & Co., 2014.

CHAPTER 5 SEXUAL REPRESSION AND THE PEEPING TOM

Brown, Dee. *Bury My Heart at Wounded Knee: An Indian History of the American West.* New York: Holt Paperbacks, 2007.

Brownmiller, Susan. *Against Our Will: Men: Women and Rape.* New York: Simon and Schuster, 1975.
de Tocqueville, Alexis. *Democracy in America.* London: Saunders and Otley, 1835-1840.
Freud, Sigmund. *Civilization and its Discontents.* Edited by L. Menand. New York: Norton & Co. Inc., 2005.
Hamilton, Marcus J., Bruce T. Milne, Robert S. Walker, Oskar Burger and James H. Brown. "The Complex Structure of Hunter–gatherer Social Networks." Proceedings of the Royal Society, July 3, 2007. Accessed July 13, 2014. http://rspb.royalsocietypublishing.org/content/274/1622/2195.full
Nesbitt, Richard E. and Dov Cohen. *Culture of Honor, the Psychology of Violence in the South.* Boulder (CO): Westview Press, 1996.

CHAPTER 6 POLITICS AND RELIGION: A MARRIAGE MADE IN HEAVEN

Adams, John. "A Defense of the Constitutions of Government of the United States of America" [1787-1788]. In *The American Enlightenment: The Shaping of the American Experiment and a Free Society.* Edited by Adrienne Koch, 258. New York: George Braziller, 1980.
Allott, Robin. "Time and Consciousness." Paper presented at European Society for the Study of Cognitive Systems, Wadham College, Oxford, August 26-29 2000.
Dawkins, Richard. *The God Delusion.* Wilmington (MA): Mariner Books, reprint edition, 2008.
Dawkins, Richard. *The Greatest Show on Earth.* New York: Free Press; 2009.
Diamond, Jared. *Guns Germs and Steel.* New York: WW Norton & Co., 1999.
Ehrman, Bart D. *Jesus, Interrupted: Revealing the Hidden Contradictions in the Bible (And Why We Don't Know About Them).* New York: HarperOne, 2010.
Harris, Sam. *Letter to a Christian Nation: A Thesis on the End of Faith.* New York: Vintage, 2008.
Hitchens, Christopher. *God is Not Great: How Religion Poisons Everything.* New York: Twelve, 2009.

Huller, Stephen. *The Real Messiah: The Throne of St. Mark and the True Origins of Christianity.* New York: Sterling Publ. Co., 2009.

James, William. *The Principles of Psychology.* New York: Dover (reprint of 1890 work), 1950.

Jefferson, Thomas. *The Writings Of Thomas Jefferson V1: Containing His Autobiography, Notes On Virginia, Parliamentary Manual, Official Papers, Messages And Addresses, And Other Writings, Official And Private, Vol. 10.* Edited by Andrew A. Lipscomb and Albert Ellery Bergh. Kila (MT): Kessinger Publishing, LLC, 2009.

Kant, Immanuel. *Critique of Pure Reason.* Translated by F. Max Muller. New York: Doubleday, 1966.

Kimball, Charles. *When Religion Becomes Evil.* New York: HarperOne, 2003.

Popper, K.R. *The World of Parmenides: Essays on the Pre-Socratic Enlightenment.* London: Routledge, 1998.

Ridley, Matt. *Genome:The Autobiography of a Species in 23 Chapters.* New York: Harper Collins Publishers, Inc., 1999.

Sagan, Carl. *Billions and Billions.* New York: Random House, 1997.

Stenger, Victor J. *God, The Failed Hypothesis: How Science Shows That God Does Not Exist.* Amherst (NY): Prometheus Books, 2008.

Tattersall, Ian. "Being Human." In *Becoming Human: Evolution and Human Uniqueness.* New York. Harcourt Brace & Co., 1998.

CHAPTER 7 THE DIVORCE OF SCIENCE FROM PHILOSOPHY

Kuhn, Thomas. *The Structure of Scientific Revolutions, Third Edition.* Chicago: University of Chicago Press, 1996.

Schmidt, Jeff. *Disciplined Minds: A Critical Look at Salaried Professionals and the Soul-Battering System that Shapes their Lives.* Lanham (MD): Rowman & Littlefield, 2000.

CHAPTER 8 WASTE NOT, WANT NOT

Kolbert, Elizabeth. *The Sixth Extinction: An Unnatural History.* New York: Henry Holt & Co., 2014.

CHAPTER 9 CONFLICT, CONFRONTATION AND VIOLENCE

Baker, Peter. *Days of Fire: Bush and Cheney in the White House*. New York: Anchor, 2014.

Bowman, John S. *The Vietnam War Day by Day*. New York: Barnes & Noble, 1989.

Brzezinski, Zbigniew. *Out of Control: Global Turmoil on the Eve of the 21st Century*. New York: Touchstone, 1995.

Drury, Bob and Tom Clavin. *The Heart of Everything That Is: The Untold Story of Red Cloud, An American Legend*. New York: Simon and Schuster, 2013.

Goldstein, Joshua S. *Winning the War on War: The Decline of Armed Conflict Worldwide*. New York: Dutton/Plume (Penguin), 2011.

Mack, Andrew (director and editor in chief, Human Security Report Project). *Human Security Report 2009/2010: The Causes of Peace and the Shrinking Costs of War*. New York: Oxford University Press, 2011.

Maslow, Abraham. *Hierarchy of Needs: A Theory of Human Motivation*. New York: Amazon Digital Services (Kindle edition), 2011.

Meredith, Martin. *The Fate of Africa: A History of Fifty Years of Independence*. New York: Public Affairs (Perseuus Book Group), 2005.

Olson, Lynne. *Those Angry Days: Roosevelt, Lindbergh, and America's Fight Over World War II, 1939-1941*. New York: Random House, 2014.

Pinker, Steven. *The Better Angels of Our Nature: Why Violence Has Declined*. New York: Penguin Group, 2011.

Wrangham, Richard and Dale Peterson. *Demonic Males: Apes and the Origins of Human Violence*. New York: Mariner Books 1997.

Wright, Ronald. *Stolen Continents: The New World Through Indian Eyes*. New York: Houghton Mifflin, 1992.

Zimmerman, Warren. *First Great Triumph: How Five Americans Made Their Country a World Power*. New York: Farrar, Strauss and Geroux, 2002.

CHAPTER 10 THE EDIFICE COMPLEX

Schumacher, E. F. *Small is Beautiful: Economics as if People Mattered*. New York: Harper Perennial, reprint edition, October 2010. Original publication: London: Blond and Briggs, 1973.

Stiglitz, Joseph E. *Globalization and its Discontents.* New York: W. W. Norton & Co., 2002.

Thomas, Evan. *The War Lovers: Roosevelt, Lodge, Hurst and the Rush to Empire, 1898.* New York: Little Brown and Co., 2010.

CHAPTER 11 TO BE OR NOT TO BE

Morrison, Reg. *The Spirit in the Gene, Humanity's Proud Illusion and the Laws of Nature (with forward by Lynn Margulis).* Ithica: Cornell University Press, 1999.

Picketty, Thomas. *Capital in the Twenty First Century.* Cambridge: Belknap Press, 2014.

Stiglitz, Joseph E. *The Price of Inequality: How Today's Divided Society Endangers Our Future.* New York: W. W. Norton and Co., 2013.

ENDNOTES

PREFACE

[1] The pickup basketball court serves well as a laboratory for the study of individual and group psychology.

[2] Omar Khayyam. "The Rubaiyat, LXXI." *The Internet Classics Archive.* Accessed July 13, 2014. http://classics.mit.edu/Khayyam/rubaiyat.1b.txt

INTRODUCTION

[3] King James version of the Bible

[4] See description of chaotic systems in Chapter 1, "Indeterminacy"

[5] Recent progress in mapping the genome may shed more light on ancestry and relationships between individuals and populations than has heretofore been possible.

[6] Noah A. Rosenberg, et. al."Genetic Structure of Human Populations," *Science* 298-5602 (2002): 2381-2385.

[7] Paul Ehrlich, and Marcus Feldman. "Genes and Culture." *Current Anthropology* 44 (1) 2003.

[8] Much current behavioral research focuses on influences of specific genes, but the complexities of genetic interrelations may well frustrate this channel of inquiry.

[9] Interactions with people of many cultures during consulting projects in most corners of the world convince me that while culture is a strong distinguishing feature among populations, it is only "skin deep." Undoubtedly there is a core behavioral repertoire that is

shared among all people, predicated on the strategic orientation of our species endowed by nature during our evolution.

[10] Robert Burns. "To a Mouse" (1786)

[11] Quote first used by Walt Kelly in a poster for Earth Day, 1970

[12] Johnny Cash, folk and western singer, in one of his songs: "I shot a man in Reno, just to watch him die!"

[13] Very late one night many years ago my wife and I came upon the wreckage of a convertible sports car under one of the elevated train lines in New York City. The car's tires were burning, and two young people were wedged in against the dashboard, a man and a woman, unconscious and apparently badly injured. Without hesitation, I quickly stopped my own vehicle, jumped out and pulled the woman out of the burning car while my wife ran to a nearby diner to call the police. The young man was completely pinned behind the wheel, so it was impossible to free him. My reaction was essentially instinctive, even though my thoughts were on imminent explosion of the vehicle. The irrepressible force of culture had trumped genes. Fortunately the fire department arrived before the flames spread to the front seat, so the probably dead young man was not immolated. We didn't stay around to find out.

[14] James Carl Nelson, in his prodigiously researched history of doughboys of WWI in France, *The Remains of Company D*, confirms through their letters and other documentation that their predominant motivations were protection of family and country and abhorrence of totalitarianism.

[15] American service casualties: WWI (1914-1918) – 117,000 deaths and 204,000 wounded; WWII (1941-1945) – 292,000 KIA, 417,000 deaths, 670,000 wounded. Total military casualties for all countries: WWI 29.5 million; WWII 59 million, (http://www.infoplease.com/ipa/A0004619.html).

[16] Positions of some philosophers on the subject are discussed in Chapter 1.

[17] The Buddha may have been onto something when he admonished us to be unmoved by blame or praise, as they constitute external influences inimical to the process of self-improvement.

[18] The five great extinctions: end of the Ordovician and Silurian Periods (440 million years ago or my) - 60 percent of terrestrial and sea life such as trilobites and brachiopods; late Devonian (367my) - 75 percent of shallow sea life; Permian (245my) - 96 percent of all species died out so that all of life forms today derive from only 4 percent of then extant species; Triassic-Jurassic (208my) - 2-3 episodes over 18my attributable to climate change or asteroid impact, which eliminated half of marine vertebrates and about 80 percent of land quadrupeds; Cretaceous - Tertiary (65my) - dinosaurs and virtually all other large land animals (e.g., pterosaurs), many flowering plants went extinct.

[19] See Bill McKibben. *Eaarth* (New Yorrk: Times Books 2010, for a thorough and alarming survey of the environmental damage resulting from greenhouse gas emissions.

CHAPTER 1 A MATTER OF CHOICE

[20] Interview at The Institute for Cognitive Science, Queen's Square, London, as reported by Tom Chivers. "Neuroscience, Free Will and Determinism: 'I'm Just a Machine,'" *The Telegraph*, October 12, 2010.

[21] Elisa Filevich, Simone Kuhn and Patrick Haggard, "There Is No Free Won't: Antecedent Brain Activity Predicts Decision to Inhibit"; *PLOS One* (February 13, 2013), accessed July 13, 2014, doi: 10.1371/journal.pone.0053053. http://www.plosone.org/article/info%3Adoi%2F10.1371%2Fjournal.pone.0053053

[22] Personal Digital Assistant

[23] The gospel of John 14, KJV

[24] Foundations in the writings of Soren Kierkegaard (1813-55), Friedrich Nietzsche (1844-1900) and Karl Jaspers (1883-1969)),

[25] The *spirit* in this context refers to a moral and/or ethical quality divinely bestowed on the individual. This contrasts with the *spirit* or *élan* of Chapter 6, which refers to the essential life force of every organism.

[26] Acknowledgement of an interventionist deity is not intended, but the possibility is allowed that nature may have a way of bestowing moral fiber to an individual organism.

[27] There is a multiplicity of possibilities describing how an indeterminate or random process evolves over time, which can be expressed as a probability distribution. The distribution, if it is known, assigns probabilities to alternative outcomes.

[28] Vladko Vedral. "Living in a Quantum World," *Scientific American*, June 2011.

[29] Chaotic systems are extremely sensitive to initial conditions. They behave randomly as a result of feedback, varying time delays and changes in external conditions. Although associated with disorder, a chaotic system can quickly transform itself between states of order and chaos. Chaotic systems are fractals, with the same structure and geometry at different geometric levels. The heartbeat is chaotic as each heartbeat is unique. (see Crystal Ives, "Human Beings as Chaotic Systems," accessed July 13, 2014. http://physics.oregonstate.edu/~stetza/ph407H/Chaos.pdf

[30] Peter Sterling and Robert G Smith. "Design for a Binary Synapse," *Neuron* 41(3) (2004): 313-315.

[31] Jean Piaget, best known for his 20th century research into childhood developmental psychology.

[32] The analysis of Reg Morrison (1999) supports the contention that the illusion of choice has significant consequences (see Chapter 11).

[33] This 'spirit' has to be differentiated from the inexorable spirit (the 'libido' or life force) that resides in every organism. For this reason, the term 'élan' (or 'élan vital' – a term first used by philosopher Henri Bergson in 1907) is used to signify the latter, and is further discussed in Chapter 6. Each of these must be distinguished from 'soul', an ethereal entity in which the spirit purportedly resides and which succeeds the material body after death (see Chapter 6 *Ensoulment*).

[34] Albert Einstein, *Albert Einstein, the Human Side: New Glimpses from his Archives*, ed. Banesh Hoffman and Helen Dukas (Princeton: Princeton University Press, 1981), 60

[35] Thinking Allowed. "Conversations On The Leading Edge Of Knowledge and Discovery; The Simple and the Complex, Part I: The Quantum and the Quasi-Classical with Murray Gell-Mann, Ph.D," accessed July 13, 2014. http://www.williamjames.com/transcripts/gell1.htm

[36] George Johnson, "Ideas & Trends: Cosmic Noise; Scaling Lofty Towers of Belief, Science Checks Its Foundations," *New York Times*, July 10, 1994.

[37] Brian Greene. *The Hidden Reality: Parallel Universes and the Deep Laws of the Cosmos.* (New York: Vintage Books, Knopf Doubleday, 2011).

[38] Thomas J. Bouchard, Director. "Minnesota Twin Family Study." University of Minnesota, 1979

[39] Morrison, op. cit.

[40] ibid.

[41] Gospel of Luke 23:34 KJV

[42] Morrison, op. cit.

[43] Heisenberg's Uncertainty Principle assures that complete knowledge of the state of a subatomic particle is not possible. The Copenhagen Interpretation of the principle, attributed to Neils Bohr and Max Born, are considered synonymous with indeterminism in physical processes.

CHAPTER 2 FECUNDITY TO A FAULT

[44] International Monetary Fund. "World Economic Outlook Data Forum," accessed July 15, 2014. http://forums.imf.org/forumdisplay.php?3-World-Economic-Outlook-(WEO)-Data-Forum

[45] World Bank. "Poverty Overview," accessed July 10, 2014.http://www.worldbank.org/en/topic/poverty/overview

[46] UNDP Global Policy Forum, "Global Trends and Statistics on Income Disparity, Development Report 1997," accessed July 15, 2014. http://www.globalpolicy.org/component/content/article/218-injustice-and-inequality/46629.html

[47] David Cay Johnson. "Income Gap Is Widening, Data Shows," *NY Times*, March 29, 2007.

[48] Many investigators have shown an inverse relationship between information dissemination and fertility. One relates televised soap operas in Brazil to fertility reduction: Eliana La Ferrara, Alberto Chong and Suzanne Duryea, "Soap Operas and Fertility: Evidence from Brazil," Bureau for Research and Economic Analysis of Development (BREAD) Working Paper No. 172, Duke University; March 2008.

[49] In an interview with Terrence McNally "Globalization has Increased the Wealth Gap" in Jan. 2007, Nobel economist Joseph Stiglitz discusses how income disparities have widened as a result of globalization, accessed July 5, 2014. http://www.alternet.org/story/45833/?page=1.

[50] The relation between destitution and fertility is widely recognized by experts in the field. Two papers on the subject are:

(1) David Lackland Sam. "Value of Children: Effects of Globalization on Fertility Behavior and Child-Rearing Practices in Ghana," *Research Review* NS 17.2 (2001) 5-16, accessed July 10, 2013. http://culturesofcare.uib.no/downloads/17_2/SAM_17.pdf

(2) Gu Baochang, et. al. "Globalization, Policy Intervention, and Reproduction: Below Replacement Fertility in China." Paper prepared for presentation at the Population Association of America annual meeting, New York City, March 29-31, 2007, accessed July 10, 2013. http://www.popline.org/node/188951

[51] *Global Issues*, Dec. 2009, accessed July 13, 2014. http://www.globalissues.org/article/4/poverty-around-the-world#WorldBanksPovertyEstimatesRevised

[52] In June, 2010 the Chinese began to allow the value of their currency, the renminbi or yuan, to decrease in value relative to the US dollar. This should tend to reduce the enormous trade surplus that the country enjoys, and possibly reduce their rate of economic growth as measured by the traditional standard of Gross Domestic Product.

[53] The Bank commenced a 'Quantitative Easing' program in 2009 by purchasing treasury notes and building up their balance sheet (with fiat money), providing banks with additional liquidity for their lending programs. Some economists fear the consequences in regard

to inflation and a spike in interest rates as the program is ultimately reversed.

[54] Jeffrey D. Sachs (2005) convinced the former Soviet states to rapidly convert to market economies. Failure to allow time for adjustment created difficult conditions for Russia and particularly for the former republics, whose umbilical cords were severed precipitously.

[55] Ibid.

[56] University of Texas, Austin. "Extinction Rate Across The Globe Reaches Historical Proportions," *Science Daily*, January 10, 2002, accessed January 19, 2012 http://www.sciencedaily.com/releases/2002/01/020109074801.htm

[57] "Victoria's Ecological Footprint," State Government of Victoria, June 2006

[58] Although some analysts attribute hunger to inadequate distribution rather than arable land availability, they fail to account for limiting factors such as depletion of irrigation and nutrient sources, and the effects of climate change.

[59] David Pimentel and Mario Giampietro. "Food, Land and Population and the US Economy." Carrying Capacity Network, Washington, D.C. 1994

[60] "Global Food Trends—Overview," UN Office for Coordination of Humanitarian Affairs, 2010

[61] U.N. Food and Agricultural Organization (FAO). "The State of Food Insecurity in the World 2013," accessed June 15, 2014. http://www.fao.org/docrep/018/i3434e/i3434e00.htm

[62] Neil MacFarquhar, "Experts Worry as Population and Hunger Grow," *NY Times*, October 21, 2009, accessed July 13, 2014. http://www.nytimes.com/2009/10/22/world/22food.html?hpw

[63] World Health Organization, "Global and regional food consumption patterns and trends," accessed July 13, 2014. http://www.who.int/nutrition/topics/3_foodconsumption/en/

[64] Néfer Muñoz, *Inter Press Service English News Wire*, February 27, 2002

[65] Hari Eswaran, Fred Beinroth and Paul Reich, "Global Land Resources & Population Supporting Capacity," USDA Resources Conservation Service, accessed July 16, 2014. http://www.nrcs.usda.gov/wps/portal/nrcs/detail/soils/use/?cid=nrcs142p2_054029

[66] US Dep't of Agriculture, "Global Land Resources & Population Supporting Capacity," *American Journal of Alternative Agriculture* 14 (1999):129-136.

[67] International Energy Agency (IEA). *World Energy Outlook 2013* (Paris: Org. for Economic Cooperation and Development, 2013)

[68] OPEC. "World proven oil reserves by country 1960-2012," accessed May 15, 2014. http://www.opec.org/library/Annual%20Statistical%20Bulletin/interactive/current/FileZ/XL/T31.HTM. US data is for 2013 based on US Energy Administration estimate.

[69] "The IEA Puts a Date on Peak Oil Production," *The Economist*, Dec 10 2009.

[70] Natural Resources Defense Council, "Risky Gas Drilling Threatens Health, Water Supplies," accessed July 9, 2014. http://www.nrdc.org/energy/gasdrilling/?gclid=CjbA1bSvkL4CFUuXOgodjhYA4Q

[71] "Has Oil and Gas Collapse Sealed Fate of Peak Oil?" accessed December 15, 2013. http://www.321energy.com/editorials/simmons/simmons042909/show042909.html?id=27

[72] Tom Whipple, "The Peak Oil Crisis: Priorities," *Falls Church News-Press*, Apr 9 2009, accessed June 12, 2010. http://www.energybulletin.net/node/48577

[73] Lester R. Brown, "The Oil Intensity of Food," in *Earth Policy Institute Book Bytes*. June 25, 2009.

[74] Global Change, "Human Appropriation of the World's Fresh Water Supply," 2006, accessed August 18, 2014. http://www.globalchange.umich.edu/globalchange2/current/lectures/freshwater_supply/freshwater.html

[75] UNEP/GRID-Arendal, "Water availability in Africa 2005," accessed July 13, 2014. http//www.grida.no/graphicslib/detail/water-availability-in-africa_3368

[76] FAO Newsroom, "Deforestation Continues at an Alarming Rate 2005," accessed September 22, 2010. http://www.fao.org/NEWSROOM/EN/news/2005/1000127/index.html

[77] Rudolf Anich, Tara Brian and Frank Laczko, "Migration Trends: Comparing the Four Pathways," in *International Organization for Migration (IOM) World Migration Report 2013* (Geneva: IOM, 2013) 52-83.

[78] Furthermore, when externalities are taken into account that are not included in GDP and other macroeconomic indicators, it's very likely that the world economy has been in 'recession' at least since the onset of neo-globalization.

[79] James G. Gimpel and Frank Morris, "Immigration, Intergroup Conflict, and the Erosion of African American Political Power in the 21st Century," Center for Immigration Studies, Jan. 2007, accessed December 21, 2010. http://www.cis.org/AfricanAmericanPoliticalPower-Immigration

[80] "Hate Crimes Against Latinos Rising Nationwide: Hate Crimes Against Latinos Flourish," *Intelligence Report, Winter 2007* (Montgomery (ALA): Southern Poverty Law Center, 2007) 128.

[81] Michael T. Klare is Professor of Peace and World Security Studies at Hampshire College. See "A Planet at the Brink: Will Economic Brushfires Prove Too Virulent to Contain?" Tuesday 24 February, 2009, accessed July 15, 2014. http://www.truth-out.org/022509B

[82] Global Footprint Network, accessed August 17, 2014. http://www.footprintnetwork.org/en/index.php/GFN/page/world_footprint/

[83] Paul Chefurka, "World Energy and Population Trends to 2100," accessed July 15, 2014. http://www.paulchefurka.ca/WEAP/WEAP.html

[84] See Daniel Burke, "The lavish homes of American Archbishops: Records Reveal that 10 of the Country's Top Church Leaders Defy the Pope's Example and Live in Residences Worth more than $1 million. CNN blog. Accessed August 6, 2014. http://www.cnn.com/interactive/2014/08/us/american-archbishops-lavish-homes/

[85] Median population figures of the UN Population Fund are: 2014 7.3 billion, 1.1 percent growth (approx. 75 million per annum); 2050, 9.3 billion, .045 percent growth (approx. 42 million per annum)

[86] Jean Leidloff (1986) explains adverse effects of a modern, "non-continuum" upbringing.

[87] See Info Please, "Births by Age and Race of Mother," accessed July 13, 2014. http://www.infoplease.com/ipa/A0005074.html

[88] Dr. Weikert's High/Scope Educational Research Foundation in Ypsilanti, MI focused on the value of pre-school education.

[89] Posit Science, "A Conversation With Bruce McEwen" with Simon Hansen, Ph.D. June 8, 2010, accessed July 13, 2014. http://brainconnection.brainhq.com/2002/03/05/a-conversation-with-bruce-mcewen/

[90] National Scientific Council on the Developing Child, Center on the Developing Child, Harvard University. "A Science-Based Framework for Early Childhood Policy: Using Evidence to Improve Outcomes in Learning, Behavior and Health for Vulnerable Children," August 2007

[91] David A. Hamburg, "The American Family Transformed," *Society* 30 (2) (1993)

[92] See, for example: Sebastián J. Lipina1, and Michael I. Posner. "The impact of Poverty on the Development of Brain Networks," *Frontiers in Human Neuroscience* 6 (2012): 238. doi: 10.3389/fnhum.2012.00238

[93] Synapses are specialized structures in the nervous system (in humans, the brain, spinal cord and retina) that permit neurons to pass signals to other cells. Neurons are core components of the nervous system, cells that process and transmit information through electrical and chemical signaling.

[94] See, for example: Jacqueline S. Johnson and Elissa L. Newport. "Critical Period Effects in Second Language Learning: the influence of maturational state on acquisition of English as a second language," *Cognitive Psychology* (1989): 21

[95] Tom DeLay (Op/Ed). "Why Kids Murder Kids: Removal of Religious Values from Public Life has Left Us Without a Moral Foundation," *Washington Post*, Mar 27, 2000, 27.

[96] As gleaned from a brief tenure as a school board member, the emphasis appears to be preparing children for roles in the economy, rather than as citizens of the community, state and world.

[97] Highly controversial health care 'reform' legislation was passed by the US Congress and signed into law by President Barack Obama in March 2010, but it falls far short of a national commitment to comprehensive health maintenance for children, or for adults as well. An effective program would, first and foremost, employ substantial national resources to essentially teach the population to maintain healthy life styles.

[98] Jean Piaget (1896-1980), Swiss biologist and psychologist: development and learning model based on the child's construction of cognitive structures for understanding and responding to physical experiences.

[99] Encyclopedia of Mental Disorders, accessed July 13, 2014. http://www.minddisorders.com/

[100] Andrea Sedlak, et. al. (1996) compares abuse of children based on family income.

[101] US Dept of Health and Human Services, "Child Maltreatment 2008," accessed July 13, 2014. http://www.acf.hhs.gov/programs/cb/pubs/cm08/cm08.pdf

[102] See: Nancy Peddle, Ph.D. et. al., "Current Trends in Child Abuse: Prevention and Fatalities: The 2000 Fifty State Suvey," Working Paper Number 808, National Center on Child Abuse Prevention Research, September 2002

[103] Dorothy Lewis, "From Abuse to Violence: Psychophysiological Consequences of Maltreatment," *Journal of the American Academy of Child and Adolescent Psychiatry.* 31 (3) (1992):383-391.

[104] See: Sarah Fass and Nancy K. Cauthen, "Who Are America's Poor Children?" National Center for Children in Poverty, *NCCP* (2006).

[105] US Department of Agriculture Economic Research Service. "Food Security of Households in 2012," accessed July 13, 2014. http://www.ers.usda.gov/topics/food-nutrition-assistance/food-security-in-the-us/key-statistics-graphics.aspx#foodsecure

[106] Marisol Bello, "Hunger is a 'Silent Crisis' in the USA," *USA Today*, April 16, 2014.

[107] "Food Banks: Hunger's New Staple," *Feeding America*, September 28, 2011.

[108] Annie E. Casey Foundation, "Reducing Youth Incarceration in the United States," (2010), accessed July 13, 2014. http://www.aecf.org/resources/reducing-youth-incarceration-in-the-united-states/

[109] ibid.

[110] Stanford J. Newman, J.D, et. al., "America's Child Care Crisis: A Crime Prevention Tragedy., 2nd ed." *Fight Crime: Invest in Kids* (2000), accessed July 13, 2014. http://www.arizonaenergy.org/Aikido/childcarereport.pdf

[111] US Environmental Protection Agency (EPA), "America's Children and the Environment,3rd Ed. ACE," (2009), accessed July 13, 2014. www.epa.gov/envirohealth/children

[112] US Public Broadcasting Service (PBS) Frontline, "The Medicated Child," (November 2009), accessed July 13, 2014. www.pbs.org/wgbh/pages/frontline/medicatedchild/

[113] ibid.

[114] EPA 2014, op. cit.

[115] Pier Alberto Bertazzi1 et. al., "Health Effects of Dioxin Exposure: A 20-Year Mortality Study," *American Journal of Epidemiology* 153 (11) (2001): 1031-1044.

[116] US Department of Health and Human Services, Substance Abuse and Mental Health Services Administration, Office of Applied Studies. Results from the 2008 National Survey on Drug Use and Health.

[117] Center for Disease Control (CDC). "Study on Overweight and Obesity, 2008," accessed July 13, 2014. http://www.cdc.gov/obesity/data/trends.html.

[118] Judy Garland, "The Plot Against Judy Garland," *Ladies' Home Journal*, August 1967.

[119] Judy Garland, "By Myself," *PBS American Masters*, Feb. 25, 2004.

[120] Gerald Clarke, *Get Happy: The Life of Judy Garland* (New York: Random House, 2001): 23.

[121] Louis B. Mayer (according to Jane Ellen Wayne). *The Golden Girls of MGM.* (New York: Carroll and Graf, 2003): 204.

[122] James Bone. "Drinking bleach and Being Bullied on 'Lord of the Flies' Reality Show," *Time* (London), August 25, 2007.

[123] Teresa Wiltz, "Child Advocates Question Safety of Reality TV," *Washington Post*, July 29, 2008; cites entertainment lawyer Robert Pafundi, who has represented reality-TV youths and child actors.

[124] Kevin Sullivan (Washington Post Foreign Service). "In Togo, a 10-Year-Old's Muted Cry: 'I Couldn't Take Any More.'" *Washington Post*, December 26, 2008, accessed July 13, 2014. http://www.washingtonpost.com/wp-dyn/content/article/2008/12/25/AR2008122501198.html.

[125] US Federal Poverty Guidelines 2014, accessed July 13, 2014. http://aspe.hhs.gov/poverty/14poverty.cfm

[126] John Biewen, "The Forgotten Fourteen Million," American Public Media, A Coproduction with National Public Radio, May 1999.

[127] Henry K. Kaiser Family Foundation, "Poverty Rate by Race/Ethnicity 2012," accessed June 22, 2014. http://kff.org/other/state-indicator/poverty-rate-by-raceethnicity/

[128] Octavio Blanco, "The Changing Face of Poverty," CNN/Money, New York, Dec. 30, 2004.

[129] Emmanuel Saez, UC Berkeley, "Striking it Richer: The Evolution of Top Incomes in the United States"(Updated with 2012 preliminary estimates), September 3, 2013, accessed May 15, 2014. http://eml.berkeley.edu/~saez/saez-UStopincomes-2012.pdf

[130] Koen Vleminckx and Timothy M. Smeeding, eds., *Child Well-Being, Child Poverty and Child Policy in Modern Nations* (Bristol, UK: The Policy Press, 2001).

[131] Robert F. Drinan, "A Global Revolution for Children," in *The Mobilization of Shame: A World View of Human Rights.* (New Haven: Yale University Press, 2001), 45-50.

[132] Anne M. Veneman (UNICEF Executive Director), (paper presented at 58th World Health Assembly, Geneva, May16, 2005).

[133] Amnesty International, "Child Soldiers: From Cradle to War (2010)," accessed January 21, 2013. http://www.amnestyusa.org/children/child-soldiers/page.do?id=1051047.

[134] Coalition to Stop the Use of Child Soldiers, "Child Soldiers—Global Report 2008."

[135] Tom Regan, "Report: Israeli Soldiers Used Children as 'Human Shields,'" *Christian Science Monitor,* March 9, 2007. Accessed February 25, 2014. http://www.csmonitor.com/2007/0309/p99s01-duts.html

[136] Fathi Hammad (Hamas MP), "We Used Women and Children as Human Shields,"Al-Aqsa TV (Hamas/Gaza), February 29, 2008. Accessed July 13, 2014. http://www.memritv.org/clip/en/1710.htm.

[137] CNN reported on June 10, 2010 that the Taliban in Afghanistan had executed a 7-year-old boy as a spy.

[138] Shannon McManimon and Rachel Stohl, "Use of Children as Soldiers," Institute for Policy Studies, *Foreign Policy in Focus* 6 (36) (2005), accessed July 13, 2014. http://www.questia.com/magazine/1G1-80949343/use-of-children-as-soldiers

CHAPTER 4 RIGHTS ARE WRONG IN DEMOCRACY

[139] Instances of 'inalienable rights' being abrogated abound. For example, during the Bush administration in the US of 2000-2008, in defiance of the Bill of Rights, one could be spied upon without a court order; due process was denied in some cases; torture was permitted; wars could be undertaken without Congressional approval; enemies could be assassinated (see Robert Parry, "The End of Inalienable Rights," *Consortium News,* Jan. 24, 2006.

[140] For further discussion, see Will and Ariel Durant, *Rousseau and Revolution* (New York: Simon and Schuster, 1967).

[141] Center for Disease Control (CDC). "Data and Statistics, Deaths and Mortality, 2010," accessed July 13, 2014. http://www.cdc.gov/datastatistics/

[142] Chris Christoff and Ilan Kolet, "American Gun Deaths to Exceed Traffic Fatalities by 2015," *Bloomberg News*, Dec 19, 2012, accessed December 21, 2012. http://www.bloomberg.com/news/2012-12-19/american-gun-deaths-to-exceed-traffic-fatalities-by-2015.html.

[143] CDC, op. cit.

[144] Garrett Hardin, "The Tragedy of the Commons," *Science*, December 13, 1968.

CHAPTER 5 SEXUAL REPRESSION AND THE PEEPING TOM

[145] Marcus Berzofsky, et. al. "Female Victims Of Sexual Violence, 1994-2010 (NCJ 240655)," *Bureau of Justice Statistics*, March 7, 2013. The estimated annual rate of female rape or sexual assault victimizations declined 58 percent, from 5.0 victimizations per 1,000 females age 12 or older to 2.1 per 1,000, accessed July 13, 2014. http://www.bjs.gov/index.cfm?ty=pbdetail&iid=4594

[146] An article in the Huffington Post "Rape Is Grossly Underreported In The US, Study Finds," November 21, 2013, discusses wide discrepancies in the number of rapes reported in the United States for the year 2010: (1) the National Crime Victimization Survey (NCVS)—a survey of households by the US Census Bureau—188,380 victims of rape and sexual assault; (2) the Centers for Disease Control and Prevention's National Intimate Partner and Sexual Violence Survey, nearly 1.3 million; the FBI (accumulated from local law enforcement agencies, 85,593. Clearly, many rapes and sexual assaults go unreported. According to the largest figure, on average about 2.5 assaults of this type occurs each minute.

[147] See Brownmiller (1975), a report of findings of research by Dr. Menachiam Amir, Israeli criminologist, and the National Institute of Law Enforcement and Criminal Justice.

[148] Freud identified the libido as the life force, assigning to it essentially a sexual connotation. Other students of the human psyche, e.g.. Jung, broadened the concept to a more general creative drive of the individual. They are merely the human manifestation, however, of a characteristic shared by all of life.

[149] The term is used as a synonym for the libido, but in the sense that Jung proposed, a life force that exists in every living thing, and not merely the sex drive.

CHAPTER 6 POLITICS AND RELIGION: A MARRIAGE MADE IN HEAVEN

[150] 'Mind and body' are used here in the vernacular, as they are fundamentally one and the same.

[151] See: Tattersall (1998). Dr. Tattersall was curator of the Museum of Natural History in New York

[152] While conducting a course in physical science, a common practice was to ask Susan to look at Charlie, and then after a few moments, ask her to look at him again to see if he was still the same Charlie. What about his metabolism in the interim, and his new awareness that she had regarded him?

[153] Dalai Lama. "Philosophical Questions on Consciousness," accessed June 9, 2010. http://hhdl.dharmakara.net/hhdlquotes3.html#time

[154] Herrmann Hesse, *Siddhartha*, (Scotts Valley (CA): Create Space, 2008).

[155] Dalai Lama, op. cit.

[156] See, for example: Sue Taylor Parker; et. al., eds., *Self-Awareness in Animals and Humans - Developmental Perspectives* (New York: Cambridge University Press, 1994).

[157] Salma Abdelaziz, et.al., "Christian in Sudan Sentenced to Death for Faith; 'I'm Just Praying,' Husband Says," CNN World, May 16, 2014, accessed July 13, 2014. http://www.cnn.com/2014/05/15/world/africa/sudan-christian-woman-apostasy/

[158] See, for example: Art Moore, "Sudan Jihad Forces Islam on Christians," WND, March 04, 2002, accessed July 13, 2014. http://www.wnd.com/?pageId=12985.

[159] For a scathing rebuttal, see Dawkins (2009)

[160] In one formulation, the uncertainty in position and velocity of a particle of matter.

[161] The idea behind putting "science" and "scientist" in quotations is explained in Chapter 7. Usually quotation marks are omitted.

[162] Conventionally, other sciences exist (e.g., biology), but the material view is that all areas of knowledge, even those involving social relations, are essentially based on physical phenomena.

[163] Survey in *Nature*, 1997

[164] Albert Einstein, from "Science, Philosophy and Religion, A Symposium," (published by the Conference on Science, Philosophy and Religion in Their Relation to the Democratic Way of Life, Inc., New York, 1941).

[165] Albert Einstein. "The Religiousness of Science," in *The World as I See It* (Minneapolis (MI): Filiquarian Publishing, LLC., 2006).

[166] See: Michael Brown. "World History Chart," accessed May 13, 2014. http://www.creation-science-prophecy.com/timeline.htm

[167] William Henry Green. "Primeval Chronology—Are There Gaps in the Biblical Genealogies?" (Dallas: Bibliotheca Sacra. April, 1890) 285-303, accessed December 14, 2013. http://www.reasons.org/interpreting-genesis/adam-and-eve/are-there-gaps-biblical-genealogies.

[168] "Crews Find Boy's Body After 30 Hours in Well," *Lansing (MI) State Journal*, March 21, 1998.

[169] As quoted in Werner Heisenberg, *Physics and Beyond, Encounters and Conversations* (New York: Harper Torchbooks, 1971) 206.

[170] See for example: Thomas Whitfield Selover (American Academy of Religion), *Hsieh Liang-tso And The Analects Of Confucius: Humane Learning As A Religious Quest* (Oxford: Oxford University Press, 2005)

[171] See: Stanford University Encyclopedia of Philosophy, "Ancient Theories of Soul," first published Oct 23, 2003; substantive revision Apr 22, 2009, accessed July 13, 2014. http://plato.stanford.edu/entries/ancient-soul/

[172] See: James Orr, John Nuelsen and Edgar Mullins, eds., *International Standard Biblical Encyclopedia* (Peabody (MA): Hendrickson Publishers, 1994).

[173] "5315 Nephesh," Bible Hub, accessed July 13, 2014. http://biblehub.com/hebrew/5315.htm.

[174] See: *Hastings Dictionary of the Bible* (Peabody (MA): Hendrickson Publishers; abridged edition, 1989)

[175] St. Augustine, "On the Immortality of the Soul" (CE 387), accessed July 13, 2014. http://puffin.creighton.edu/phil/Stephens/Augustine/On%20the%20Immortality%20of%20the%20Soul.htm

[176] Hendrik Lorenz, "Ancient Theories of Soul," in *Stanford Encyclopedia of Philosophy* (Stanford: Stanford University Press, Apr. 2009)

[177] See: Innvista: http://www.innvista.com/culture/religion/bible/contraot.htm, typical of such lists published on the Internet.

[178] Although religion is inherently predicated on fantasy, this would not necessarily be grounds for condemnation if devotees of ROs did not usually function in slavish obeisance to their holy edicts and canons, often obviating sensible solutions to societal issues.

[179] Thomas Paine, "Of The Religion Of Deism Compared With The Christian Religion," Fordham University Modern History Sourcebook, accessed July 13, 2014. http://www.fordham.edu/halsall/mod/paine-deism.asp.

[180] Thomas Paine, "The Age of Reason," US History Organization, accessed July 13, 2014. http://www.ushistory.org/paine/reason/.

[181] Paul Tice, *Jumpin' Jehovah—Exposing the Atrocities of the Old Testament God, 3rd ed.* (San Diego: The Book Tree, 2007): Quoting Steve Allen.

[182] Solipsism : a philosophical concept that no knowledge is reliable except what exists in the mind, and that the claim to external knowledge is unjustified—a dangerous myth in Hitchens' view as a departure from reality.

[183] See: Dawkins (2008), from Chapter 1, "A Deeply Religious Non-Believer."

[184] See: Dawkins (2009), op. cit.

[185] Contender Ministries, accessed May 17, 2011. http://contenderministries.org/prophecy/endtimes.php

[186] See: "Christianity and Violence: Crusades," accessed July 14, 2014. http://atheism.about.com/library/FAQs/christian/blfaq_viol_crusades.htm

[187] Monica Mark, "Missing Nigerian schoolgirls: Boko Haram claims responsibility for kidnapping," *The Guardian*, May 5, 2014.

[188] A statement from qaidat al-jihad regarding the mandates of the heroes and the legality of the operations in New York and Washington, accessed July 15, 2014 http://triceratops.brynmawr.edu/dspace/bitstream/handle/10066/4796/QAE20020424.pdf?sequence=3

[189] Sheryl Henderson Blunt, "Election 2000: Partisanship in the Pews: Race, Religion Played Decisive Roles in the Presidential Vote," *Christianity Today*, April 2, 2001, accessed July 15, 2014. http://www.christianitytoday.com/ct/2001/april2/15.29.html.

[190] Ironically, the US backed president of Afghanistan, Hamid Karzai, reportedly negotiated with Taliban terrorists because he "lost faith in the US strategy in Afghanistan and is increasingly looking to Pakistan to end the insurgency," according to those close to Afghanistan's former head of intelligence services. See "Potential Allies: Karzai, Pakistan and the Taliban?" *Reuters News Service* Jun 11, 2010. Accessed July 15, 2014. http://blogs.reuters.com/afghanistan/2010/06/11/potential-allies-karzai-pakistan-and-the-taliban/

[191] Alan Cooperman and Thomas B. Edsall, "Evangelicals Say They Led Charge For the GOP," *Washington Post*, November 8, 2004, A01.

[192] See: Laurie Goodstein, "Seeing Islam as 'Evil' Faith, Evangelicals Seek Converts," *New York Times*, May 27, 2003.

[193] See, for example: Seth Mydans, "Churches Attacked Amid Furor in Malaysia," *New York Times*, January 10, 2010.

[194] The use of gender (she/he) in describing a deity seems misplaced. Gods most likely do not have to resort to sexual means to reproduce or recreate, as the Romans apparently believed of their Pantheon. It would be a great disappointment to learn that the Romans were correct, but even if true, this doesn't apply to the common god of Christians, Jews and Muslims.

[195] Sam Harris; *Letter to a Christian Nation—A Thesis on the End of Faith* (New York: Vintage, January 2008).

[196] Carolyn Tuft, "Meyer Received Millions, Records Show," *St. Louis Post-Dispatch*, April 30, 2005.

[197] Jonathan Wynne-Jones (Religious Affairs Correspondent), "Disney Accused by Catholic Cleric of Corrupting Children's Minds," *The Telegraph*, Nov 29 2008. Accessed July 16, 2014. / http://www.telegraph.co.uk/news/newstopics/religion/3534960/Disney-accused-by-Catholic-cleric-of-corrupting-childrens-minds.html.

CHAPTER 7 THE DIVORCE OF SCIENCE FROM PHILOSOPHY

[198] The term *science* is intended to describe the activities of academic, industrial and government researchers who are engaged in the pursuit, acquisition and application of knowledge via the *scientific method*, involving observation, hypothesis and confirmation through experimentation.

[199] Michael Agnes, *Webster's New World Dictionary of American English* (New York: Pocket, 2003).

[200] Some may bridle at the assertion that all quests for knowledge are ultimately utilitarian. This is consistent with a material view of existence, that humans are part and parcel of nature and driven by its forces, as is any other species, with choice, or free will, an illusion (see Chapter 2).

[201] See: Thomas Kuhn (1996), p. 88.

[202] Andrew Janiak, "Newton's Philosophy," in Stanford Dictionary of Philosophy, October, 2006. Accessed July 13, 2014.http://plato.stanford.edu/entries/newton-philosophy/.

[203] Source: http://ircamera.as.arizona.edu/NatSci102/NatSci102/lectures/ptolemy.htm.

[204] Qur'an 6:97.

[205] Nicolaus Copernicus, *Dedication of the Revolutions of the Heavenly Bodies to Pope Paul III* (1543), (Cambridge: The Harvard Classics 1909–14).

[206] Nicolaus Copernicus, "*On the Revolutions of the Heavenly Spheres, Preface*" (Amherst (NY): Prometheus Books 1995).

[207] Kepler's interests extended into many other areas: his studies in optics resulted in discoveries concerning reflection, refraction and imaging. His book *Stereometrica Doliorum* was the basis of integral

calculus later developed by Isaac Newton and Gottfried Liebniz. He used stellar parallax to measure the distance to stars, and revealed that the sun rotates around its own axis, among other mathematical and astronomical discoveries.

[208] Sir Isaac Newton, *The Mathematical Principles of Natural Philosophy*, trans. Andrew Motte (London: H. D. Symonds, 1803).

[209] Sir David Brewster. *Memoirs of the Life, Writings, and Discoveries of Sir Isaac Newton, 1855*, II (27) (Boston: Adamant Media Corporation, 2001).

[210] The period from about mid-17th through the 18th century characterized by scientific and socio-political revolutions in the Western world and based on principles of reason rather than superstition; which overturned medieval hierarchical social and political structures. A turning point was the French Revolution, which virtually destroyed the powers of the ruling class and Catholic Church; traditional political and social institutions were replaced by a new socio-political order seeking Liberté, Egalité, Fraternité (liberty, equality, brotherhood).

[211] See: John van Wyhe, "Charles Darwin: Gentleman Naturalist, A Biographical Sketch," The Complete Works of Charles Darwin Online. Accessed July 15, 2014. http://darwin-online.org.uk/darwin.html.

[212] Charles Darwin. *The Descent of Man* (XXI: General Summary and Conclusion). (New York: Create Space, 2011).

[213] See: The Stanford Encyclopedia of Philosophy, "Einstein's Philosophy of Science," first published Feb 11, 2004. Accessed July 15, 2014. http://plato.stanford.edu/entries/einstein-philscience/#7.

[214] Albert Einstein, "The Born-Einstein Letters, Letter to Max Born (4 December 1926)," trans. Irene Born (New York: Walker and Company, 1971. Einstein refers to statistical descriptions in quantum mechanics, which he considered merely a device to cover temporary ignorance of cause and effect.

[215] Albert Einstein, "Physik und Realität," trans. Jean Piccard, *Journal of The Franklin Institute*, 221 (1936): 313-47 and 348-82.

[216] Albert Einstein, "Ernst Mach," *Physikalische Zeitschrift*, 17 (1916): 101-4.

[217] Letter of Albert Einstein to Robert Thornton, December 7, 1944, accessed July 15, 2014. http://plato.stanford.edu/entries/einstein-philscience/.

[218] See: Philip Hunter, "Is Political Correctness Damaging Science?" *European Molecular Biology Organization* 6(5) (2005): 405–407. Accessed July 13, 2014. http://www.ncbi.nlm.nih.gov/pmc/articles/PMC1299305/.

[219] See: Paul Arthur Schilpp. ed., "Remarks Concerning the Essays Brought together in this Co-operative Volume," in *Albert Einstein: Philosopher-Scientist* (Evanston, IL: The Library of Living Philosophers, 1949, 7): 665-688.

[220] Paul Arthur Schilpp, ed., *Albert Einstein: Philosopher-Scientist.* Living Philosophers vol. 7. (New York: MJF Books, 2001).

[221] Ronald William Clark. *Einstein: The Life and Times.* (New York: Harper Perrenial, 2007).

[222] ibid, p. 752.

[223] Dr. Maury Seldin, Chairman of the Board of The Hoyt Group, "Roots of Modern Disciplines, Philosophical Foundations," accessed January 17, 2014. http://hoytgroup.org/wp-content/uploads/2012/12/Spring-2003-Roots-of-Modern-Disciplines.pdf

[224] In mitosis, the two "daughter" cells are replicas of the "parent"; in the domain of science, the split results in disciplinary subdivisions.

[225] NationMaster, "List of academic disciplines," accessed December 18, 2013. http://www.statemaster.com/encyclopedia/List-of-academic-disciplines.

[226] World Health Organization, "Children's' Environmental Health: Chemical Hazards," accessed June 17, 2013. http://www.who.int/ceh/risks/cehchemicals/en//

[227] Monika Gisler and Didier Sornette, "Exuberant Innovations: The Apollo Program," *Society Journal*, Springer 46 (1) (2009).

[228] ibid.

[229] Positions of commentators on the manned space program are posted on a blog maintained by Stephen J. Dubner for the NY Times: "Is Space Exploration Worth the Cost? A Freakonomics

Quorum," January 11, 2008. Accessed January 15, 2014. http://freakonomics.blogs.nytimes.com/2008/01/11/is-space-exploration-worth-the-cost-a-freakonomics-quorum/

[230] Dubner, op. cit.: Mike Hollis, Jan 29 2010.

[231] J.R. Wilson, "Space Program Benefits: NASA's Positive Impact on Society," accessed July 15, 2014. http://spinoff.nasa.gov/Spinoff2008/tech_benefits.html

[232] The problem of space junk that each launch missile and artificial satellite eventually becomes has to be taken into account in deciding on a particular mission.

[233] Dubner, op. cit. G. Scott Hubbard, professor of Aeronautics and Astronautics at Stanford University and former director of the NASA Ames Research Center, January 11, 2008

[234] Suzanne Presto, "Russia Plans to Leave International Space Station by 2020, Official Says," Cable News Network (CNN), May 14, 2014. These comments appeared related to US sanctions on Russia for its takeover of Crimea from Ukraine and further involvement in nationalist uprisings in Eastern Ukraine.

[235] Astronomers at the University of California-Berkeley and the University of Hawaii, using data from NASA's Kepler space telescope, have estimated that there are billions of planets in our own galaxy (the Milky Way) that might be able to support the kind of life with which we are familiar—possible venues for human expansion? There are, of course, possibilities for other forms of life. However, we are still faced with the reality of the damage wrought on this one planet that we have occupied for only two thousand centuries, a flick of the eye in cosmic terms. See Brad Lendon, "Tens of Billions of Planets Out There are Like Earth, Study Finds," CNN, November 5, 2013, accessed July 16, 2014. http://www.cnn.com/2013/11/05/tech/innovation/billions-of-planets/.

[236] NASA, "The Future of Human Space Flight," accessed July 15, 2014. http://www.nasa.gov/externalflash/human_space/

[237] ibid.

[238] Extinction is inevitable, if not by our own hand then ultimately at the burnout of our sun a few billion years hence, when Earth will be swallowed up in the resulting supernova. But why rush it?

[239] Mariah Blake, "Are Any Plastics Safe?" *Mother Jones*; March-April 2014.

[240] Jennifer Washburn, "Science's Worst Enemy: Corporate Funding," *Discover*, October 2007, accessed July 15, 2014. http://discovermagazine.com/2007/oct/sciences-worst-enemy-private-funding.

[241] Alexander Pope (1688-1744), "An Essay on Criticism," (1709), Poetry Foundation, accessed July 15, 2014. http://www.poetryfoundation.org/learning/essay/237826.

[242] Deficiencies in the system of higher education is supported by the analysis of Jeff Schmidt (2000)

[243] Ibid.

[244] ibid.

[245] Graham P. Collins, "Within Any Possible Universe, No Intellect Can Ever Know It All," *Scientific American*, Feb 16, 2009.

CHAPTER 8 WASTE NOT, WANT NOT

[246] Keynes may have employed a bit of hyperbole to emphasize that what happens in the short term is of vital importance.

[247] This has been the practice in some countries for centuries, e.g., Korea. Properly composted to remove pathogens, human waste is an excellent fertilizer.

[248] Source: United Nations Economic Commission for Europe (UNECE), accessed July 15, 2014. http://www.unece.org/statistics/news/newswaste-statistics.html.

[249] Daniel Hoornweg and Perinaz Bhada -Tata, "What a Waste: A Global Review of Solid Waste Management," *The World Bank*, March 2012. Accessed July 15, 2014. http://documents.worldbank.org/curated/en/2012/03/16537275/waste-global-review-solid-waste-management

[250] Ibid.

[251] Ibid.

[252] million US short tons, unless otherwise specified.

[253] US Environmental Protection Agency, "Municipal Solid Waste in The United States: Facts and Figures 2009," accessed July 15, 2014. http://www.epa.gov/osw/nonhaz/municipal/pubs/msw2009rpt.pdf

[254] OECD Environmental Data Compendium, 2002.

[255] "Improving Recycling Markets," OECD, 2006. Accessed July 15, 2014. http://www.oecd.org/env/waste/improvingrecyclingmarkets.htm.

[256] Dimitrios Zekkos, et. al., "Unit Weight of Municipal Solid Waste," *ASCE Journal of Geotechnical and Geoenvironmental Engineering*, October 2006.

[257] Although about half of MSW generated in developed countries is landfilled, in most of the world the percentage is probably far greater. Also, this calculation does not nearly take into account the total amounts of waste reported from various sources, including hazardous waste, which could total as much as seven times the level assumed in this calculation. If the maximum amount of waste and fifty percent recycling is assumed, the annual pile of annual grows to 5 miles on a side.

[258] Daniel Hoornweg, et. al., "Environment: Waste Production Must Peak this Century," Nature, *International Weekly Journal of Science*; October 2013. Accessed February 12, 2014. http://www.nature.com/news/environment-waste-production-must-peak-this-century-1.14032.

[259] "Waste Generation," World Bank, Urban Development Series Knowledge Papers, accessed July 15, 2014. http://siteresources.worldbank.org/INTURBANDEVELOPMENT/Resources/336387-1334852610766/Chap3.pdf.

[260] "Ocean Trash Plaguing Our Sea," Smithsonian Museum of Natural History, accessed April 14, 2014. http://ocean.si.edu/ocean-news/ocean-trash-plaguing-our-sea?gclid=CKL06_LF3bwCFUYOOgodSloATw.

[261] Christopher K. Pham, et. al., "Marine Litter Distribution and Density in European Seas, from the Shelves to Deep Basins," *PloS One* 5 (2014), accessed August 15, 2014, doi: 10.1371/journal.pone.0095839. Study

led by University of Azores, in collaboration with Mapping the Deep Project led by Plymouth University and the European Union-funded HERMIONE Project, coordinated by the National Oceanography Centre.

[262] Simon Romero and Christopher Clarey, "Note to Olympic Sailors: Don't Fall in Rio's Water," *New York Times*, May 18, 2014.

[263] Under United Nations auspices, the Inter-Governmental Conference on the Convention on the Dumping of Wastes at Sea met in London in November 1972 at the invitation of the United Kingdom and adopted this Convention for protecting the marine environment from human activities; its effective date was August 30, 1975. Since 1977, it has been administered by International Maritime Organization (IMO).

[264] The National Aeronautic and Space Administration (NASA) of the US is a typical offender. They deploy rockets and satellites with little to no concern about the ultimate disposition of the materials (many of them toxic) that ultimately descend back to earth.

[265] In the materialist view these new substances can be considered 'natural' in the sense that all matter and 'mind' are subject to nature's rules, and nothing else.

[266] Polymers, which are large molecules comprised of repetitive monomers (smaller structures) occur 'naturally', but also have been synthesized in the laboratory and produced commercially by industrial enterprises.

[267] Autism now afflicts about 1 in 68 children, according to a report of the Center for Disease Control of March 27, 2013, up from 1 in 88 two years ago.

[268] Research suggests environment influences in development of ASD. Environmental vulnerability to particular stressors and exposures appears to be affected by some gene variants related to this disorder. De-novo gene mutations (present for the first time in one family member in an egg or sperm of one of the parents or in the fertilized egg) also suggest a role for environment in development of ASD. Systemic and central nervous system disorders can be consistent with a role for environmental influences (e.g., from air pollution, organophosphates, heavy metals): see Martha R. Herbert,

"Contributions of the environment and environmentally vulnerable physiology to autism spectrum disorders (ASD)"; Current Opinion in Neurology 2010, 23:000–000.

[269] "Draft Update Toxicological Profile for Chlorinated Dibenzo-p-dioxins," Agency for Toxic Substances Disease Registry (ATSDR), Research Triangle Institute study commissioned by US Department of Health and Human Services, 1998.

[270] Brahima Sanou, "ICT Facts and Figures 2013," International Telecommunications Union (ITU), accessed May 9, 2014. http://www.itu.int/en/ITU-D/Statistics/Documents/facts/ICTFactsFigures2013-e.pdf.

[271] "Solving the e-waste problem," U.N. Environmental Program (UNEP), StEP e-waste World Map (data for 2012), accessed January 17, 2014. http://www.step-initiative.org/index.php/WorldMap.html. This estimate differs from other sources that give e-waste tonnage in the 3 million range, and may be due to the inclusion of large electronic or electrical appliances in the higher figure.

[272] "Recycling—From E-waste to Resources," UNEP July 2009, accessed February 13, 2014. http://www.unep.org/pdf/pressreleases/E-waste_publication_screen_finalversion-sml.pdf

[273] John Vidal, "Toxic e-waste Dumped in Developing Nations, Says United Nations," *The Guardian, The Observer*, December 14, 2013, accessed January 18, 2014. http://www.theguardian.com/global-development/2013/dec/14/toxic-ewaste-illegal-dumping-developing-countries.

[274] Basel Convention on the Control of Transboundary Movements of Hazardous Wastes and their Disposal, adopted on 22 March 1989 and entered into force on 5 May 1992. Number of Signatories: 53 (including the US); Number of Parties: 181

[275] op. cit.

[276] "Exporting Electronic Waste - The Question is.... to Where?" 1800ewaste, accessed August 15, 2014. http://www.ewaste.com.au/exporting-electronic-waste-where/.

[277] U.N. Environmental Program (UNEP); "Recycling—From E-waste to Resources—Final Report, July 2009," accessed May 18, 2014. http://www.unep.org/pdf/Recycling_From_e-waste_to_resources.pdf.

[278] T Zhang, et.al., "PCDD/Fs, PBDD/Fs, and PBDEs in the Air of an E-waste Recycling Area (Taizhou) in China: Current Levels, Composition Profiles, and Potential Cancer Risks." *Journal of Environmental Monitoring* (Dec 2012): 14(12):3156-63. Accessed June 20, 2014. doi: 10.1039/c2em30648d (Epub Nov 5, 2012).

[279] T Xianjin, et. al., "PBDEs and PCDD/Fs in Surface Soil Taken from Taizhou e-waste Recycling Area, China," *Chemistry and Ecology* 30 (3) (2014), accessed February 17, 2014. http://dx.doi.org/10.1080/0275754 0.2013.844798.

[280] Aside from the rapid depletion of our natural capital, a report of the Intergovernmental Panel on Climate Change of March 2014 predicts that climate change attributable to carbon emissions into the atmosphere from burning fossil fuels will result in massive forced migrations as a rise in sea level floods coastal areas, widespread food insecurity as climatic conditions impact on crop production, and attendant economic shocks leading to increases in the incidence of poverty with dire social consequences.

[281] See letters of John Wesley, The Wesley Center Online, accessed March 17, 2014, http://wesley.nnu.edu/john-wesley/the-letters-of-john-wesley/wesleys-letters-1772b/; also http://igd.com/Waste_not_want_not; the phrase was first cited in the United States in 1932 by Gregory Y. Titelman, "'Topper Takes a Trip' by T. Smith," Random House Dictionary of Popular Proverbs and Sayings (New York: Random House, 1996).

[282] Contemporary democracies are "nominal" because they do not even approach the ideal. A true democracy requires commitment to preparation of citizens to participate fully by being well informed and open minded, which is cynically suppressed by wielders of power and influence abetted by legislator collaborators.

[283] The national income is approximately the GDP, some of which flows into investment, presumably to enhance future consumption.

[284] US Environmental Protection Agency (EPA), "Municipal Solid Waste Generation, Recycling, and Disposal in the United States: Tables and

Figures for 2012," Feb 2014, accessed March 17, 2014. http://www.epa.gov/waste/nonhaz/municipal/pubs/2012_msw_dat_tbls.pdf .

[285] "Rethinking Recycling," *Sappi eQ Journal* (005), April 2, 2013, accessed July 15, 2014. http://www.na.sappi.com/aboutus/news/2013-04-02.

[286] "Recycling of Plastics," University of Cambridge ImpEE Project, 2005, accessed January 12, 2014. http://www-g.eng.cam.ac.uk/impee/topics/RecyclePlastics/files/Recycling%20Plastic%20v3%20PDF.pdf .

[287] A zero waste policy would include provisions for minimum use of non-renewable resources; require that products be readily disassembled into their constituent parts; and that all product constituents be either infinitely recyclable or biodegradable.

[288] Items that would be reprocessed with no addition to the waste stream.

[289] OECD countries with EPR regulations include Austria, Belgium, Denmark, Finland, France, Germany, Greece, Ireland, Italy, Luxembourg, the Netherlands, Norway, Sweden, Switzerland and the UK. Others are Canada, Japan, Korea and Taiwan.

[290] S.G. Lee, X Xiu; "Design for the environment: life cycle assessment and sustainable packaging issues," *International Journal of Environmental Technology and Management*, 5 (1) (2005).

CHAPTER 9 CONFLICT, CONFRONTATION AND VIOLENCE

[291] The toll of victims of an unremitting wave of violence continues: on a typical weekend, say July 19-20, 2014, 47 people were shot in Chicago, five fatally (60 were shot over the July 4th holiday weekend); three boys in Albuquerque, NM were arrested for randomly selecting homeless people and beating them to death, accessed July 22, 2014, http://www.cnn.com/2014/07/21

[292] Thomas Hobbes, "Of the Natural Condition of Mankind As Concerning Their Felicity, and Misery," Chapter XIII. Leviathan, accessed July 15, 2014. http://oregonstate.edu/instruct/phl302/texts/hobbes/leviathan-c.html

[293] Ibid.

[294] Maplecroft, "Conflict and Political Violence Intensifies in 48 Countries Since 2013, Ukraine Sees Biggest Increase in Risk," accessed August 11, 2014, http://reliefweb.int/report/world/conflict-and-political-violence-intensifies-48-countries-2013-ukraine-sees-biggest.

[295] "Global Burden of Armed Violence 2011," Geneva Declaration on Armed Violence and Development (adopted by 42 states on June 7. 2006), accessed January 20, 2014. http://www.genevadeclaration.org/the-geneva-declaration/what-is-the-declaration.html.

[296] "Global Study on Homicide: UNOCD Homicide Statistics 2013," accessed July 15, 2014. https://www.unodc.org/gsh/en/data.html.

[297] See "United States Crime Rates," accessed July 15, 2014. http://www.disastercenter.com/crime/uscrime.htm.

[298] Piero Scaruffi, "Wars and Casualties of the 20th and 21st Centuries," accessed February 21, 2014. http://www.scaruffi.com/politics/massacre.html.

[299] Alsace-Lorraine, created by Germany after its victory in the Franco-Prussian war of 1870-1, was returned to France. Belgium, Czechoslovakia, Poland and Denmark were ceded territories previously within the German sphere. Part of East Prussia along the Baltic Sea, was given over to Lithuanian control. The historically Prussian city of Danzig (Gdansk) was proclaimed a free city administered by the League of Nations. Germany lost 13 percent of its European territory (more than 27,000 square miles) and one-tenth of its population (between 6.5 and 7 million people). Germany also lost all of its colonies.

[300] In July 2014 the Palestinian political-military faction, Hamas, "went for broke" in its undertaking of war with Israel, whose military prowess is far superior. By some accounts the economy in Gaza was in such dire condition that they felt they had little to lose. But it's unlikely that their gains will justify the devastation wrought on the people and infrastructure of that minute strip of territory. See Ann Bernard, "Hamas Gambled on War as Its Woes Grew in Gaza," *New York Times*, July 22, 2014.

[301] See, for example: Gary A. Cziko, "Unpredictability and Indeterminism in Human Behavior: Arguments and Implications for Educational

Research," American Educational Research Association, *Educational Researcher*, 18 (3) (1989): 17-25, accessed August 14, 2014. http://www.sscnet.ucla.edu/polisci/faculty/chwe/austen/cziko.pdf.

[302] See Martin Meredith. *The Fate of Africa: A History of Fifty Years of Independence*, Chap. 17 "The Great Plunder" (New York: Public Affairs (Perseuus Book Group) 2005). A masterful work on the history and consequences of colonialism.

[303] Costy Constantinos. "Sub-Saharan Africa Resource Wars: Exploitation and Imperatives for regulation in the Great lakes region of Africa," Sub-Saharan Resource Wars, 2012, accessed June 13, 2014. http://www.academia.edu/1555166/Sub-Saharan_Africa_Resource_Wars_Exploitation_and_Imperatives_for_regulation_in_the_Great_lakes_region_of_Africa.

[304] International Conference on the Great Lakes Region, Regional Initiative Against Illegal Exploitation of Natural Resources, Sept. 2006, accessed March 17, 2014. http://www.lse.ac.uk/collections/law/projects/greatlakes/2.%20Democracy%20and%20Good%20Governance/2b.%20Projects/Project%202.2.2.Illegal%20Exp.%20of%20Resources%20Eng%2030.09.06.pdf.

[305] Ajit Varki1 and Tasha K. Altheide, "Comparing the human and chimpanzee genomes: Searching for needles in a haystack," (Cold Spring Harbor: Laboratory Press (Genome Research), 2005), accessed January 18, 2014. http://genome.cshlp.org/content/15/12/1746.long.

[306] J.M. Williams, et. al., "Causes of death in the Kasekela chimpanzees of Gombe National Park, Tanzania," *American Journal of Primatology* 70 (8) (2008): 766-77.

[307] Martin Surbeck and Gottfried Hohmann, "Primate Hunting by Bonobos at Lui Kotale, Salonga National Park," *Current Biology* 18 (19) (2008): R906-7.

[308] Martin, Surbecki, et. al., "Evidence for the Consumption of Arboreal, Diurnal Primates by Bonobos (Pan paniscus)," *American Journal of Primatology* 71 (2009): 171–174.

[309] Sonja Koski and Jorge Publication in "Chimps of a Feather Sit Together: Chimpanzee Friendships are Based on Homophily in Personality,"

Evolution and Human Behavior (October 2013), accessed January 20, 2014. http://dx.doi.org/10.1016/j.evolhumbehav.2013.08.008.

[310] Richard Wrangham and Dale Peterson. "Paradise Lost," in *Demonic Males: Apes and the Origins of Human Violence* (New York: Mariner Books, 1997).

[311] Curiously, primates tended to be more intimate after a non-lethal confrontation, with grooming and more intimate body contact. This is reminiscent of the outcome of fistfights in filmdom, where gallant adversaries shake hands and quickly become fast friends.

[312] Camilo Mora, et.al., "How Many Species Are There on Earth and in the Ocean?" *PLOS Biology* (2011).

[313] Carmine D. Clemente and Donald B. Lindsley, "Aggression and Defense: Natural Mechanisms and Social Patterns," *UCLA Press* (1967). Comments by G. A. Bartholowmew, UCLA Department of Ecology and Evolutionary Biology

[314] J.M.G. van der Dennen,. "The origin of war: the evolution of a male-coalitional reproductive strategy," *Rijksuniversiteit Groningen* (Netherlands) (1995)

[315] M Enquist and O Leimar, "The Evolution of Fatal Fighting," *Animal Behaviour* 39 (1) (1990): 1-9

[316] Josephine Johnson, "Conflict of Interest in Biomedical Research," in *From Birth to Death and Bench to Clinic: The Hastings Center Bioethics Briefing Book for Journalists, Policymakers and Campaigns*, ed. Mary Crowley (Garrison NY: The Hastings Center, 2008), 31-34, accessed July 15, 2014. http://www.thehastingscenter.org/Publications/BriefingBook/Detail.aspx?id=2156

[317] "Wolf advocates fear poisoning," News from Norway, July 15, 2013, accessed February 27, 2014. http://www.newsinenglish.no/2013/07/15/wolf-advocates-fear-poisoning/

[318] See, for example: Jodi Burack, "Uniting Mind and Music," *American Music Teacher* 55 (1) (2005): 84

[319] A building epitomizing classic Byzantine architecture, built in the sixth century. It served as a cathedral for the Eastern Orthodox Church

until the fifteenth century, except for the period 1204 - 1261, when it was converted to a Roman Catholic cathedral. After the Ottoman Turks conquered Constantinople in 1453 the building was converted to a mosque, and became a museum in 1935.

320 World Health Organization. "World Report on Violence and Health," Geneva, accessed May 17, 2014. http://www.who.int/violence_injury_prevention/violence/world_report/en/abstract_en.pdf

321 A gripping survey, from the perspective of Native Americans, of their virtual annihilation in the United States, primarily during the 19th century

322 See: Nesbitt (1996)

323 Max Fisher, "What Makes America's Gun Culture Totally Unique in the World, in Four Charts," Washington Post, December 15, 2012, accessed November 22, 2013, http://www.washingtonpost.com/blogs/worldviews/wp/2012/12/15/what-makes-americas-gun-culture-totally-unique-in-the-world-as-demonstrated-in-four-charts/

324 Nothing scares a Washington politician more than a hot-button issue where she is not sure which button provides the most constituent votes.

325 "Gun Homicides and Gun Ownership Listed by Country," UN Office on Drugs and Crime (UNODC) 2012, accessed July 15, 2014, http://www.theguardian.com/news/datablog/2012/jul/22/gun-homicides-ownership-world-list

326 See Zimmerman 2002, p.219; cited from three volume series *The Winning of the West*

327 Wright, op. cit.

328 Brad J. Bushman and Craig A. Anderson, "Media Violence and the American Public Scientific Facts Versus Media Misinformation," Joint statement of American Psychological Association (APA), the American Academy of Pediatrics, the American Academy of Child and Adolescent Psychiatry, the American Medical Association, the American Academy of Family Physicians, and the American Psychiatric Association, July 2000: "at this time, well over 1,000 studies ... point overwhelmingly to a

causal connection between media violence and aggressive behavior in some children," accessed July 15, 2014, http://www.psychology.iastate.edu/faculty/caa/abstracts/2000-2004/01BA.ap.pdf

[329] The decline in rate of violent crime appears to have reached its nadir in 2012, and is currently on the rise, at least in the US

[330] Morgan Winsor, "Terrifying 'Knockout' Game Assaults Spreading," CNN Nov. 24, 2013, accessed July 15, 2014, http://www.cnn.com/2013/11/22/justice/knockout-game-teen-assaults/index.html?hpt=hp_t2

[331] Maite Garaigordobil, "A Comparative Analysis of Empathy in Childhood and Adolescence: Gender Differences and Associated Socio-emotional Variables," *International Journal of Psychology and Psychological Therapy*, Volume 9 Num. 2, June 2009

[332] Nicole M. McDonald and Daniel S. Messinger, "The Development of Empathy: How, When, and Why," in A. Acerbi, et. al., "Free Will, Emotions and Moral Actions: Philosophy and Neuroscience in Dialogue," IF-Press, accessed August 13, 2014. http://www.psy.miami.edu/faculty/dmessinger/c_c/rsrcs/rdgs/emot/McDonald-Messinger_Empathy%20Development.pdf

[333] Years of incumbency as president of the United States

[334] "First World War Casualties," accessed July 15, 2014, http://www.historylearningsite.co.uk/FWWcasualties.htm

[335] Source: Encyclopedia Britannica plus a variety of others; much of the statistics are rough estimates

[336] Howard Zinn's short history of the war in Vietnam from the beginning of the Communist insurgency in 1957 until the defeat of US and South Vietnamese forces in 1975.

[337] Interview published in the Vancouver, B.C. weekly *The Straight*, on November 12, 2009

[338] Alternatively designated as ISIL - Islamic State of Iraq and the Levant

[339] Stephen Daggett, "Costs of Major US Wars," Congressional Research Service, June 29, 2010. These costs do not include post-war expenditures for medical, social and other services for veterans, infrastructure

improvements to accommodate military logistics, and expenditures by states and localities for veterans' benefits. Accessed July 15, 2014, https://www.fas.org/sgp/crs/natsec/RS22926.pdf

[340] William James, professor of psychology and philosophy was considered one of the great thinkers of his time in the late 19th century.

[341] Evan Thomas. *The War Lovers: Roosevelt, Lodge and Hearst and the Rush to Empire, 1898* (New York: Little Brown & Co. 2010).

[342] Tutsi and Hutu are actually of the same ethnic origin, although time and practice have tended to increase physical differences. They speak the same language. There were many marriages between people identified with the two groups.

[343] A number of first hand accounts of the Cambodian Genocide have been published, e.g.: Loung Ung. *First They Killed My Father: A Daughter of Cambodia Remembers.* (New York: Harper Perennial, 2006)

[344] See Pinker (2011), Goldstein (2011) and Mack (2011)

[345] Federal Bureau of Investigation (FBI), "Crime in the United States 2012," accessed June 12, 2014, http://www.fbi.gov/about-us/cjis/ucr/crime-in-the-u.s/2012/crime-in-the-US-2012/violent-crime/violent-crime

CHAPTER 10 THE EDIFICE COMPLEX

[346] With apologies to Robert Frost.

[347] Michael J. Lewis. "Ego, vanity & megalomania," *New Criterion* (2002)

[348] See: Hans-Peter Martin, Harald Schumann and Patrick Camillier. *Die Globalisierungsfalle: Der Angriff auf Demokratie und Wohlstand.* published in English as *The Global Trap: Civilization and the Assault on Democracy and Prosperity* (New York: St. Martin's Press, 1997). Political analyst Zbigniew Brzezinski, among others, has noted this mechanism employed by controllers of capital for diverting the masses with sterile, deadening, least common denominator "entertainment".

[349] There's nothing unholy about capital investment. It only rears its ugly head when its owners either neglect or deliberately compromise the real needs and wants of the host community.

[350] Religionists are shown to function in a similar vein.

[351] See "Troubled Asset Relief Program (TARP) Monthly Report to Congress, January 2013," accessed June 1, 12014, http://www.treasury.gov/initiatives/financial-stability/reports/Documents/January%20 2013%20Monthly%20Report%20to%20Congress.pdf

[352] Edmund L. Andrews and Peter Baker, "A.I.G. Planning Huge Bonuses After $170 Billion Bailout," *New York Times*, March 14, 2009.

[353] US Senator Henry Cabot Lodge and Publisher William Randolph Hurst were Roosevelt's confidants before and during his presidency.

[354] World Record Almanac: The Palace of the Romanian Parliament has a floor area of 360,000 m^2, setting the world record for the Largest administrative building for civilian use. The largest building for military use is the Pentagon in Arlington, Virginia, USA, with a floor area of 604,000 m^2. Accessed June 5, 2014. http://www.worldrecordacademy.com/biggest/largest_administrative_building_world_record_set_by_the_Palace_of_the_Romanian_Parliament_80185.htm

[355] On one occasion in the 1990's, the author travelled by train from Copsa Mica to Bucharest with a prominent Romanian engineer from the Ceausescu era. As we passed by large factories it became clear that the self-sufficiency criterion ran wide and deep, even down to the fabrication of nuts, bolts, bearings, etc.

[356] The term originally referred to a factory set up in Mexico by a US manufacturer to produce either component parts or products that would then be exported into the US Here the term is used more generally as a company set up in a developing country by a foreign investor on the basis of production cost advantage .

[357] Scott Thurm and Kate Linebaugh, "More US Profits Parked Abroad, Saving on Taxes," *Wall Street Journal*, March 10, 2013. These funds are unavailable for paying dividends, share buy-back or investment in the US

[358] See the review by Madeleine Bunting, "Small is Beautiful: an Economic Idea That has Sadly Been Forgotten," *The Guardian*,

November 10, 2011, accessed June 8, 2014, http://www.theguardian.com/commentisfree/2011/nov/10/small-is-beautiful-economic-idea

CHAPTER 11 TO BE OR NOT TO BE

[359] There is a U.N. Arts Initiative already functioning (see www.unarts.org)

[360] Center for Disease Control . "Worldwide Injuries and Violence," accessed June 9, 2014, http://www.cdc.gov/injury/global/index.html

[361] Etienne G. Krug, et. al., eds. "World Report on Violence and Health," Geneva: World Health Organization, 2002

[362] ibid.

[363] Pinker, op. cit.

[364] NPR interview with Steven Pinker (author of *The Better Angels of Our Nature*, and Joshua Goldstein, author of *Winning the War on War*, December 7, 2011, "War And Violence On The Decline In Modern Times," accessed June 10, 2014, http://www.npr.org/2011/12/07/143285836/war-and-violence-on-the-decline-in-modern-times

[365] Some analysts have asserted that globalization is having the effect of reducing global income inequality, suggesting that while income inequality *within* nations has been increasing over the past two decades, inequality *between* nations has been falling. It is true that globalization has allowed some countries, such as China and India, to greatly increase their GDPs. But the increase has been by no means egalitarian. In fact, while some moguls in these countries have become extremely wealthy, income disparity remains. For the entire global population, income disparity has to be increasing. The apparent improvement in a few developing countries in per capita GDP or income is not spread among the population, but rather is accruing to the few entrepreneurs who have been able to secure a role in the distribution channels handling the intensive demand for goods and services from a consolidating industrial and commercial behemoth.(see Tyler Cowan, "Income Inequality Is Not Rising Globally. It's Falling," New York Times, July 19, 2014)

[366] "Global Burden of Armed Violence," Geneva Declaration on Armed Violence and Development, 2011, accessed June 9, 2014, http://www.genevadeclaration.org/fileadmin/docs/GBAV2/GBAV2011-Ch2-Summary.pdf

[367] Julian Jaynes, in *The Origin of Consciousness in the Breakdown of the Bicameral Mind,* postulates that the human brain existed in a bicameral state within the last few thousand years, in which people were not conscious in the sense with which we are familiar. Rather, the impressions of the right brain were transmitted to the left via auditory hallucinations. It was only with the acquisition of metaphorical language that self-consciousness arose.

[368] Some philosophers postulate a variety of self-conscious states, some more primitive and not necessarily reflective. Here the reference is to the reflective form of self-consciousness. For further discussion see Shaun Gallagher and Dan Zahavi, "Phenomenological Approaches to Self-Consciousness," Stanford Encyclopedia of Philosophy, August, 2006, accessed June 11, 2014, http://plato.stanford.edu/entries/self-consciousness-phenomenological/

[369] Much of what is known about the division of functions in brain hemispheres is attributable to Roger Sperry, who won a Nobel Prize for his experiments in1973.

[370] Morrison 1999, op. cit.

[371] ibid.

[372] ibid.

[373] US Department of Labor and Bureau of Labor Statistics data

[374] "Work longer, have more babies," *The Economist*, September 23, 2003.

[375] "China's one-child policy to change in the new year," *The Independent*, June 6, 2014, accessed July 13, 2014, http://www.independent.co.uk/life-style/health-and-families/health-news/chinas-onechild-policy-to-change-in-the-new-year-9028601.html

[376] "World Population Prospects, The 2012 Revision - Key Findings and Advance Tables" UNFPA June, 2013, accessed July 13, 2014, http://esa.un.org/wpp/documentation/pdf/WPP2012_%20KEY%20FINDINGS.pdf

[377] The President of the Nature Conservancy, Mark R. Tercek, in the Spring 2010 issue of his organization's publication of the same name: "You need reliable science on which to base pragmatic conservation decisions that will yield tangible results." Nature did a reasonably good job for all but about the last 10 millennia, when humanity began to apply its science.

INDEX